D1292438

ILLUSION AND REALITY

Sprigg Christopher St. John

ILLUSION AND REALITY

A STUDY OF THE SOURCES OF POETRY

By

CHRISTOPHER CAUDWELL, pseud.

LONDON

LAWRENCE & WISHART

First published in 1937
by Messrs. Macmillan
New Edition published in 1946
by Messrs. Lawrence & Wishart Ltd
Reprinted 1947
Reprinted 1950

COPYRIGHT

Printed in Great Britain by
The Camelot Press Ltd., London and Southampton (T.U.)

CONTENTS

32749

"Freedom is the recognition of necessity."

ENGELS

BIOGRAPHICAL NOTE

THIS is one of the great books of our time. It is not easy reading. It is a book to be studied and annotated and returned to again and again. The reader will then find that, however often he takes it up, it will always give him fresh food for thought.

The author, Christopher St. John Sprigg, was born in Putney on October 20, 1907. He was educated at the Benedictine school at Ealing. He left school at sixteen and a half and worked for three years as a reporter on the *Yorkshire Observer*. Then he returned to London and joined a firm of aeronautical publishers, first as editor and later as a director. He invented an infinitely variable gear, the designs for which were published in the *Automobile Engineer*. They attracted a good deal of attention from experts. He published five textbooks on aeronautics, seven detective novels, and some poems and short stories. All this before he was twenty-five.

In May, 1935, under the name of Christopher Caudwell, he published his first serious novel, *This My Hand*. It shows that he had made a close study of psychology, but he had not yet succeeded in relating his knowledge to life.

At the end of 1934 he had come across some of the Marxist classics, and the following summer he spent in Cornwall immersed in the works of Marx, Engels, and Lenin. Shortly after his return to London he finished the first draft of *Illusion and Reality*. Then, in December, he took lodgings in Poplar and later joined the Poplar Branch of the Communist Party. Many of his Poplar comrades were dockers, almost aggressively proletarian, and a little suspicious at first of the quiet, well-spoken young man who wrote books for a living; but before long he was accepted as one of themselves, doing his share of whatever had to be done.

A few months after joining the Party he went over to Paris to get a first-hand experience of the Popular Front, and he came back with renewed energy and enthusiasm. Besides continuing to write novels for a living, he re-wrote *Illusion and Reality*, completed the essays published subsequently as *Studies in a Dying Culture*, and began *The Crisis in Physics*. He worked to the clock. After spending the day at his typewriter, he would leave the house at five and go out to the Branch to speak at an open-air meeting, or sell the *Daily Worker* at the corner of Crisp Street Market.

Meanwhile, the Spanish Civil War had broken out. The Poplar Branch threw itself into the campaign, with Caudwell as one of the leading spirits. By November they had raised enough money to buy an ambulance, and Caudwell was chosen to drive it across France. After handing it over to the Spanish Government, he joined the International Brigade, and was killed in action on the Jarama on February 12, 1937.

In a letter from Spain he wrote: "I'm beginning to feel an old soldier, and already act as machine-gun instructor to our section. I'm political delegate to the group, joint editor of the wall newspaper, and have another political job, so you see I have my spare time fairly well filled." He goes on to ask for news from Poplar, no matter how small. "Out here", he continues, "where our Labour Party group meets in the Communist Political Commissar's room in the offices of the local Anarchist Trade Unions, it's difficult to imagine the frame of mind of the Labour Party leadership at home."

His death was reported by a fellow Brigader, one of his best friends, who has since been killed in the Second World War. "On the first day, John's section was holding a position on a hill crest. They got it rather badly from all ways: first artillery, then aeroplanes, then three enemy machine guns. The Moors then attacked the hill in large numbers. As there were only a few of our fellows left, including John, who had been doing great work with his machine gun, the Company Commander gave the order to retire. I got in touch later with one of his section who was wounded while retiring, and he told me the last he saw of John was covering the retreat with the Moors less than thirty yards away. I enquired of all our chaps for him for the next seven days, while I was on that front, but no one had seen him again. It was obvious he never managed to get off the hill."

Except for the novels and textbooks on aviation, all Caudwell's books are posthumous. *Illusion and Reality* was in the press when he left for Spain; *Studies in a Dying Culture* appeared in 1938, *Poems* and *The Crisis in Physics* in 1939.

In a review of *The Crisis in Physics*, Professor J. B. S. Haldane wrote: "Caudwell has something to say about science, and something very important indeed, though he only half-said it. I believe that the book will be a quarry of ideas for philosophers for generations to come." The same may be said of *Illusion and Reality*. It marks an entirely new departure in literary criticism. It is the first comprehensive attempt to work out a Marxist theory of art, and, while some parts of the argument will doubtless be modified by further research, it is as a whole a permanent contribution to the subject, destined to become a classic.

Caudwell was a man of genius, but he might have been that and still not achieved what he did in his short life. A naturally gifted thinker, he became a man of action. It was not an accident that his most productive period as a writer coincided with his political activity in Poplar. And his death was a tragedy in the true sense of the word, because in it his life was consummated. He lived and died a Communist.

G. T.

INTRODUCTION

THIS is a book not only about poetry but also about the sources of poetry. Poetry is written in language and therefore it is a book about the sources of languages. Language is a social product, the instrument whereby men communicate and persuade each other; thus the study of poetry's sources cannot be separated from the study of society.

It is a common assumption of literary criticism that the sources of literature are irrelevant or unimportant, and that literature can be completely criticised in terms of literature. There was for some time a similar philosophy about the study of nature—the mechanical materialism of d'Holbach, adopted unconsciously by most scientists to-day. It was supposed that matter could be completely described in terms of itself, and since man is made of matter, these terms would describe him also. This philosophy began by divesting matter of all those qualities which have a subjective or mental component—colour, solidity, taste. Mass, size, time and space were regarded as objective material qualities—matter described in terms of itself; until Einstein proved that the observer also entered into the determination of these. Einstein, however, made the same attempt to produce an absolute term, the tensor, which, in its turn, has been shown by the quantum physicists' Principle of Indeterminacy to depend on the observer. Nothing is left absolute by modern physics but equations—and these are thoughts. Obviously this unexpected outcome of mechanical materialism is not due to the fact that it was materialistic, but to the fact that it was not materialistic enough. By giving thoughts and sensuous qualities a purely subjective and fictitious existence, excluded from the reality of matter, the mechanical materialists at once established a field of non-material reality which contradicted the basis of their procedure.

While mechanical materialism was developing the objective or contemplated aspect of matter, idealism was developing its active or subjective side. Idealism became the study of *sensuousness*, and sensing is an active process. The world as known to man was shown to consist only of sensory qualities—forms, concepts, ideas. At first Kant admitted an unknown thing-in-itself, but Hegel exploded this and left only the idea, not existing in man's head but out of it—the absolute Idea. Being absolute, it was objective; being objective, it was material. Idealism had become materialism, but because from the start it had excluded objective, contemplated matter it was the rigid, ghostly materialism of Hegel's Logic, with a self-sufficient structure determined by thought.

This had only come about because in materialism the object had been separated from the subject and regarded contemplatively, while in idealism the subject had certainly been considered actively, but active on a nothing, on mere appearance. Marx's realisation of this led to the conception of the subject-object relation as an active one—man's *theory* as the outcome of *practice* on the *object*, *sensing* as the sensing of *something*. Theory was seen to be generated by the struggle of man the subject with nature the object.

But this conception could not rest there. For, once it had become plain that the errors of philosophy were due to its abstraction of subject from object, it also became clear that the active subject-object relation was nothing but man living in nature. Not an abstract man in abstract nature, but men as they really live and behave, who must live concretely before they come to speculate abstractly, and whose abstract speculations therefore will bear the marks of their concrete living. Marx saw that the separation of subject in enjoyment and object in contemplation which had occurred in philosophy was the abstract reflection of a similar cleavage in concrete living between the conscious existence of the philosophising class and the unconscious actions of the remainder of society. Theory and practice were sundered in consciousness because they were divided in social reality.

Thus the understanding of concrete living came to appear to Marx as primary to the understanding of the products of concrete living, of which philosophy is one. There is concrete living itself, which includes both theory and practice, and there is the theory of concrete living, which attempts to reduce to theory the concrete relation of theory and practice.

Concrete living is not solid crystal. At any one time men are doing different things and therefore stand in relation to one another. The study of these human relations in a general form is sociology. This sum of human relations is not changeless in time but changes rapidly. The general laws determining the relations of human beings at a given period, and the change of these relations from period to period, form the theory of historical materialism.

Mechanical materialism and idealism are not peculiar to philosophy but are expressed in the science, aesthetics and history of men. If poetry is approached by a mechanical materialist in psychology, it will be regarded as a form of behaviour; if by one in philosophy, as nothing but the gratification of the "aesthetic" sense inherent in matter organised in a human body. The idealist position is generally regarded as a more suitable approach to poetry, which is then explained in terms of the Beautiful, the True or the Good.

It is not very difficult for anyone genuinely interested in art to repel these attacks, although they are often as insidious as they are confused. But the same cleavage of approach is also seen in the methods of those who remain entirely within the province of art and refuse to accept any but "pure" aesthetic considerations.

The mechanical materialists of art regard the art work as the detached object, and attempt to elicit a theory of art from which the subject or artist is excluded, a theory written in terms of the technique or forms of the art. It is supposed that when the devices, technique and "abstract" qualities of the art which can be examined independently of the artist have all been extracted and reduced to theory, art will have been described in its own terms. This is the theory of "formalism", and it is evident that as a theory it corresponds in aesthetics to mechanical materialism in philosophy. Like these philosophers, the formalists are left at the end with merely subjective realities—with concepts, ideas, schemes and rules.

The idealists of art regard the art work as subjective, as the "feeling" in the mind of the appreciator or artist, and attempt to write a theory of art entirely on this basis. They believe that the aesthetic emotion is ultimately final and unquestionable, that it is wholly inside them, that any criticisms of art are personal and subjective. This is the theory of "emotionism".

Not only does this theory correspond to that of the idealists of philosophy, but like theirs it ends in a phantom materialism. As Ogden's and Richards' theories show,[1] ultimately the aesthetic emotion is reduced to coenaesthesia and this in turn is the excitation of certain nerves. Just as formalism becomes "ideas", emotionism becomes "physiology".

When Hegel had brought the contradiction to the limit where it was finally resolved on a new plane by Marx, it was still possible for a bastard compromise to arise, the compromise of positivism or phenomenalism. This solved the problem of the subject-object relation by making the relation alone real. Only phenomena existed.

This solution was no solution. Since only appearances exist, there is no reality (such as the mind or matter) which can serve to organise or value appearances and all have equal validity. As the number of appearances is infinite, those organisations of appearances, known as science, theory or truth, are arbitrary and unfounded.

In fact, positivism is always dishonest and from the very start smuggles another reality (usually the mind) into the system in order to organise it and provide some standard of validity. This reality will be concealed under some such name as "convenience" or "probability". Positivism is thus in fact generally shamefaced idealism or occasionally (in the form of agnosticism) shamefaced materialism. Positivism in philosophy marks a degradation as compared even with Hegelianism, and more so as compared with the real resolution of the problem achieved in dialectical materialism.

Positivism, therefore, also appears in aesthetics as the pure act of enjoyment of the art work, as "art for art's sake". Of course this would give absolutely no standard of discrimination between art works or between enjoyments of art works, and, therefore, in fact all aesthetic positivists smuggle in some organising principle, generally emotionist (integration of the

[1] Cf. Ogden and Richards, *Meaning of Meaning*, and Richards, *Principles of Literary Criticism.*

personality or reality of the emotion) but occasionally formal (rhythm or "form").

If well-known English works on aesthetics are examined, it will be found that even those writers who remain purely aesthetic in their approach adopt the emotionist standpoint in one part and then in another part use formalist criteria without any attempt to reconcile the obvious contradictions of the two viewpoints. But it is, in fact, rare to find an English writer on aesthetics who maintains a rigidly aesthetic approach. Generally he imports also, from outside the field of art, considerations which are psychological, historical or even biological in origin, and as some of the considerations may be idealist in their theory (as, for example, psycho-analysis) and others materialist (as, for example, physiology or Darwinian biology), and as these may be mixed with metaphysical theories drawn from sources as far apart and hopelessly in opposition as Descartes, Spinoza, Hegel and even Marx, the result is remarkable. Specialisation is useful; integration is essential; eclecticism, which avoids both, makes the worst of both worlds and is a characteristic feature of modern thought.

As regards this study of poetry, we reject from the outset any limitation to purely aesthetic categories. If anyone wishes to remain entirely in the province of aesthetics, then he should remain either a creator or an appreciator of art works. Only in this limited field is aesthetics "pure".

But as soon as one passes from the enjoyment or creation of art works to the criticism of art, then it is plain that one passes outside art, that one begins to look at it from "outside". But what is outside art? Art is the product of society, as the pearl is the product of the oyster, and to stand outside art is to stand inside society. The criticism of art differs from pure enjoyment or creation in that it contains a *sociological* component. In art criticism, values are ranged and integrated in a perspective or world-view which is a more general view of art from outside. It is an active view, implying an active living relation to art and not a cold contemplation of it, and implying therefore a view of art as active, with an explosive, energetic content. And it is a view of art, not of society or of the mind.

But physics, anthropology, history, biology, philosophy and

psychology are also products of society, and therefore a sound sociology would enable the art critic to employ criteria drawn from those fields without falling into eclecticism or confusing art with psychology or politics. There is only one sound sociology which lays bare the general active relation of the ideological products of society with each other and with concrete living—historical materialism. Historical materialism is therefore the basis of this study.

Although the other arts are discussed in their general relation to society, it was thought better to concentrate primarily on one particular art, that of poetry, because its ancient history and somewhat obsolescent appearance to-day raises crucial problems for the student of aesthetics, while, in addition, the fact that it was the art most attractive to the writer gave him a special interest in the task.

I

THE BIRTH OF POETRY

I

POETRY is one of the earliest aesthetic activities of the human mind. When it cannot be found existing as a separate product in the early literary art of a people, it is because it is then coincident with literature as a whole; the common vehicle for history, religion, magic and even law. Where a civilised people's early literature is preserved, it is found to be almost entirely poetical in form—that is to say, rhythmical or metrical. The Greek, Scandinavian, Anglo-Saxon, Romance, Indian, Chinese, Japanese and Egyptian peoples are instances of this generalisation.

This poetry is not "pure" poetry in any modern sense. We may describe it as a heightened form of ordinary speech, without committing ourselves to this as an adequate definition of poetry. This heightening is shown by a formal structure—metre, rhyme, alliteration, lines of equal syllabic length, regular stress or quantity, assonance—devices that distinguish it from ordinary speech and give it a mysterious, perhaps magical emphasis. There are repetitions, metaphors and antitheses which, because of their formality, we regard as essentially poetic.

This generalisation is commonly accepted, and there is no need to give more than a few instances. Hesiod thought it natural to use a poetical framework for a theological work and a farmers' guide. Solon cast his political and legislative maxims into metre as a matter of course. The metaphysical speculations of the Aryan race in India were versified. Egyptian astronomy and cosmogony were poetical in form. Religion spoke always in rhythm or metre, and just as the epic grew out of a poetic theogony glorifying aristocratic history, so the early agricultural ritual, cast in metrical form, became the Athenian tragedy and comedy, and finally, after various vicissitudes, survives as poetical drama to-day in the opera and the Christmas pantomime.

Ethnological researches have further shown how any words worth preserving—weather saws, farmers' wisdom, magical spells or the more refined subtleties of ritual and religion—tend among all races, in all ages, to a heightened language. This heightened language, as the people becomes self-consciously literary, is eventually set on one side as the specific vehicle of a department of literature known as Poetry, and distinguished to varying extents in different ages from the other uses of writing and speech. The form peculiar to poetry in a civilised age is the primitive form of all literature. A consideration of poetry must therefore be fundamental for a consideration of literary art.

Among primitives we usually meet with a heightening of language on formal occasions which disappears when the phrases are written down. This heightening is effected by accompanying the words with music or rude rhythm—by chanting them. It is tempting to assume, though by no means certain, that rhythmical or metrical language, before the invention of writing, was always accompanied by some rude music. Indeed one could make out a case for the supposition that music itself was generated at the same time as primitive poetry and that an aboriginal physical rhythm, expressed in gestures and leaps, in shouted words and meaningless ejaculations, and in artificial noises made by beating sticks and stones, was the common parent of dance, poetry and music. Much evidence for this theory could be found in Africa. Significant, for instance, are the Ashanti talking drums described by Rattray, which transmit messages—not by code, an abstraction impossible to a primitive people lacking letters, but by mimicking the rhythm and pitch of speech on drums, so that the drums literally talk.

However, it would be dangerous to build our foundations on a hypothesis of this sort, which, however attractive, is too sweeping to be capable of rigorous proof. All that is assumed, therefore, is the general evolution of a written civilised literature from a special form of heightened language. At first monopolising nearly all traditional literature, this heightened language, as civilisation progresses, becomes confined to a niche of its own.

In its early stages this heightened language is usually in association with music and the dance. Even such a self-conscious literature as that of Periclean Athens does not seem to have seen any real distinction between poetry and music. Every form of Greek poetry had its appropriate musical, and in the case of dramatic poetry, its choreographic, accompaniment. This liaison persists in a shadowy form to-day. Music and poetry have long existed in their own right, but the frontiers overlap in the region of song and dance music.

This differentiation and specialisation of language with increasing civilisation is of course characteristic of all civilised functions. The development of civilisation consists of a continually differentiating division of labour, which is not opposed to but is the cause of a continually integrating web of social economy. Just as the human body, because of the specialisation of its parts, is more highly integrated by an elaborate nervous system than a jelly-fish, from which parts can be severed which will continue to live, so the productive basis of society grows in elaborateness and differentiation at the same time as it becomes more and more unified. This is seen in any civilisation taken as a whole, which, as its economic basis elaborates and interpenetrates, becomes increasingly differentiated in all its cultural superstructure. Poetry, maid-of-all-work in a simple tribal economy, becomes in the rich elaboration of a modern culture an activity which exists side by side with the novel, history and the drama. This development will give us the clue, not merely to the meaning of poetry, but also, if we follow the successive trails as they open up, to the significance in man's life of all art and science. As man's society develops, we must expect his art to show a corresponding development, and therefore to reveal with increasing clarity the implicit qualities of man, society and culture which made this development possible.

2

How are we to judge whether a given society is more highly developed than another? Is it a question of biological evolution? Fisher has pointed out that there can be only one definition of "fitness" justified by biological considerations, and that is increase of numbers at the expense of the environment, including other species. In man this increase must depend on the level of economic production—the more advanced this is, the more man will dominate his environment.

But there is only one species of man—*Homo sapiens*—and his level of economic production is unequal at different points and develops in self-contained systems of various sizes. This inter-specific difference in mankind is just what separates humanity from other species, and makes biological standards no longer the most important in the very department in which we are interested—that of culture. The non-biological change of man, superimposed upon his relatively constant biological make-up during historic times, is the subject of literary history. This development is non-biological just because it is economic. It is the story of man's struggle with Nature, in which his increasing mastery of her and himself is due, not to any improvement in his inborn qualities but to improvements in systems of production, including tools, the technique of using them, language, social systems, houses, and other transmissible external structures and relations. This inheritance is the vast concrete accumulation of "human qualities" which are not transmitted somatically but socially. Mother wit is needed for their use, but it is a plastic force which inflates these developing and transmitted forms. Looked at in this way, culture cannot be separated from economic production or poetry from social organisation. They stand together in sharp opposition to the ordinary biological properties of species.

Poetry is to be regarded then, not as anything racial, national, genetic or specific in its essence, but as something economic. We expect cultural and therefore poetical development to increase with the complexity of the division of labour on which it is based. As yet no aesthetic standards have been introduced. Complexity is not an aesthetic criterion. It is a quality

associated only with division and organisation of labour.
Among primitives—peoples with whom economic production has not passed its early stage of food-gathering or
hunting and fishing—there is less differentiation in function
than among more historically-developed peoples. The only
differences of importance are sexes, age-grades and marriage
classes or totemic groups. Each member of the tribe can
perform the social, magical and economic offices proper to his
sex, age or totem, providing of course that he is not ceremonially impure or outcast. Hence it is not surprising that their
formal language and their art are equally undifferentiated, and
that poetry, or heightened language, is the common medium
of collective wisdom.

As to the exact process of differentiation, there is difference
of opinion among anthropologists. Even the Australian
aborigines possess a culture obviously resulting from a considerable period of historical development. Indeed the diffusionists see in it traces of indirect Egyptian influence. Frazer
visualises the process as one by which the clever primitive
appropriates to himself magical offices, and by this means
becomes a priest or god-king. This view is confused, for
individual cleverness could not create permanent classes, unless
they played some part in the mechanism of social production.
This in fact the god-king did, being an important class in
agricultural organisation, but Frazer does not mention this.

Extrapolating into the past, Durkheim sees the primitive
tribe as a homogeneous unit with a group consciousness, and
Lévy-Bruhl regards this group consciousness as "prelogical".
Durkheim imagines such a primitive tribe to be almost
entirely undifferentiated, so that one can consider the members
as without character or individuality except the common
impress of the tribe's collective representations, which are
coercive and overcome the individual's free thoughts.

This is an abstract conception, since no such homogeneous
tribe can be found to-day. Abstractions of this kind are limits
to which society never fully attains. If this school had a clearer
idea of the connection between economic function and genetic
make-up in creating characters or "types", they would not
confuse, as do so many other anthropologists, *differentiation*

B

with *individuation*. Individual differences are genetic, the result of a particular pack of genes. Biologically speaking, they are "variations". But social differentiation means that an individual plays a particular rôle in social production. This differentiation may be the very antithesis of individuation, for by it the individual may be pressed into a mould—whether that of miner, bank clerk, lawyer or parson—which is bound to suppress some part of his native individuality. He becomes a *type* instead of an individual. An inherited character is forced into an acquired mould. The greater the differentiation, the more specialised will be the mould and the more painful the adjustment. Psychologically, as Jung has shown, the process takes place by the exaltation of one psychic function—that most marked genetically, and therefore most likely to prove economically remunerative. The hypertrophy of this function and its accommodation to the purposes of the chosen professional type result in the wilting of the other psychic functions, which eventually become largely unconscious, and in the unconscious exercise an opposing force to the conscious personality. Hence the typical "modern" unease and neuroses. Twentieth-century civilisation, the creation of a gospel of unadulterated economic individualism, has thus finally become anti-individualistic. It opposes the full development of genetic possibilities by forcing the individual to mould a favoured function along the lines of a type whose services possess exchange-value; so that for a refreshing contrast we turn (like T. E. Lawrence) to a nomad civilisation such as that of the Bedouins. Here genetic individuality, the character of a man, is most respected and most highly developed; and yet it is just here that economic differentiation is at a minimum.

Does this mean that biological individuality is opposed to economic differentiation, and that civilisation fetters the "free" instincts—as the followers of Freud, Adler, Jung and D. H. Lawrence by implication claim? No, it is precisely economic differentiation, by the possibility of specialisation that it affords, which gives opportunity for the most elaborate development of the peculiarities or "variations" constituting the "difference" of a biological individual. But this opportunity presupposes a free choice by any individual of the complete range of economic functions. There is no such free choice in modern civilisation, because of its class structure. Not only is an individual heavily weighted in the direction of following an occupation approximately equivalent in income and cost of training to that of his parents, but also a marked bent for a slightly remunerative occupation (such as poetry) will be sacrificed to a slight bent for a markedly remunerative occupation (such as company promoting), while the career of being unemployed, the involuntary function of so many millions to-day, muffles all useful variations.

It is not civilisation as such which by its differentiation stifles genetic individuality; on the contrary, its complexity gives added scope for its development and increases the sum of "standard deviation". One incident of civilisation—the development of classes in society and the increasing restriction of choice of function for the individual—holds back the very development of individuality which the existing productive forces could allow in a more fluid system of social relations. Capitalism, by making all talents and gifts a commodity subject to the inexorable and iron laws of the "free" market, now restrains that free development of the individual which its vast productive forces could easily permit, if released. This gives rise to the complaints of the instincts tortured by civilisation which are investigated by Freud, Jung and Adler.

It is not surprising that a civilisation in which this rigidity has become pathological and individuality has almost vanished —as in the declining Egyptian and Roman Empires—collapses before "barbarians" at a lower stage of economic production in which, however, individuality has a freer rein. This class rigidity is itself the reflection of a complete disintegration of the economic foundations of a culture, in which the productive forces, like men's imprisoned characters, are wasting themselves in a sterile quarrel with the iron fetters of obsolete social relations.

Durkheim's conception of a tribe whose consciousness is solid crystal and undifferentiated, corresponding to its undifferentiated economy, in its absoluteness misses the significance of genetic individuality as the basis of economic differentiation, just as the conception of the instincts of civilised man fighting the constraints of society ignores the importance of economic differentiation as a fruitful outlet for individuality. Biologists will notice here a significant parallel to the famous dispute on their own science over "acquired" and "innate" characters.

Durkheim distinguishes the collective representations of the tribe which constitute its collective mind, from individual representations which constitute the individual mind, because of the coercive character of the former. This error is only the fundamental error of contemporary philosophy which, by its false conception of the nature of freedom, continually generates the same stale antithesis. The consciousness made possible by the development of society is not by its nature coercive; on the contrary this consciousness, expressed in science and art, is the means whereby man attains freedom. Social consciousness, like social labour, of which it is the product and auxiliary, is the instrument of man's freedom. And it is not the instincts unadapted by society which are of their essence free; on the contrary the unmodified instincts deliver man into the slavery of blind necessity and unconscious compulsion.

Yet social consciousness is sometimes felt by men as coercive —why is this? Because it is a consciousness which no longer represents social truth; because it is no longer generated freely in the whole process of social co-operation. Such a consciousness is the product of a class antagonism; it is the consciousness of a class which by the development of the division of labour and absolute property-right has become isolated from economic production, and is therefore maimed and obsolete. This consciousness now becomes the bulwark of privilege instead of the spontaneous expression of social fact, and must therefore be coercively enforced on the rest of society. Durkheim does not see that this coercive type of group consciousness is least common with a primitive people, and most common with a sophisticated civilisation.

We cannot help noticing already the connection of early poetry—poetry which is also tribal wisdom and rude chronology —with a state of society in which economic differentiation due to division of labour hardly exists. In primitive society man's

genetic individuality realises itself simply like a physical trait
—a wide forehead or a splay foot. Remembering that there
seems in all ages something simple and direct about poetry,
that good poetry can be written by the comparatively im-
mature, that it has a more personal and emotional core than
other forms of literary art, we may already guess that poetry
expresses in a special manner the genetic instinctive part of
the individual, as opposed, say, to the novel, which expresses
the individual as an adapted type, as a social character, as the
man realised in society. Such an art form as the novel could
therefore only arise in a society where economic differentiation
gives such scope for the realisation of individual differences
that it is useful and valuable to tackle man, the individual,
from this angle. There is no essential difference; it is a difference of aspect. But it is an important difference, and one to
which we will return again and again. In this sense poetry is the
child of Nature, just as the developed novel is the child of the
sophistication of modern culture.

We must repeat the warning against mechanically separating
genetic individuality from social differentiation. One is a
means of realising the other. In tragedy, in dramatic verse,
and in the epic they unite, because these flourish at a time of
rapidly-changing society, a society in which older class-
distinctions are cracking and man's genetic individuality, his
passions, his instincts, his blind desires, are the means by
which new economic functions, new differentiations, new
standard types, are being idealised and realised. Odysseus,
Oedipus and Hamlet are such figures of a social poetry, and
the problems these epics and tragedies resolve are the problems
peculiar to such a period of change.

All such problems are problems concerning the nature of
freedom, and hence tragedy poses with overwhelming poignancy
the question of necessity, although in each culture the necessity
wears a different aspect, for in each culture necessity presses
on men through different channels. The necessity that drives
on Oedipus is wholly different from that which torments
Hamlet, and this difference expresses the difference between
Athenian and Elizabethan cultures. The same necessity, but
posed in a metaphysical way and with its solution postponed

to another world, is the constant theme of religion—the problem it has set itself immediately it begins to talk of good and evil. A religion expresses by its definition of "sin" the stage of development of the society which generated it.

3

All peoples present, to ethnologists who live among them, distinct individualities, as indeed do animals. Among the Australian aborigines, as Gillen and Spencer have observed, men acquire reputations for special types of socially useful dexterity and exercise it to an extent which shows that differentiation already exists. Some division of labour has appeared but it is still mainly genetic. It is not produced by a complex which moulds each generation, and leads to the formation of a class.

Thus, as a rough type of the matrix in which poetry was born, we take the average food-gathering or hunting tribe of to-day where poetry is charm, prayer and history. This undifferentiated group shares social functions and therefore thoughts in common, and is bound by that "primitive passive sympathy" which Köhler has observed in anthropoid apes, and which McDougall considers a specific human instinct. With this group appears a heightened language, the common vehicle of all that seems worthy of preservation in the experience of men.

We must think of this language, not as it looks recorded in arid script, but as it was originally born, and as from age to age it lived its group life, accompanied by the rhythmic beating of drums, by dance and gesture, by the violent emotions of the group festival, a fountain of tradition in which not only the living group participated, but also all the ghosts of dead ancestors which are a tribe's chief strength. From this undifferentiated society the class-types proper to the priest, lawyer, administrator and soldier arise by division of labour, and, in the same way, the heightened language of the primitive corroboree splits into science, history, theology, law, economics and other appropriate divisions of cultural capital. In doing so each department evolves a special phraseology and method of literary attack which not only differs from those of other departments but also from those of spoken speech. But the departments are not watertight compartments. Their development affects each other and also spoken speech, mutually and continuously, because all are rooted in the one developing complex of real social life.

For the sake of convenience we talk of *heightened* language. But at this stage the adjective should not be allowed to carry any tincture of a value-judgment. For any given people at any given stage of evolution the precise heightening adopted can be defined in objective terms of prosody, musical or choreographic accompaniment, or the use of special words not permitted for profane purpose. As yet we have found no reason why an imposed rhythm should improve a language. The reading of almost any manual of prosody will give grounds for supposing that poetry is inferior to unhampered speech as a vehicle of expression, but we claim as yet neither superiority nor inferiority for prosody, only a qualitative difference, and if it be asked why the language should be made different, if it was not intended to make it better, an answer can be given. The function of rhythm may be purely mnemonic. This is evidently the case in rhymed wisdom such as:

> Red at night,
> The shepherd's delight.
> Red in the morning,
> The shepherd's warning,

or

> Ne'er cast a clout
> Till May is out.

It was at one time supposed that the "faculty of attention" was weak in primitive peoples, and that the rhythmic pattern held their wandering attention. Few modern anthropologists would accept this view. Attention is not a "faculty" but an instinctive component of psychic life, and if anything is more powerful where intelligence is less. A cat stalking a bird, or an Eskimo watching a seal blow-hole, show at least as much attention as a modern scientist watching an experiment. On any matter that interests them—a ritual, dramatic performance or a hunt—primitive peoples show greater capacity for sustained attention than more civilised groups. Rivers has recorded how, during his researches among the Melanesians, he found that an interrogation which left him exhausted and mentally dispersed, found his source of information still fresh and ready to keep up the supply. Yet as between two civilised people, it is almost invariably the interrogated, rather than the interrogator, who tires first.

We call the primitive's heightened language, which is as it were speech in ceremonial dress, *poetry*, and we saw how in the course of evolution it became prosaic and branched into history, philosophy, theology, the story and drama. This raises a question whether poetry was ever anything but a reflection of the undifferentiated economy in which it was born, and whether poetry in its own right has now any real justification for existence. The fact that it still continues to exist is no complete answer, since evolution is full of vestigial organs, and poetry may be one of these. Poetry has an increasingly small "public". Alone in literature, it clings tenaciously to heightened language. This might be merely the stigma of degeneration, as if poetry, like a mental deficient, still babbled in a childish tongue outgrown by the rest of the family, which has had to earn its living in an adult world.

We know there is a certain accident in the survival of poetry. Men speak, tell ancient tales, repeat bits of wisdom, and this vanishes. Poetry in its heightened language survives, and therefore we think of it as "literature", making too artificial a separation from the rest of social speech. This in turn may lead us to overlook why poetry has a heightened language, why it survives, why it has a relative changelessness and eternity.

Primitive poetry is not so much the matrix of subsequent "literature", as one pole of it. Because of its collective and traditional nature, it is the one which survives, and leads us, who see in it the sole literature of a primitive people, to imagine a kind of golden age in which even the oracles speak the language of epics.

What is the nature of this other pole? A modern mind, surveying the primitive scene, and noticing all the vague aspirations, religious phantasies, mythological cosmologies and collective emotions collecting at the pole of rhythmical language, would be disposed to think of the other pole as the scientific pole. This would be the pole of pure statement, of collections of facts uncoloured by emotion: pedigrees, astronomical calculations, censuses and all other literary productions which aim at a strong grasp of simple reality.

But science is not likely to seem the opposite of poetry to the primitive mind. He does not know of science as a branch of literature. He knows science only as a practice, a technique, a way of building boats and planting trees which can best and most easily be learned through a kind of dumb imitation, because the practice is common to all the members of a tribe. The idea of a statement devoid of prejudice and intended only to be the cold vehicle of sheer reality is quite alien to that mind. Words represent power, almost magical power, and the cold statement seems to divest them of this power and substitute a mirror-image of external reality. But what difference, save of inferiority, is there between the real object and its mirror-image? The image of reality which the primitive seeks in words is of a different kind: it is a magic *puppet image*, such as one makes of one's enemies. By operating on it, one operates on reality.

The primitive would defend in this way his lack of interest in the "photographic" scientific statement. It is a late abstraction in the history of thought, a limit to which all sciences work, but only fully achieve in their mathematic content, perhaps not even then, except in so far as it is translated into the logistic of *Principia Mathematica*.

This colourless statement is alien to a mind shaped by primitive culture, and the primitive does not understand language without a purpose. The purpose of rhythmical language is obvious—to give him that feeling of internal strength, of communication with the gods, that keeps him in good heart. The purpose of non-rhythmical language is equally obvious. There is no question of finding a function for it. The function itself, as in all biological development, created the organ and was shaped by it. The need to extend his personality, to bring it to bear on his neighbours, to bend their volitions into harmony with his, whether in flight, immobility or attack, would have given birth to the gestures and then the grunts which finally became articulate speech. Indeed Sir Richard Paget's plausible theory of the origin of human speech is based on the assumption that man, with tongue and other movable portions of his vocal organs, attempted to imitate in gesture the images he wished to impose on his fellows' minds.

The function of non-rhythmical language, then, was to persuade. Born as a personal function, an extension of one individual volition, it can be contrasted with the collective spirit of rhythmical language, which draws in primitive society all its power from its collective appearance. Poetry's very rhythm makes its group celebration more easy, as for example in an infants' class, which imposes prosody upon the multiplication table it recites, making mathematics poetical.

As with all polar opposites the two interpenetrate, but on the whole the non-rhythmical language, based on everyday speech, is the language of private persuasion, and rhythmical language, the language of collective speech, is the language of public emotion. This is the most important difference in language at the level of primitive culture.

4

Poetry is characteristically song, and song is characteristically something which, because of its rhythm, is sung in *unison*, is capable of being the expression of a collective emotion. This is one of the secrets of "heightened" language.

But why should the tribe *need* a collective emotion? The approach of a tiger, of a foe, of rain, of an earthquake will instinctively elicit a conditioned and collective response. All will be menaced, all will fear. Any instrument to produce such a collective emotion is therefore unnecessary in such situations. The tribe responds dumbly, like a frightened herd of deer.

But such an instrument is socially necessary when no visible or tangible cause exists, and yet such a cause is *potential*. This is how poetry grows out of the economic life of a tribe, and how illusion grows out of reality.

Unlike the life of beasts, the life of the simplest tribe requires a series of efforts which are not instinctive, but which are demanded by the necessities of a non-biological economic aim—for example a harvest. Hence the instincts must be harnessed to the needs of the harvest by a social mechanism. An important part of this mechanism is the group festival, the matrix of poetry, which frees the stores of emotion and canalises them in a collective channel. The real object, the tangible aim—a harvest—becomes in the festival a phantastic object. The real object is not here now. The phantastic object is here now—in phantasy. As man by the violence of the dance, the screams of the music and the hypnotic rhythm of the verse is alienated from present reality, which does not contain the unsown harvest, so he is projected into the phantastic world in which these things phantastically exist. That world becomes more real, and even when the music dies away the ungrown harvest has a greater reality for him, spurring him on to the labours necessary for its accomplishment.

Thus poetry, combined with dance, ritual, and music, becomes the great switchboard of the instinctive energy of the tribe, directing it into trains of collective actions whose immediate causes or gratifications are not in the visual field and which are not automatically decided by instinct.

It is necessary to prepare the ground for harvest. It is necessary to set out on an expedition of war. It is necessary to retrench and retract in the long scarcity of winter. These collective obligations demand from man the service of his instinctive energy, yet there is no instinct which tells him to give them. Ants and bees store instinctively; but man does not. Beavers construct instinctively; not man. It is necessary to harness man's instincts to the mill of labour, to collect his emotions and direct them into the useful, the economic channel. Just because it is economic, *i.e.* non-instinctive, this instinct must be *directed*. The instrument which directs them is therefore economic in origin.

How can these emotions be collected? Words, in ordinary social life, have acquired emotional associations for each man. These words are carefully selected, and the rhythmical arrangement makes it possible to chant them in unison, and release their emotional associations in all the vividness of collective existence. Music and the dance co-operate to produce an alienation from reality which drives on the whole machine of society. Between the moments when the emotion is generated and raised to a level where it can produce "work", it does not disappear. The tribal individual is changed by having participated in the collective illusion. He is educated—*i.e.* adapted to tribal life. The feasts or corroborees are crises of adaptation —some general and intended to last throughout life, such as the initiation or marriage ceremonies, others regularly renewed or directed to special ends, such as the harvest and war festivals or mid-winter Saturnalias.

But this collective emotion organised by art at the tribal festival, because it sweetens work and is generated by the needs of labour, goes out again into labour to lighten it. The primitive conducts such collective tasks as hoeing, paddling, ploughing, reaping and hauling to a rhythmic chant which has an artistic content related to the needs of the task, and expressing the collective emotion behind the task.

The increasing division of labour, which includes also its increasing organisation, seems to produce a movement of poetry away from concrete living, so that art appears to be in opposition to work, a creation of leisure. The poet is typically now the solitary individual; his expression, the lyric. The division of labour has led to a class society, in which consciousness has gathered at the pole of the ruling class, whose rule eventually produces the conditions for idleness. Hence art ultimately is completely separated from work, with disastrous results to both, which can only be healed by the ending of classes. But meanwhile the movement has given rise to a rich development of technique.

These emotions, generated collectively, persist in solitude so that one man, alone, singing a song, still feels his emotion stirred by collective images. He is already exhibiting that paradox of art—man withdrawing from his fellows into the world of art, only to enter more closely into communion with humanity. Once made fluid, this collective emotion of poetic art can pervade the most individual and private transactions. Sexual love, spring, a sunset, the song of the nightingale and the ancient freshness of the rose are enriched by all the complex history of emotions and experience shared in common by a thousand generations. None of these reactions is instinctive, therefore none is personal. To the monkey, or the man reared like Mowgli by a wolfish foster-mother, the rose would be something perhaps edible, a bright colour. To the poet it is the rose of Keats, of Anacreon, of Hafiz, of Ovid and of Jules Laforgue. For this world of art is the world of social emotion— of words and images which have gathered, as a result of the life experiences of all, emotional associations common to all, and its increasing complexity reflects the increasing elaboration of social life.

The emotions common to all change with the development of society. The primitive food-gathering or hunting tribe projects himself into Nature to find there his own desires. He changes himself socially to conform with Nature. Hence his art is naturalistic and perceptive. It is the vivid drawings of Palaeolithic man or the bird- and animal-mimicking dances and songs of the Australian aborigine. Its sign is the totem— the man really Nature. Its religion is mana.

The crop-raising and herd-rearing tribe is an advance on this. It takes Nature into itself and changes Nature to conform with its own desires by domestication and taming. Its art is conventional and conative. It is the arbitrary decoration of Neolithic man or the elaborate rituals of African or Polynesian tribes. Its sign is the corn-god or the beast-god—Nature really man. Its religion is one of fetishes and spirits.

The introduction of Nature into the tribe leads to a division of labour and so to the formation of chiefs, priests and ruling classes. The choreagus detaches himself from the ritual and becomes an actor—an individual. The art depicts noble persons as well as gods. The chorus becomes an epic—a collective tale about individuals—and, finally, the lyric—an individual utterance. Man, already conscious, first of his difference, and then of his unity with Nature, now becomes conscious of his internal differences, because for the first time conditions exist for their realisation.

Thus the developing complex of society, in its struggle with the environment, secretes poetry as it secretes the technique of harvest, as part of its non-biological and specifically human adaptation to existence. The tool adapts the hand to a new function, without changing the inherited shape of the hands of humanity. The poem adapts the heart to a new purpose, without changing the eternal desires of men's hearts. It does so by projecting man into a world of phantasy which is superior to his present reality precisely because it is a world of superior reality—a world of more important reality not yet realised, whose realisation demands the very poetry which phantastically anticipates it. Here is room for every error, for the poem proposes something whose very reason for poetical treatment is that we cannot touch, smell or taste it yet. But only by means of this illusion can be brought into being a reality which would not otherwise exist. Without the ceremony phantastically portraying the granaries bursting with grain, the pleasures and delights of harvest, men would not face the hard labour necessary to bring it into being. Sweetened with a harvest song, the work goes well. Just because poetry is what it is, it exhibits a reality beyond the reality it brings to birth and nominally portrays, a reality which though secondary is yet higher and more complex. For poetry describes and expresses not so much the grain in its concreteness, the harvest in its factual essence— which it helps to realise and which are the conditions for its own existence—but the emotional, social and collective complex which is that tribe's relation to the harvest. It expresses a whole new world of truth—its emotion, its comradeship, its sweat, its long-drawn-out wait and happy consummation— which has been brought into being by the fact that man's relation to the harvest is not instinctive and blind but economic and conscious. Not poetry's abstract statement—its content of facts—but its dynamic rôle in society—its content of collective emotion—is therefore poetry's *truth*.

II

THE DEATH OF MYTHOLOGY

I

WE have reached the birth of religions. This collective phantasy of poetry which passes into the individual life of each because it is secreted in the web of society, again emerges (as that web is differentiated out by division of labour) in the form of an elaborate outgrowth, a world of religion separate from the material world of terrestrial life.

Poetry is the nascent self-consciousness of man, not as an individual but as sharer with others of a whole world of common emotion. This emotion, because it is common, has for each individual an objective, and therefore pseudo-external existence. This social objectivity is confused by primitive man with material objectivity, so that the phantastic world, because it is presented to the individual "from outside" by outside manipulation, is confused with the material world against which he bumps himself. Other men confirm by their actions the objectivity of a material world; similarly they seem to confirm a like reality for the phantastic world whose sanctions they recognise.

Man's emotions are fluid and confusing. They are projected into the outside world in animism, orondism and mana at his primitive stage of culture, not because he is one with his environment, but because he has consciously separated himself from it in order to seek his desires in it by hunting or crop-gathering. Because the environment is already something consciously distinct from himself, he is concerned with locating "things" out there or in himself. Because these collective emotions, unlike a pain or a wound but like a sunset or a thunder-storm, are manifestly experienced by all, they gain the sanction of objectivity and therefore of material reality and are located "out there", in the object which arouses them.

Man enters into nature: nature becomes "animated"—endowed with man's subjective soul.

What in fact is this emotional complex of tribal poetry? Is it material reality or completely ideal illusion? It is neither. It is a *social* reality. It expresses the social relation of man's instincts to the ungathered fruit. These instincts have generated these emotions just because they have not blindly followed the necessities of the germ plasm, but have been moulded by the objective necessities of collective action to a common economic end. The phantasy of poetry is a social image.

Therefore the phantastic world of poetic ritual, myth or drama expresses a social truth, a truth about the instincts of man as they fare, not in biological or individual experience, but in associated experience. Such truths are necessarily phrased therefore in the language of the emotions. A pianola roll is pierced with holes. Those holes are real concrete entities. But they are not the music. The music is what happens when it is played. The poem is what happens when it is read.

Hence tribal poetry, and that part of religion from which it is at first indistinguishable, is man's confused knowledge of society and of his relation to it.

And magic? Man, conscious of his personal emotions, locates the irregularity in the object which stimulates them, because such conscious affects as terror and desire are due to the common experience of a tribe, are impressions common to all individuals of the tribe in relation to certain things. The emotion then seems located in these things and, because of its immediate vividness, seems the soul, the essential reality of these things. Force, the kin-aesthetic sensation of muscular effort, even up to a late date dominated the thought of science, and yet expresses this primitive animistic way of regarding nature.

Man's emotions are also in him. They therefore seem under his control. They therefore seem to be the means whereby he can dominate reality—through the emotional essence of things. He, the individual, can dominate reality by his *will*. By evoking—through charms, ceremonies and sympathetic magic—the emotions proper to the achieved act, he believes the act accomplished. It seems to him that he can control outer reality by returning into himself. So indeed he can, but only if this thought is scientific thought and, acting as a guide to action, returns out again to grapple with reality.

Because society stands as *environment* to individual man, and as *associated men* to the environment, magic and religion overlap, and blend more closely in a primitive economy, where society is only slightly developed and is therefore a thin blanket between the individual and outer reality.

Magic gives birth to science, for magic commands outer reality to conform to certain laws, and reality refuses, so that knowledge of the stubborn nature of reality is impressed on the magician. He does not try to walk upon the water with spells, or if he does, the spells fail. Rainmakers are not found in the desert, but in regions where rain sometimes comes. No magician makes spells for a winter harvest. Thus certain stubbornnesses in reality for which stronger spells are needed are gradually recognised; and so it becomes accepted that certain laws can only be overridden by mighty forces—by gods, by Fate, and eventually Fate dissolves into that very decree that these forces may not be overborne by anyone. Even Jove is subject to Fate. Fate is law. Magic has turned into its opposite, scientific determinism.

In proportion as man, by the development of economics, discovers more and more of the nature of reality, magic sets itself bolder and more elaborate tasks, and more and more is corrected by experience. It proposes to man phantastic possibilities, which man realises. But he does not realise them by magic. Without the absurd ambitions of the *shaman* and the impossible hopes of the alchemist, the modern chemistry which fulfils them would not be. Always the magician is defeated by "fate", by the inexorable determinism of things, and it is precisely when he has become conscious of that determinism, and magic has turned into science, that he is able to do in reality the things magic only feigned. Illusion thus plays into the hands of reality. Magic, promising freedom by a blind pressure of the affects, is realised when the emotional content vanishes, when the magician's eyes are opened, and he becomes conscious of the passionless causality of reality.

Magic can only exist, as a confused perception of outer

C

reality, because man is himself confused about his relations with it. He has not distinguished himself from his environment—subjective affects are confused with objective qualities. How does he clear up this confusion? Not by mere contemplation, refusing to handle the pitch lest he become soiled. He separates himself consciously from his environment by struggling with it and actively interpenetrating it, in the course of the development of economic life. When man has grasped the nature of outer reality by his constant struggle with it in economic production, then he understands clearly the distinction between environment and self, because he understands their unity. He learns that man, as a machine, is subject also to necessity, and that the universe, as a process, is the theatre of free development.

2

How can we separate religion from poetry in the childhood of the race? Both have an economic function and a social content.

We can distinguish them because we find in poetry, in all ages, a characteristic we do not find in religion the more and more clearly it emerges as "true" religion. Poetry is productive and changeful. The poetry of one age does not satisfy the next age, but each new generation (while appreciating the old poetry) demands poems which more peculiarly and specially express its own problems and aspirations. Thus we have the constant generation of a mass of songs, stories, myths, epics, novels, as a peculiarity of poetic life, which reveals art as something organic and changeful, a flower on the social plant developing and growing with the plant as a whole, because it sucks the same sap, and performs an office that benefits the whole plant.

This incessant change of poetic art is only possible because the appreciator accepts the illusion as illusory. He accepts the phantasy as expressing objective reality while immersed in the phantasy, but, once the phantasy is over, he does not demand that it be still treated as part of the real world. He does not demand a correspondence of all stories and all poetic statements as he demands a correspondence between the experiences of what he calls his real life.

The world may be fairyland in one story, hell in another. Helen may be seized by Paris in one epic, in another she may elude him and die an honoured death in Egypt. Because of this the poet and his hearer are not faced with the problem of integrating the mock worlds of poetry with the real world of everyday existence on the basis of the logical laws of thought—which by no means implies that no integration of any kind takes place. But the poem or novel is accepted as an illusion. We give to the statements of poetic art only a qualified assent, and therefore reality has no vested interest in them. Because of this there is no barrier to the fluent production which is the life of art in all ages.

This too is the characteristic of religion, but only in the early stage, when it is still merged with poetry. Religion is then mythology and shows all the spontaneous inventiveness. and recklessness of self-contradiction which is characteristic of mythology.

Why does mythology show this organic characteristic? Because it *is* organic. Because it is still organically connected with society, penetrating every pore. Native races who see an aeroplane presently have a great white bird figuring in their mythology. Early Christianity shows the same insurgent proliferation of mythology so characteristic of art.

A new form of religion begins when the mythologising era ends. The mythology is taken over, but it ossifies. Religion has become "true" religion.

It is plain that mythology, because of the contradictions it contains, can gain only a special kind of consent from the primitive. It demands from him assent to the illogical. So far Lévy-Bruhl is correct. But this same illogical assent is given by twentieth-century man to the productions of poetry and literary art. Hamlet lives for him. So do the Furies. So does the Inferno. Yet he does not believe in an after-existence in hell or in personal agents of retribution.

True, the assent is not of the same strength with twentieth-century man. The gods live for the primitive in the collective festival and the collective emotion. Because so little division of labour exists, because society is still so undifferentiated, the collective world of emotion in which the gods live penetrates every hour of the individual's life. Not so with the worlds of the theatre or the novel, which segregate themselves from the more complex social life of men. The world of twentieth-century art is more withdrawn—so much so that philosophers continually conceive of it as entirely separate, and advance "purely" aesthetic criteria—art for art's sake.

But though the strength of the assent differs, the quality is the same. The world of literary art is the world of tribal mythology become sophisticated and complex and self-conscious because man, in his struggle with Nature, has drawn away from her, and laid bare her mechanism and his own by a mutual reflexive action. Mythology with its ritual, and art with its performances, have similar functions—the adaptation of man's emotions to the necessities of social co-operation. Both embody a confused *perception* of society, but an accurate *feeling* of society. Mythology, it is true, has other functions. But we are concerned here with the poetic content of myth-ology, which afterwards separates itself out as a distinct sphere.

Because mythology so interpenetrates the daily life of the primitive, it demands no overt, formal assent. No Holy Inquisition rams it down people's throats, because in the collective festival it rises vividly from their hearts. Therefore it is flexible. It yields and changes as the tribe's relation to the environment or itself changes. The incursion of an aeroplane or a conqueror produces a corresponding adaptation of the collective mind by a recasting of the always fluid mythology. Hence mythology has a "self-righting" tendency; it remains on the whole true; it reflects accurately the collective emotional life of the tribe in its relations with the environment to the degree in which the tribe's own interpenetration of its en-vironment in economic production makes accuracy possible.

Why does the age of mythology as a real organic growth give place to the age of dogma and "true" religion when, because the mythology must now be accepted as true, it ceases to reflect the continual movement of reality and tends to become ossified and dead? Mythology ceases to grow and change and contradict itself, and is set up as something rigid and absolutely true. Faith, a virtue unknown to the primitive, is necessary for its acceptance. Faith was not necessary to the primitive because of his simple direct experience in the world of collective emotion. Faith is not necessary to the novel-reader, because of his immediate direct experience in the world of art. Faith becomes necessary when mythology ossifies into "true" religion. Faith and dogma are the signs of lack of faith and suspicion of doctrine. They show that mythology has in some way separated itself from society.

How has this come about? Only because society has separated itself from itself; because the matrix of religion has become only a part of society, standing in antagonism to the rest of society. Because of this, religion becomes isolated from the rest of society. "True" religion marks the emergence of economic classes in society. The end of mythology as a developing thing is the end of undifferentiated tribal life.

3

Marx has explained how the division of labour demands a class of overseers, village headmen, managers of irrigation works, etc., whose supervision, as differentiation proceeds, gradually passes from administration of the social means of production to that special right or privilege known as owner-ship of them. The emergence of the ownership of the means of production, as an absolute right, distinct from elective administration of them at society's behest, marks a definite stage in the development of society, the stage of class society. These class divisions rend society in twain, and yet are the only means by which society can pass to higher stages of pro-ductive development until a stage is reached generating a class whose economic circumstances enable it to end classes.

The special rôle of the members of the ruling class as supervisors gives them the means of directing into their own lives all the goods produced by society, save for those needed to ensure the continued existence of the exploited class. Originally chosen as supervisors for "intellectual" ability, their rôle, even when it becomes an absolute right and is therefore independent of mental capacity, yet demands primarily mental work, just as the working of the means of production demands primarily manual work. At the same time the privileged conditions and leisure afforded by consumption of the lion's share of the social product encourages the cultivation of thought and culture among this class, while the hard-driven and beastly condition of the other class discourages this culture.

This rapidly generates a position of increasing instability, like that which causes "critical" vibration in engineering and in the world of Nature produces in certain species a flare-up of unfavourable adaptions—enormous crests, huge hides, colossal tails and huge protuberances. Like a snowball, the organism increases its own impetus to disaster.

In the same way, once the formation of classes due to division of labour passes a certain stage, the process of cleavage is accelerated. The differentiation of the classes produces on the one hand an exploiting class more and more isolated from reality, more and more concerned with thought, with pleasure, with culture, and on the other hand an exploited class more and more isolated from thought, more and more laborious, more and more subject to circumstances.

This specialisation of function, at first beneficial, eventually becomes pathological. Thought originally separated itself from action, but it only develops by continually returning upon action. It separated from action to guide it. Once from supervisors and leaders the exploiting class turn to mere enjoyers and parasites, thought has finally separated itself from material reality, and ossifies in a barren formalism or scholasticism. And once from partners and fellow-tribesmen the exploited class turns to mere slaves, action has finally separated itself from thought and becomes blind mechanism. This is reflected in the life of society as a whole by the decay of culture, science and art in formalism and Alexandrine futility, and the decay of economic production in inefficiency and anarchy. Egypt, China, India, the declining Roman Empire, are all examples of this degeneration.

This division of the undifferentiated tribe into a class of supervisors who exercise thought, and a class of workers who only work, is reflected by a similar dichotomy in religion and art. Religion and art cease to be the collective product of the tribe, and become the product of the ruling class who impose a religion just as they impose an act.

A tribe does not give orders to its members to work; their work naturally arises from the collective functioning of the group as a whole, under the pressure of tradition and religion whose genesis we have already examined. Any problem or job can only be solved according to the interests of the tribe as a whole because the tribe is a whole. But when interests are divided, the ruling class orders the ruled. The relation is now coercive.

In the same way religion becomes dogma. As the class society forms, religion, which continues to function as a confused perception of society, produces a new and more elaborate world of phantasy but one now with a class structure. There is a supreme god in a monarchical society, or family of gods in an autocracy, or a pantheon in a state such as Egypt formed by the syncresis of various developed class units already godded. There are heavenly peers, scribes, priests and captains, corresponding to the division of the earthly ruling class.

Meanwhile the unequal division of goods and the opposed class interests have created an antagonism which divides society. There are outbreaks, rebellions and revolts which must be crushed. Absolute ownership of the means of production, not being thrown up as a natural response to the task confronting the tribe as a whole, is arbitrary, and depends therefore ultimately on violence. It is not made necessary by things and is therefore enforced by men. In the same way class religion, no longer expressing the collective adaptation of society, must be equally arbitrary. It becomes dogma. A challenge to it is a challenge to the State. Heresy is a civil crime.

The ruling class now seems to dispose of all social labour. With a highly-developed agricultural civilisation a god-king is formed at the top of the pyramid, and he seems to wield all social power. The slave by himself seems very small compared with the might of social labour wielded by the god-king. In association the slave wields a tremendous power, the power of building pyramids. But this power does not seem to the slave to be his; it seems to belong to the god-king who directs it. Hence the slave humiliates himself before his own collective power; he deifies the god-king and holds the whole ruling class as sacred. This alienation of self is only a reflection of the alienation of property which has produced it. The slave's humility is the badge not merely of his slavery, but of the power of a society developed to a stage where slavery exists and yields a mighty social power. This power is expressed at the opposite pole to the slave by the divine magnificence of the god-kings of Egypt, China, Japan, and the Sumerian, Babylonian and Accadian city-states. In a syncretic empire like that of Rome, other religions can exist beneath the State cult of the worship of the Emperor. These local cults express local forms of exploitation on which Imperialist exploitation has been imposed, and only a challenge to the god-Emperor is a challenge to Imperial exploitation and therefore a crime in Roman law. As Marx, studying the phenomenon of religion, had perceived as early as 1844: "This State, this society, produces religion—an inverted consciousness of the world— because the world is itself an *inverted world*. Of *this* world Religion is the general theory, its encyclopaedic compendium, its logic in popular form, its spiritual *point d'honneur*, its enthusiasm, its moral sanction, its solemn complement, its general consolation and justification. It is the phantastic realisation of man, *because* man possesses no true realisation. . . . Religious misery is at once the expression of real misery and a protest against that real misery."[1]

As society, increasingly rent by this class division, enters on a period of failing economy like that of the declining Roman Empire, the goods produced become less and the share-out more and more coercive. Therefore religion too becomes more and more coercive, more rigid, more tremblingly alive to heresy.

At first the ruling class believes its religion, for differentiation from a primitive mythology has only just taken place. It endeavours therefore to appropriate for itself all the goods of religion, as it is already doing those of society. The best seats

[1] Marx, *On Hegel's Philosophy of Law.*

in Heaven are taken, or—as with the early rulers of Egypt and the aristocracy of Greece—the Elysian fields are monopolised by them. But as this ruling class is challenged by a restive exploited class, the exploiting class appeases it by sharing with it its own spiritual goods, for these, unlike material goods, do not grow less for being shared. Hence in Egypt immortality was gradually extended even to slaves; and mystery religions, in the decaying Empire, offered to the meanest the deification at first peculiar to the god-Emperor. Thus the increasing misery of the exploited class is reflected in the increasing loveliness of its after-life, provided it leads the good life—*i.e.* one obedient to its employers. The harvest of phantasy, which in tribal life is always eventually reaped, is for the majority in a class society postponed to a phantastic after-life, because the real harvest also is not consumed by the majority.

This increasing consciousness of the function of religion leads to scepticism on the part of the ruling class itself, which coercively enforces a religion it no longer believes in, and itself takes refuge in an elegant idealism or esoteric philosophy.

Beneath the official religion, which can no more be changed than the system of productive relations which has generated it, lurks a whole undergrowth of "superstition" and "legend". This "superstition" is simply the mythology of the people, playing its old collective rôle, but now regarded as something vulgar and ungentlemanly by the ruling class. This superstition itself bears signs that, although collective, its collectiveness is the emasculated homogeneity of an emasculated class. It has a childishness and servility which distinguishes it from the barbarian simplicity of the creations of an undivided society. Sometimes tolerated, sometimes condemned, this superstition shows the adaptive powers of mythology, but it is now an adaptation to the rôle of an exploited class and is tainted with the idiocy of exploitation. It is full of luck and gold and magic meals and lucky sons—all the fortune this class so conspicuously lacks. But it is genuine, and believed without the need for Faith, precisely because it is not coercively enforced but is the spontaneous production of a collective spirit, and, if not of an undivided society, at least of an un-divided class. It is the poetry of religion at a time when religion itself ceases to be poetic. It is the art of the oppressed. Though it fulfils the function of poetry in adapting man's instincts to social life, it cannot be great poetry, for it is no lie that great poetry can only be written by the free. This poetry moves within the boundaries of wish-fulfilment. Its creators have too little spontaneity in their life to be greatly conscious of necessity. It is not therefore ever *tragic* poetry.

Tribal mythology was free and poetic because the un-differentiated economy of the tribe made its members' actions *relatively* free. This freedom was true freedom—the conscious-ness of necessity. The job demanded evidently such actions, and they were done spontaneously—by the individual's con-sciousness of their necessity. Of course this freedom is only relative. It reflects the limited consciousness produced by a limited economy. The divisions of class society were necessary to break the soil for a deeper consciousness and a higher freedom. But still primitive freedom is freedom—such freedom as human society in that stage can know, a stage where, because the economy is undifferentiated, the limited freedom, like the limited product, is at least equally shared by all. Poetry or poetic mythology, fluid and spontaneous, grows in such soil.

In a class society the workers do their tasks blindly as they are told by supervisors. They build pyramids but each contri-butes a stone; only the rulers know a pyramid is being built. The scale of the undertakings makes possible a greater con-sciousness of reality, but this consciousness all gathers at the pole of the ruling class. The ruled obey blindly and are unfree.

The rulers are free in the measure of their consciousness. Therefore the exercise of art becomes more and more their exclusive prerogative, reflecting their aspirations and desires. Religion is ossified by the need of maintaining a class right and therefore art now separates itself from religion. Moreover, religion is already disbelieved by the ruling class because of its openly exploitive character. The ossification of religion and the growth of scepticism in a class society is therefore always accompanied by a flourishing of art, the art of the free ruling class, an art which sucks into itself all the fluid, changeful and adaptive characteristics of primitive religion. Religion is now primarily an expression of class coercion, an expression of real misery and a protest against that real misery, while art is now the emotional expression of the ruling class. Sophisticated art of the exploiters sets itself up against the fairy tale and folk art of the exploited. Both flourish for a time side by side.

This stage itself is only transitory. For as the ruling class becomes more and more parasitic, and delegates increasingly its work of supervision, it itself becomes less free. It repeats formally the old consciousness of yesterday, yet the reality it expressed has changed. The class is no longer truly conscious of reality, because it no longer holds the reins, whose pressure on its hands guided it. The exercise of art, like the exercise of supervision, becomes a mechanical repetition by stewards and servants of the forms, functions and operations of the past. Art perishes in a Byzantine formality or an academic conventionality little better than religious dogma. Science becomes mere pedantry—little better than magic. The ruling class has become blind and therefore unfree. Poetry grows in no such soil.

The exploited class too, as this occurs, become more exploited and more miserable. The decay of economy, due to the decay of the ruling class, produces a sharper and more bitter exploitation. The cleavage between the rulers and the ruled makes the life of the ruled more mechanical and slavish, and unfree. A peasant or small landholder economy changes to an economy of overlords and serfs. To produce even "folk" art and "superstition" a limited spontaneity is necessary. Unlike a class of nomads, smallholders or burghers, a class of slaves has no art. The still essential function of adaptation is now performed for men's minds by a religion whose fixed dogmatism and superstitious faith expresses the lack of spontaneity of the ruled and their diminished consciousness.

Such collapses are not necessarily complete, for between the ruling class and the class which bears the brunt of the exploitation, other classes may develop, in turn to become the ruling class as a result of a revolution. Ossified religions are challenged by heresies which succeed precisely because they express the interests of another class formed secretly by the development of economy and soon to supersede the old. Such heresies are fought as what they are—a challenge to the very existence of the ruling class.

4

Poetry, then, cannot be separated from the society whose specifically human activity secretes it. Human activity is based on the instinctive. But those forms of human activity which are most changeful and least dependent on instinct are highest and most human. These activities, because they are based on the inheritance from generation to generation of developing forms and systems which are real and material and yet are not environmental in the biological sense, mould in a different way each new generation, which is not however mere clay, for its own inner activity drives on the movement of the external system. This contradiction between individual or natural man, and associated or civilised man, is what makes poetry necessary, and gives it its meaning and its truth. Poetry is a productive or economic activity of man. To separate it from this foundation makes its development impossible to understand.

How far do men's own estimates of the function of poetry at various times agree with our analysis? It has been generally realised by poets such as Milton, Keats, Shelley or Wordsworth that the poet as "seer", "prophet" or "teacher" had a social function of importance. This was not expressed precisely but in a metaphorical way, a *poetic* way, in which the resounding magnitude of the claims concealed a certain vagueness and poverty of social insight. Indeed the conditions of bourgeois economy—under which poetry tends, like everything else hitherto thought sacred, to become a commodity, and the poet, hitherto thought inspired, tends to become a producer for the anonymous free market—these conditions make it almost impossible for any critic who remains within the categories of bourgeois thought to penetrate the idealistic veils with which poetry in the modern era has concealed her commercialised shame.

Yet it is impossible to appeal to primitive self-appraisement, for literary criticism cannot exist among the unself-conscious primitives—the undifferentiated state of their society makes it

unnecessary. The criticism is direct and dumb and efficacious
—the valuation of the poet is expressed by the place he is
voluntarily accorded in tribal society, the valuation of the
poems by their repetition and survival.

In Athens of the fifth century B.C. a society had emerged
which, although it was still sufficiently near to primitive society
to be conscious of the social function of poetry, was also
sufficiently differentiated to be able to separate poetry off as a
distinct "sphere" of culture. Poet as producer is not yet a
trade, because Athens is not a capitalistic town engaged chiefly
in commodity production. It is a port, a centre of exchange.
The vending of poems is therefore a trade—the trade of
rhapsodist or paid reciter.

It is a society in ferment, in *revolution*. The developing com-
merce of the Aegean is producing a class of merchants and
slave-owners who are displacing the old land-owning aristocracy.
In Athens already the qualifications for rule have ceased to be
based on land, and are now based on money income; and this
brings it in sharp opposition to Sparta. From a market town
and residence of nobles which was a mere appendage of the
estates of Attica, Athens has become a town in its own right,
a centre of merchants and artisans. This is regarded by the
Hellenes as a change from an "oligarchy" to a "democracy".
As in later transitions of the same kind, it has taken place
through a transitional period of strong, centralised government
or "tyranny" like the Tudor monarchy. The "democracy" of
course is extremely qualified—it is a democracy of men of
property. The proletariat has no franchise.

Unlike a somewhat similar stage in medieval economy—the
transition from feudalism to capitalism—this is not a class
struggle which ends with the clear victory of the revolutionary
class, but rather with the "mutual ruin of the contending
classes". The struggle between the oligarchs and the democrats,
between Athens and Sparta, tears Greece to fragments. It is a
struggle between town and country, between slave latifundia
and slave-town. Because it remains within the categories of
slave-owning, it is incapable of a final solution. No decisive
stroke is possible such as the freeing of the tied serfs which
provides the basis of the bourgeois revolution. Neither class can

completely undermine the foundations of the other, for both are based on slavery, and slavery of a similar character.

Culture is still sufficiently undifferentiated for one man to survey the whole, and Plato and Aristotle stand out as philosophers surveying the whole field of culture, including that of literary art. Both were fortunate in that they were born before the class struggle was reaching its final sterile issue in Greece. There had recently been an alliance between the classes against the common enemy, Persia, and the alliance was still dynamic and creative. Plato, spokesman of the oligarchic class, reacts creatively upon Aristotle, who voices the aims and aspirations of the newer class, more tough-minded, more practical, more in touch with reality. It was no accident that Aristotle of Stagira had been so closely allied with Philip and Alexander, for if at last his class were to score a more solid triumph, and to emerge somewhere as conquerors, it was only by bursting the confines of the city and ruling beyond the bounds of Greece in the Hellenistic empires of Alexander's heirs.

Aristotle clearly sees the primitive distinction between private and public speech, between non-rhythmical and rhythmical language, between individual persuasion and collective emotion. Indeed to a Greek of that time the distinction appeared so self-evident and practical that it needed no explanation. On the one hand was the great instrument of Rhetoric whereby an individual swayed his fellow men; on the other hand the world of Poetics wherein men were collectively moved to emotion. Aristotle writes about both like a man writing a text-book on a useful and important human activity.

Aristotle's view of Rhetoric is simply this—the art of Persuasion. But he makes it clear that he has chiefly in mind the obvious and impressive public occasions where the art of persuasion is needed—in the law courts and the political assemblies. This conception of Rhetoric as individual speech used for formal "public" occasions, must be distinguished from the publicity of poetry. It is the publicity of *State* occasions where State is distinguished from society. Both are one in primitive life, but the class development of Athens has already separated the city from men. The occasions when men use the State machinery and State occasions to persuade others are by

Aristotle considered as separate from the occasions when one man speaks to others to persuade them about the normal incidents of daily life. The development of classes has made the city a "tamer of men", something already towering above society as a structure separate and imposed on it, a view which was to reach its zenith with the Hegelian conception of the absolute State. But it is already implicit in Socrates' refusal to flee the city's judgment of death. In this refusal, Socrates forecasts that the class struggle was doomed to destroy Greece, because the city could not generate a class or even one man able to look beyond the city.

Aristotle's treatment of Poetics requires a more detailed consideration. He deals with a primitive poetry already in process of differentiation in odes, dramas, epics and love poetry, and already distinct from rhetoric; and he therefore looks for a characteristic common to poetic creations which will distinguish them as a species from the non-poetic. An obvious characteristic of poetry to the Greeks was that it told some sort of story. It made some statement about the ways of gods or men or the emotions of the poet which, even though it was not true, seemed true. The epic is a false history, and the drama a feigned action. Even in love poetry the poet may justly say "I die for love of Chloe" when no Chloe exists. The essence of poetry therefore seemed to the Greeks to be illusion, a conscious illusion.

To Plato this feature of the poet's art appeared so deplorable that he would not admit poets to his Republic, or at least only if their productions were strictly censored. Such reactionary or Fascist philosophies as Plato's are always accompanied by a denial of culture, particularly contemporary culture, and Plato's contemporary culture was pre-eminently poetic. He therefore hates poetry as a philosopher even though he is charmed by it as a man. In a revolutionary period culture expresses the aspirations of the revolution or the doubts of the dispossessed. The philosophers of the dispossessed regard both the aspirations and the doubts as "dangerous", or "corrupt", and want a culture which shores up their rottenness. Such a culture idealises the past in which they were strong. This ideal past does not bear much likeness to the real past, for it is one carefully arranged so that, unlike the real past, it will not again generate the present. For Plato this past is idealised in his *Republic*, ruled by aristocrats and practising a primitive communism which is the way Plato hopes to undermine the trade by which the rival class has come to power.

The Greeks reasoned that poetry was designed to create an illusion. Evidently then the poet made something which created the illusion, even if the something was fabulous. He made stories actually visible on the stage or, as in the Homeric cycle, a history more real than the transactions of the market-place, the reallest thing in the collective life of the Hellenes. This creation the Greeks took to be the special mark of the poet. The very name etymologically was derived from "making", just as was the Anglo-Saxon word for poet—*makar*:

> To build from matter is sublimely great,
> But only gods and poets can create.

However, the Greeks did not suppose that a poet could create something out of nothing by words, which are only symbols of reality. They considered the poet created an artificial imitation of reality, a *mimesis*. For Plato the poet is essentially a man who mimics the creations of life in order to deceive his hearers with a shadow-world. In this the poet is like the Demiurge, who mocks human dwellers in the cavern of life with shadows of reality.

This theory of mimesis gives Aristotle the specific mark to differentiate between the class of rhetoric and the class of poetry. Though it is, to our modern minds, imperfect as a distinction, owing to the differentiation which has taken place in literature since then, it was an adequate distinction in Aristotle's day.

We separate poetry from the novel and drama; he did not. But the categories of literature are not eternal, any more than the classifications of systematic biology; both must change, as the objects of systematisation evolve and alter in the number and characteristics of their species. Culture changes faster than species, and cultural criticism must be correspondingly flexible. Aristotle's theory of mimesis, as our analysis will show, so far from being superficial, is fundamental for an understanding of the function and method of art.

Aristotle, with his extraverted mind turned firmly on the object, was more interested in the created thing, *e.g.* the play— than in the man who was influenced by it or who produced it. Thus his angle of attack is aesthetically correct; he does not approach literature like a psychologist or a psycho-analyst.

Plato, with the more intuitive, introverted mind, is interested in the poet and in his hearer rather than the composition itself. His conception of the productive and receptive states of the poetic mind is primitive, corresponding to the more reactionary character of Plato's thought, but behind the barbarity is a cultured snigger which is characteristically Platonic. The barbarity rather than the culture makes Plato to some extent a spokesman of the primitive view of the poet's rôle, at a time when poetry is passing, as a result of the invention of writing, from a collective to a private phase.

Plato, belonging to the older world of Athens, is not aware of the change. He does not see that the development of Hellenic economy makes the poem an object of exchange between cities and people, like Athenian vases. The poem is no longer, as in old Athenian tragedy, rooted in a collective festival where actors and audience are simultaneously plunged into an associated world of art. Neitzsche's passage from the Dionysian to the Apollonian in art has already taken place as a result of the passage of Athens from the primitive to the sophisticated, *i.e.* the differentiated. Poems are now separate from the body of society, to be enjoyed by individuals or groups separate from society. And the invention of writing, made necessary by the development of economy to a stage where records and messages were essential because records were no longer the collective memory of the tribe and men no longer lived in common, led to written poems, not simply because writing was invented, but because the needs that demanded writing also demanded that poetry be detached from the collective festival and be enjoyed by men alone. With Euripides even drama becomes a closet art. Plato, however, was only conscious of this in a general way, as expressed in his condemnation of books and the art of writing. Plato's criticisms

D

are like D. H. Lawrence's, they reach back to the past, to the time of an undifferentiated society and collective emotion. They are correct but useless because the critic is unaware that what he condemns is a product of a class differentiation rooted in economy. He does not therefore reach forward to a solution of present difficulties, but backwards to a time before those difficulties arose. But one cannot put back the clock of history.

Plato is the most charming, humane and civilised of Fascist philosophers, corresponding to a time before the aftermath of the Peloponnesian War had made reaction murderously bitter. In this respect he is an Athenian Hegel. No reactionary philosopher of to-day could attain Plato's urbanity or charm. This is Plato's conception of the poet:

Socrates is speaking to Ion, a rhapsodist:

It is a divine influence which moves you, like that which resides in the stone called Magnet by Euripides, and Heraclea by the people. For not only does this stone possess the power of attracting iron rings, but it can communicate to them the power of attracting other rings; so that you may see sometimes a long chain of rings and other iron substances, attached and suspended one to the other by this influence. And as the power of the stone circulates through all the links of the series, and attaches each to each, so the Muse, communicating through those whom she has first inspired, to all others capable of that first enthusiasm, creates a chain and a succession. For the authors of those great poems which we admire, do not attain to excellence through the rules of any art, but they utter their beautiful melodies of verse in a state of inspiration, and, as it were, possessed by a spirit not their own. Thus the composers of lyrical poetry create those admired songs of theirs in a state of divine insanity, like the Corybantes, who lose all control of their reason in the enthusiasm of the sacred dance; and, during this supernatural possession, are excited to the rhythm and harmony which they communicate to men. Like the Bacchantes who, when possessed by the god, draw honey and milk from the rivers, in which, when they come to their senses, they find nothing but simple water. For the souls of the poets, as poets tell us, have this peculiar ministration in the world. They tell us that these souls, flying like bees from flower to flower, and wandering over the gardens and the meadows and the honey-flowing fountains of the Muses, return to us laden with the sweetness of melody; and, arrayed as they are in the plumes of rapid imagination, they speak truth. For a poet is indeed a thing ethereally light, winged and sacred, nor can he compose anything worth calling poetry until he becomes inspired, and, as it were, mad, or whilst any reason remains in him. For whilst a man retains any portion of the thing called reason, he is utterly incompetent to produce poetry or to **vaticinate**. Every rhapsodist or poet, whether dithyrambic, enconiastic,

choral, epic, or iambic, is excellent in proportion to the extent of his participation in the divine influence, and the degree in which the Muse itself has
descended upon him. In other respects, poets may be sufficiently ignorant
and incapable. For they do not compose according to any art which they
have acquired, but from the impulse of the divinity within them; for did
they know any rules of criticism according to which they could compose
beautiful verses upon any one subject, they would be able to exert the same
faculty in respect to all or any other. The god seems purposely to have
deprived all poets, prophets, and soothsayers of every particle of reason and
understanding, the better to adapt them to their employment as his
ministers and interpreters; and that we, their auditors, may acknowledge
that those who write so beautifully, are possessed, and address us inspired by
the god.[1]

Here Plato shows poetry to be something different in kind
from conscious rhetoric, the art of persuasion, which, according
to Greek views, could be reduced to rule and learned. But
poetry can never be learned, for according to Plato it is not
a conscious function, with rules of criticism, but an inpouring
of the god, and he is sufficiently near to primitive culture to
place the poet beside the prophet and the soothsayer. Moreover,
according to Plato's view this inspiration is not only essential
for the poet, but for his reader. The rhapsodist who declaims
him, and the auditor who is affected by him, must also be
inspired by the god. In other words, not only the writing but
also the appreciation of poetry is an unconscious (or irrational)
function. To Plato all deception is a form of enchantment.
Poets are wizards wielding quasi-religious powers. Plato's
symbol of the magnetised rings well expresses the collective
character of primitive poetry. In contrast to Aristotle, Plato
the idealist is concerned with the enjoyment rather than the
function of poetry.

Aristotle, however, is uninterested in the poet's mind, and
does not concern himself with whether or not the creation
and appreciation of poetry is a conscious function. He judges
it by results, by poems. He systematises them, analyses them,
and reduces them to rule. He finds that mimesis is the dis-
tinguishing features of Poetics, and he investigates the rules
for producing a convincing and successful mimesis.

Unlike Plato, he goes further. As befits a philosopher who

[1] *Ion*, translated by Shelley.

studied the constitutions of existing states, he asks: what is the social function of tragedy?

His answer is well known. Its effect is *cathartic*—purging. The answer is somewhat enigmatic, once one attempts to go behind it. It is tempting to give to the expression a modern interpretation. It has been suggested, for example, that this is merely the basic therapy of Freudism—therapy by abreaction —in a Greek dress. This is on the one hand an over-refinement of Aristotle, and on the other hand a misunderstanding of what therapy by abreaction actually is. Poetic creations, like other phantasies, may be the vehicle of neurotic conflicts or complexes. But a phantasy is the cloak whereby the "censor" hides the unconscious complex. So far from this process being cathartic, it is the opposite according to Freud's own principles. To cure the basic complex by abreaction the phantasy must be stripped of its disguise and the infantile and archaic kernel laid bare.

Thus the poetic construct, according to Freud's own empirical discoveries, cannot represent an abreactive therapy even for the poet. But Aristotle visualises tragedy as cathartic for the *spectators*. Even if the poetic phantasy did have an abreactive effect on the poet, it is impossible that every spectator should have, not only the same complex as the poet, but the same associations, which analysis shows are generally highly personal.

Hence followers of Freud who suggest that Aristotle's *catharsis* is the equivalent of Freud's *therapy by abreaction*, not only misunderstand Aristotle, but also are imperfectly acquainted with the empirical discoveries on which psychoanalysis rests.

It is best, in fact, not to go behind Aristotle's simple conception, until we ourselves are clear as to the function of poetry, and can compare Aristotle's ideas with our own. How Aristotle arrived at his definition is fairly clear. On the one hand he saw tragedy arousing unpleasant emotions in the spectator—fear and anxiety and grief. On the other hand these same spectators went away feeling the better for it, so much so that they returned for more. The emotions, though unpleasant, had done them good. In the same way unpleasant medicaments do people good, and perhaps Aristotle went further, and visualised the tragedy concentrating and driving out of the mind the unpleasant emotions, just as a purge concentrates and drives out of the body the unpleasant humours. This highly practical attitude towards tragedy is not only, as it seems to me, healthy, and good literary criticism, but essentially Greek. If the tragedy did not make the Athenians feel better, in spite of its tragedy, it was bad. The tragic poet who made them weep bitterly at the fate of their fellow Hellenes in Persia was fined. A similar imposition suggests itself for our own purely sentimental war literature.

This, then, was the intelligent Greek view of literature as the differentiation, carried so far in our own culture, had just begun. On the one hand Rhetoric, the art of persuasion, exercised consciously and appreciated consciously, an art which was simply ordinary conversation hypostatised by the hypostasis of the city-state. On the other hand Poetics, a mimesis whose success in imitating reality can be judged by the poignancy of the emotions roused, just as if the auditors were really concerned in it. Both Plato and Aristotle agree here. But in Plato's view no rules can be laid down for achieving that poignancy, for both creation and appreciation come from outside the conscious mind. Plato, moreover, sees no social justification for poetry. "The emotions aroused", retorts Aristotle, "serve a social end, that of *catharsis*."

Such a definition of poetry is insufficient in literature to-day, not because the Greeks were wrong but because literature, like society, has changed. If he were systematising literature to-day, Aristotle would see that the criterion of mimesis was insufficient to distinguish the existing species of literature, not because of any weakness in the original definition, but simply because in the course of social evolution new forms of literature had arisen. Mimesis is characteristic also of the modern novel and prose play. What we nowadays agree to call poetry is something apart from both play and novel, for which fresh specific differences must be sought. Our next task is to find them.

But Aristotle's definition reminds us that we cannot, in studying the sources of poetry, ignore the study of other forms of literature, because there is a time when all literature is poetry. A materialistic approach to culture avoids any such error. We have already seen that there is a time when all religion as well as all literature is poetry. Yet as moderns, as men living in the age of capitalism, our concern must be principally with bourgeois poetry. Our next section therefore will be devoted to a general historical study of the development of modern poetry.

III

THE DEVELOPMENT OF MODERN POETRY

I

WHEN we use the word "modern" in a general sense, we use it to describe a whole complex of culture which developed in Europe and spread beyond it from the fifteenth century to the present day. There is something "modern" in Shakespeare, Galileo, Michael Angelo, Pope, Goethe and Voltaire which we can distinguish from Homer, Thales, Chaucer and Beowulf, and compare with Valery, Cézanne, James Joyce, Bergson and Einstein. This complex rests on an economic foundation. The complex itself is changeful—no epoch of human history has been so variegated and dynamic as that from the Elizabethan age to ours. But then, the economic foundations too have changed, from feudal to "industrial". This culture complex is the superstructure of the bourgeois revolution in production— a revolution whose nature was first analysed completely by Marx in *Das Kapital*. Modern poetry is *capitalist* poetry.

It is impossible to understand modern poetry unless we understand it historically—in motion. We can only bring back dead formulae from a study of poetry as static "works of art", as something frozen and ossified. This is particularly true where poetry is the organic product of a whole society violently in motion.

Yet to study the poetry of bourgeois culture as a whole during that time is a formidable task. Many nations and many languages have been caught up into the bourgeois movement, and yet it is the characteristic of poetry that it demands for its appreciation a more intimate knowledge of the language in which it was written than any other form of literature.

But as it happens, England pioneered the bourgeois revolution in economy. Italy preceded it—but its development was stifled early. America outstripped it—but only at a late date. In England alone the greater part of the bourgeois revolution unfolded itself, and from there spread to the rest of the globe.

In France during the period 1789–1871 the bourgeois revolution moved through many stages with greater speed, greater precision and more relentless logic than here, but its very speed made the ideological superstructure more confused. For a study of bourgeois literary art in general, France during that short period is more valuable; but for the study of poetry in particular; England—where the revolution unfolded itself so much more evenly and in so much more detail—is a better field.

Owing to its earlier and fuller development, the decay of English bourgeois economy arrived later than in other countries. Therefore during the period of Imperialism the poetic symptoms come to light at first in other countries than England— in France, Germany and Russia. With the exception, therefore, of this concluding period, our historical survey of modern poetry will be confined to one country—England.

It is no accident that this same country, England, has also been notable for the volume and variety of its contribution to modern poetry. The fact that England for three centuries led the world in the development of capitalism and that, during the same period, it led the world in the development of poetry, are not unrelated coincidences but part of the same movement of history.

The bourgeoisie, historically, has played a most revolutionary part.

The bourgeoisie, wherever it has got the upper hand, has put an end to all feudal, patriarchal, idyllic relations. It has pitilessly torn asunder the motley feudal ties that bound man to his "natural superiors," and has left no other nexus between man and man than naked self-interest, than callous "cash payment".

The bourgeoisie cannot exist without constantly revolutionising the means of production, and thereby the relations of production, and with them the whole relations of society. Conservation of the old modes of production in unaltered form was, on the contrary, the first condition of existence for all earlier industrial classes. Constant revolutionising of production, uninterrupted disturbance of all social conditions, everlasting uncertainty and agitation distinguish the bourgeois epoch from all earlier ones. All fixed fast-frozen relations, with their train of ancient and venerable prejudices and opinions, are swept away, all new-formed ones become antiquated before they can ossify. All that is solid melts into air, all that is holy is profaned, and man is at last compelled to face with sober senses his real conditions of life and his relations with his kind.[1]

Capitalist poetry reflects these conditions. It is the outcome of these conditions. The birth of poetry took place from the undifferentiated matrix of the tribe, which gave it a mythological character. It separated itself from religion as the art of a ruling class in class society, but, except in moments of revolutionary transition like that of fourth century B.C. Greece, this art led a quiet existence, mirroring the slow rise and slow collapse of a class "whose first condition of existence is conservation of its mode of production in unaltered form". Then a class developed beneath the quiet, stiff art of feudalism, whose vigour is first announced by the Gothic cathedrals. This class in turn became a ruling class, but one whose condition of existence is a constant revolution of the means of production, and thereby the relations of production, and with them the whole relations of society.

Its art is therefore in its essence an insurgent, non-formal, naturalistic art. Only the art of revolutionary Greece in any way forecasts the naturalism of bourgeois art. It is an art which constantly revolutionises its own conventions, just as bourgeois economy constantly revolutionises its own means of production. This constant revolution, this constant sweeping-away of "ancient and venerable prejudices and opinions", this "everlasting uncertainty and agitation", distinguishes bourgeois art from all previous art. Any bourgeois artist who even for a generation rests upon the conventions of his time becomes "academic" and his art lifeless. This same movement is characteristic of English poetry.

The characteristic of capitalist economy is that it apparently sweeps away all directly coercive relations between men— and seems to substitute for them the coercive relations of men to a thing—the State-upheld right to property. Men are no longer coercively tied together, as in a feudal society serf is tied to lord and lord to overlord, but they produce independently for the free market, and buy independently from this same free market. They take not merely their products but

---

[1] Marx and Engels, *The Communist Manifesto*, 1848.

their abilities to the market and are entitled to sell their labour-power there without let or hindrance to the highest bidder. This unreserved access to an unrestricted market constitutes the "freedom" of capitalist society.

Thus there appear to be no coercive relations between men, but only force-upheld relations between men and a thing (property) which result in relations between an individual and the market. The market seems to be a part of Nature, a piece of the environment, subject to natural "laws" of supply and demand. Its coercion does not seem the coercion of men, but of blind natural forces, like a gale or volcanic eruption.

In fact the market is nothing but the blind expression of real relations between men. These relations are relations of coercion, the characteristic exploitation of capitalism by ownership of the means of production and the purchase of the labour-power of the free labourer—free of all property but his bare hands. But just because it is a *blind* expression, it is coercive and anarchic, and acts with the violence and uncontrolled recklessness of a natural force. Just because the coercive relations between capitalist and wage-labourer are veiled, they are so much the more brutal and shameless.

Capitalist economy, therefore, is the economy of a sham individualism and a hollow freedom for the majority. The condition of existence of the bourgeois class as a ruling class, and therefore the condition of its freedom in society, is the absence of directly coercive relations between man and man. Such coercive relations are restrictions—like the feudal restrictions which bind serf to lord. But freedom without social relations would be no freedom at all, but only a blind anarchy in which society must perish. In addition, therefore, to the absence of direct relations between men, bourgeois society must include the presence of rights to absolute ownership of means of production—the right of "private property". This absolute right is maintained by the device of a coercive State power, with its laws and police and army, which, because it enforces a property right and not any direct ownership of men by men, seems to tower over society as something mediating and independent. But in fact, since this property right gives the bourgeois coercive power over the "free" labourer through ownership of the means of production, both the State and the bourgeois economy it enforces veil a coercive society for the majority, and the only freedom it contains is the freedom of the bourgeois from nature—due to his monopolisation of the social product—and his freedom from human coercion—due to the elimination from society of all directly coercive relations of a feudal character. Seen from the viewpoint of the bourgeois, bourgeois society is a free society whose freedom is due to its individualism, to its completely free market and its absence of direct social relations, of which absence the free market is the cause and expression. But to the rest of society bourgeois society is a coercive society whose individualism and free market is the method of coercion. This is the basic contradiction of bourgeois society, which must be grasped to understand the whole movement which secures the development of capitalist culture.

We saw in our analysis of the birth of poetry that early poetry is essentially collective emotion, and is born in the group festival. It is not collective emotion of an unconditioned, instinctive kind, such as might be roused in a herd by a foe; it is the collective emotion of a response conditioned by the needs of economic association.

Now bourgeois culture is the culture of a class to whom freedom—man's realisation of all his instinctive powers—is secured by "individualism". It might therefore seem that bourgeois civilisation should be anti-poetic, because poetry is collective and the bourgeois is an individualist.

But this is to take the bourgeois *at his own valuation*. Certainly we must first of all do this, whether to understand him as capitalist or as poet. The bourgeois sees himself as an heroic figure fighting a lone fight for freedom—as the individualist battling against all the social relations which fetter the natural man, who is born free and is for some strange reason everywhere in chains. And in fact his individualism does lead to a continual technical advance and therefore to an increasing freedom. His fight against feudal social relations permits a great release of the productive forces of society. His individualism expresses the particular way in which the bourgeois economy continually revolutionises the base on which it stands, until the base becomes too much for the superstructure, and bourgeois economy explodes into its opposite.

And, in the same way, the bourgeois poet sees himself as an individualist striving to realise what is most *essentially* himself by an expansive outward movement of the energy of his heart, by a release of internal forces which outward forms are crippling. This is the bourgeois dream, the dream of the one man alone producing the phenomena of the world. He is Faust, Hamlet, Robinson Crusoe, Satan and Prufrock.

This "individualism" of the bourgeois, which is born of the need to dissolve the restrictions of feudal society, causes a tremendous and ceaseless technical advance in production. In the same way it causes in poetry a tremendous and ceaseless advance in technique.

But both capitalist and poet become darker figures—first tragic, then pitiful and finally vicious. The capitalist finds his very individualism, his very freedom, producing all the blind coercion of war, anarchy, slump and revolution. The machine in its productiveness finally threatens even him. The market in its blindness becomes a terrifying force of nature.

By means of the market, capitalist constantly hurls down fellow capitalist into wage-labour or relegates him to the ranks of the temporarily privileged "salariat". The artisan of yesterday is the factory hand of to-day. The shop-owner of this year is the chain-store manager of the next year. Last week, owner of a small business—to-day, salaried executive in a large trust: this is the dramatic process whereby capitalism revolutionises itself. It does so by means of the very free market on which the bourgeois depends for freedom. This guarantee of individualism and independence produces the very opposite—trustification and dependence on finance capital. This golden garden of fair competition produces the very opposite of fairness: price-cutting, wars, cartels, monopolies, "corners" and vertical trusts. But all these evils seem to the bourgeois, who is hurled from his freedom by them, to be—as indeed they are—direct and coercive social relations and he revolts against them as the very opposite of his ideal recipe, the free market. He therefore revolts against them by demanding a fairer market and keener competition, without realising that since these ills are created by the free market, to demand the intensification of its freedom is to demand an intensification of the slavery he hates. He therefore drives on the movement he detests, and can only escape by escaping from the bourgeois contradiction. The bourgeois is always talking about liberty because it is always slipping from his grasp.

The bourgeois poet treads a similar circle. He finds the loneliness which is the condition of his freedom unendurable and coercive. He finds more and more of his experience of the earth and the universe unfriendly and a restraint on his freedom. He ejects everything social from his soul, and finds that it deflates, leaving him petty, empty and insecure.

How has this come about? We can only discover why if we now cease to take the bourgeois at his own valuation, and lay bare the economic motion of which his own valuation of himself is the reflection. At each stage the bourgeois finds that his abolition of social "restrictions" leads to their intensification. His drive towards a free market exposes the producer to a gale of competition of which the only outcome is—an amalgamation. His destruction of feudal "complexities" in favour of the simple bourgeois right to property produces all the staggering elaboration of the bourgeois law of contract. His hate of feudal rule and social coercion produces the strongly-centralised, bourgeois State with its endless petty interferences with the liberty of the individual. Individualism has produced anti-individualism. The very economy whose mission it seemed to be to sweep away all social relations, produces a society more overwhelmingly complex than any hitherto known. His demand for freedom is a negation of freedom. He is a "mirror-revolutionary" and continually revolutionises society by asking for that which will procure the opposite of what he desires.

This self-contradictory movement is given in the fundamental law of capitalist production. It is a result of the same law which brings about a price-cutting war, in which each capitalist is compelled to ruin the other, and cannot do otherwise, for to delay the final ruin of all would ensure his earlier extinction. This movement produces the continual increase of constant capital in every industry, which leads to a falling rate of interest and causes the familiar capitalist crisis, from which recovery is only possible by means of the destruction of a large portion of the country's wealth. This same contradiction produces also the expansive growth of capitalism, its constant revolution of its own basis and its eager pressure into every corner of the world. It produces a continual amalgamation and trustification which, by increasing the proportion of constant capital, only accelerates the falling rate of profit.

This contradiction in capitalist production, which secures its revolutionary expansion, also brings about its revolutionary decline. When the expansive powers of capitalism have laid the whole world under tribute, the rival centres of advance clash against each other in concealed or open war, only to intensify in each other the causes which demand expansion. The productive forces strain at the productive relations. There is a final crisis of "over-production". The falling rate of profit, unavoidable fruit of the self-contradiction in the heart of capitalism, becomes apparent in mass unemployment, a world crisis, a general slowing-down of capitalist expansion, war and revolution. And this final movement, in which the bourgeois finds his charter of freedom the very bond that seals him slave to necessity, is reflected also in his poetry, in the poetry of Imperialism and Fascism.

The very destruction of all direct social coercion—which was the condition of bourgeois pre-eminence and therefore freedom—is the condition of slavery for the exploited and expropriated, because it is the means of maintaining the indirect coercion of capital, and for this uses the openly coercive machinery of the State. Therefore in the latter part of capitalist development, the bourgeois finds himself confronted by a class, the means of whose freedom is an organisation into trade unions, which alleviate the rigour of the free market. These can only secure freedom for themselves by imposing coercive restrictions on him. This class is the class of wage-labourers or proletarians. Organising themselves first as Chartists, then in the trade unions, and finally led by a conscious political party, they impose on the capitalist coercive restrictions, such as the Factory Acts, social insurance and the like, which are the conditions of such liberty as they can obtain within the categories of bourgeois economy. But each class's freedom secures the unfreedom of the other—that is the contradiction which now comes nakedly to light.

Bourgeois production imposes on this class the means of organisation. Bourgeois economy groups its members in towns and factories and makes them work in co-operation. The bourgeois class temporarily buried the competition of men and appealed to the brotherhood of men whenever it required their alliance to overthrow feudal restrictions; and this gave the wage-labourers a political education and led to the formation of their political party.

This new class finally secures its own freedom by a complete executive organisation of itself as a *ruling* class—the Soviets of workers' power—and imposes on the bourgeoisie the final "freedom" of release from ownership of private property, thus exposing the lie on which the bourgeois notion of freedom was based. But with the disappearance of the bourgeoisie the last coercive relation rooted in the necessities of economic production disappears, and man can set about becoming genuinely free.

This proletarian revolution is accomplished in circumstances which necessarily uproot and proletarianise numbers of the bourgeoisie themselves.

"Just as therefore, at an earlier period, a section of the nobility went over to the bourgeoisie, so now a portion of the bourgeoisie goes over to the proletariat, and in particular a portion of the bourgeois ideologists who have raised themselves to the level of comprehending theoretically the historical movement as a whole. They thus defend not their present, but their future interests; they desert their own standpoint to place themselves at that of the proletariat."[1]

This desertion of the bourgeois ideologists to defend their future interests, in the final movement of capitalism, is also reflected in English poetry.

We cannot therefore understand the fundamental movement of capitalist poetry unless we understand that the self-contradiction which drives on the development of bourgeois poetry so rapidly and restlessly is the ideological counterpart of the self-contradiction which produces the increasing movement

[1] *The Communist Manifesto.*

of capitalist economy and is the cause of the growth of constant capital, the falling rate of profit, and the recurrent capitalist crisis. What the bourgeois encounters in real life necessarily moulds his ideal experience. The collective world of art is fed by the collective world of real society because it is built of materials which derive their structure and emotional associations from social use.

2

To the bourgeois, freedom is not the consciousness of necessity but the ignorance of it. He stands society on its head. To him the instincts are "free", and society everywhere puts them in chains. This is the reflection, not only of his revolt against feudal restrictions, but of capitalism's continual revolt against its own conditions, which at every step drives it forward to revolutionise its own base.

The bourgeois is a man who believes in an inborn spontaneity which secures man's free will. He does not see that man is only free in so far as he is conscious of the motive of his actions —as opposed to involuntary actions of a reflex character, like a tic, or imposed actions of a coercive character, like a shove in the back. To be conscious of the motive is to be conscious of the cause, that is of the necessity. But the bourgeois protests against this, because determinism seems to him the antithesis of free will.

To be conscious of one's motives is to will freely—to be conscious of the necessity of one's actions. Not to be conscious is to act instinctively like an animal, or blindly like a man propelled by a push from behind his back. This consciousness is not secured by introspection but by a struggle with reality which lays bare its laws, and secures to man the means of consciously using them.

The bourgeois refusal to acknowledge this is paralleled by his attitude to society, in which he thinks he is free if he is free from overt social duties—the restrictions of feudalism. But at the same time the conditions of capitalist production demand that he enter into an increasingly complex series of relations with his fellow men. These, however, appear as relations to an objective market controlled by the laws of supply and demand. He is therefore unconscious of their true nature and ignorant of the real determinism of society that has him in its grasp. Because of this he is unfree. He is ruined by blind forces; he is subject to crises, wars, and slumps and "unfair" competition. His actions produce these things, although he is undesirous of producing them.

In so far as man understands the laws of outer reality—the determinism or necessity of dead nature as expressed by science—he is free of nature, as is shown by machines. Freedom here too is the consciousness of necessity. The bourgeois is able to attain to this freedom, which is lacking in earlier class societies. But this freedom is dependent not on the individual but on associated men. The more elaborate the machine, the more elaborate the association needed to operate it. Hence man cannot be really free of nature without being conscious of the laws of association in society. And the more the possibility of being really free develops with the development of machinery, the more rudely he is reminded of the slavery of ignorance.

In so far as man understands the nature of society—the determinism which connects the consciousness and productive relations of men—he can control society's impact upon himself as an individual and on nature as a social force. But the very conditions of bourgeois economy demand that social relations be veiled by the free market and by the forms of commodity production, so that relations between men are disguised as relations to things. The bourgeois regards any demand that man should control economic production and become conscious of determinism as "interference with liberty". And it is an interference with liberty in this respect, that it interferes with his status as a bourgeois and his privileged position in society —the privilege of monopolising the products and therefore the freedom of society.

Thus the root of the bourgeois illusion regarding freedom and the function of society in relation to the instincts, is seen to spring from the essential contradiction of bourgeois economy —private (*i.e.* individual) property in social means of production. The bourgeois ceases to be bourgeois as soon as he becomes conscious of the determinism of his social relations,

E

for consciousness is not mere contemplation, it is the product of an active process. It is generated by his experiments in controlling social relations, just as his consciousness of Nature's determinism is generated by his experiments in controlling her. But before men can control their social relations, they must have the power to do so—that is, the power of control the means of production on which social relations rest. But how can they do this when these means are in the power of a privileged class?

The condition of freedom for the bourgeois class in a feudal society is the non-existence of feudal rule. The condition of the freedom of the workers in a capitalist society is the non-existence of capitalist rule. This is also the condition of freedom for a completely free society—that is, a classless society. Only in such a society can all men actively develop their consciousness of social determinism by controlling their associated destinies. The bourgeois can never accept this definition of freedom for all until he has ceased to be a bourgeois and comprehended the historical movement as a whole.

The nature of this contradiction in the bourgeois notion of freedom only becomes apparent in so far as bourgeois society decays, and the freedom of the bourgeois class becomes increasingly antagonistic to the freedom of society as a whole. The freedom of society as a whole consists in its economic products. These represent the freedom man has won in his struggle with Nature. In proportion as these expand, not only does the bourgeois feel himself free, thanks to the conditions of bourgeois economy, but the rest of society, which shares these products, is not proposed to challenge these conditions in a revolutionary way. It also—passively—accepts them. All this seems therefore a confirmation of the bourgeois theory of freedom. In these particular circumstances the bourgeois theory of freedom is true. It is an illusion, a phantastic illusion, which at this stage *realises* itself in practice. Man *is* gaining freedom by denying the relations of society, for these were feudal relations, already made obsolete by the development of bourgeois economy in their pores.

"But in order to oppress a class, certain conditions must be assured to it under which it can, at least, continue its slavish existence. The serf, in the period of serfdom, raised himself to membership in the commune, just as the petty bourgeois, under the yoke of feudal absolutism, managed to develop into a bourgeois. The modern labourer, on the contrary, instead of rising with the progress of industry, sinks deeper and deeper below the conditions of existence of his own class. He becomes a pauper, and pauperism develops more rapidly than population and wealth. And here it becomes evident that the bourgeoisie is unfit any longer to be the ruling class in society and to impose its conditions of existence upon society as an over-riding law. It is unfit to rule because it is incompetent to assure an existence to its slave within his slavery, because it cannot help letting him sink into such a state, that it has to feed him instead of being fed by him. Society can no longer live under this bourgeoisie: in other words, its existence is no longer compatible with society."[1]

At this point, therefore, the contradictory nature of the bourgeois definition of freedom discloses itself because the advance of society has objectively negated it. This, therefore, gives way to a definition of freedom as a consciousness of determinism, and the condition of man's freedom is now seen to be the consciousness and the control of the determining causes of social relations—the productive forces. But this is a revolutionary demand—a demand for socialism and pro-letarian power, and it is opposed by the bourgeois as the negation of freedom—as indeed it is for him, as a bourgeois. He attempts to speak here in the name of all society, but the revolutionary movement of the bulk of society itself denies him this right.

Thus the bourgeois illusion regarding freedom, which counterposes freedom and individualism to determinism and society, overlooks the fact that society is the instrument whereby man, the unfree individual, in association realises his freedom and that the conditions of such association are the conditions of freedom. This illusion is itself the product of a particular class-society, and a reflection of the special privilege on which bourgeois rule rests, and which rends society in two as long as it persists.

[1] *The Communist Manifesto.*

Other class societies have their own illusions. Thus a slave-owning society sees freedom, not in the absence of coercive relations, but in a special coercive relation, that of Will, in which the lord directs, and the slave blindly obeys as of right. In such a society, to be free is to will. But the development of classes sunders the consciousness that directs the will from the reality with which the slave, who blindly obeys the will, must actively struggle. The economic decline which results from this is a reflection of unfreedom due to man's increasing unconsciousness of necessity, due to the increasing inactivity of the class which is supposed to be the vehicle of consciousness and therefore of freedom. Consciousness is generated by man's active struggle with Nature, and perishes in a blind formalism once that grapple ceases.

To be aware of the true nature of freedom—that it involves consciousness of the determinism of the environment and of man and of the society which expresses their mutual struggle —to be aware of this, not as a result of contemplation, which cannot generate consciousness, but in active struggle, is to be engaged in a struggle to end those very relations of blind coercion or exploitation in society which obstruct the development of this consciousness. To end them is to end classes and give men the means of becoming truly free: but this can only happen because capitalism has evolved its own grave-digger— the class whose conditions of existence not only drive it to revolt and make possible a successful rule, but also ensure that its rule can only be based on an extinction of all rights which can produce classes.

3

The gradual self-exposure of this illusion is the history of bourgeois freedom. We may find it as tragic as Macbeth, as comic as Falstaff, as inspiring as Henry V, or as disgusting as the world of Timon of Athens—all these aspects are reflected in its development, corresponding to a similar development in the economic foundations.

Have we not said that tragedy is always a problem of necessity? To Oedipus tragedy appears in the very guise by which freedom seems to be secured in a slave-owning society

—as Will, as Fate visualised in the form of a divine, superior will overriding all human wills.[1] To Macbeth tragedy appears in the cloak of bourgeois freedom: man's free desires intemperately issuing forth are reflected back upon him by circumstances and now appear as their opposite—Macbeth's wishes, granted by the three Witches, reappear as those wishes inverted, as a contradiction of their very essence. Birnam Wood comes to Dunsinane and he is slain by a man not of woman born.

All bourgeois poetry is an expression of the movement of the bourgeois illusion, according as the contradiction rooted in bourgeois economy emerges in the course of the development of capitalism. Men are not blindly moulded by economy; economy is the result of their actions, and its movement reflects the nature of men. Poetry is then an expression of the real essence of associated men and derives its truth from this.

The bourgeois illusion is then seen to be a phantasy and bears the same relation to truth as the phantasy of primitive mythology. In the collective festival, where poetry is born, the phantastic world of poetry anticipates the harvest and, by so doing, makes possible the real harvest. But the illusion of this collective phantasy is not a mere drab copy of the harvest yet to be: it is a reflection of the emotional complex involved in the fact that man must stand in a certain relation to others and to the harvest, that his instincts must be adapted in a certain way to Nature and other men, to make the harvest possible. The collective poetry or the festival, although it is a confused perception of the real harvest-to-be, is an accurate picture of the instinctive adaptations involved in associated man's relation to the harvest process. It is a real picture of man's heart.

In the same way bourgeois poetry reflects, in all its variety and complexity, the instinctive adaptations of men to each other and Nature necessary in those social relations which will produce freedom—for freedom, as we saw, is merely's man's phantastic and poetic expression for the economic product of society which secures his self-realisation. We include of course

[1] "The God to whom men pray, whether it be Compulsion or blind Fate, or all-fathering Zeus" (Euripides).

in this economic product not merely the commercial or saleable product of society, but the cultural and emotional products, including men's consciousnesses themselves. Hence this bourgeois illusion regarding freedom, of which bourgeois poetry is the expression, has a reality in so far as it produces, by its existence, freedom—I do not mean in any formal sense, I mean that just as primitive poetry is justified by the material harvest it produces, which is the means of the primitive's freedom, so bourgeois poetry is justified by the material product of the society which generates it in its movement. But it is a freedom not of all society, but of the bourgeois class which appropriates the major part of society's products.

For freedom is not a state, it is a specific struggle with Nature. Freedom is always relative, relative to the success of the struggle. The consciousness of the nature of freedom is not the simple contemplation of a metaphysical problem, but the very act of living and behaving like a man in a certain state of society. Each stage of consciousness is definitely won; it is only maintained as a living thing by social movement—the movement we call labour. The working-out of the bourgeois illusion concerning freedom, first as a triumphant truth (the growth and increasing prosperity of capitalism), next as a gradually revealed lie (the decline and final crisis of capitalism) and finally as its passage into its opposite, freedom as the life-won consciousness of social necessity (the proletarian revolution), is a colossal movement of men, materials, emotions and ideas, it is a whole history of toiling, learning, suffering and hoping men. Because of the scale, energy and material complexity of the movement, bourgeois poetry is the glittering, subtle, complex, many-sided thing it is. The bourgeois illusion which is also the condition of freedom for the bourgeoisie is realised in their own poetry, because bourgeois poets, like the rest of the bourgeoisie, realise it in their lives, in all its triumphant emotion, its tragedy, its power of analysis and its spiritual disgust. And the consciousness of social necessity which is the condition of freedom for the people as a whole in classless, communist society, will be realised in communist poetry because it can only be realised in its essence, not as a metaphysical formula, but by living as men in a developing

communist society, which includes living as poets and readers
of poetry.

4

The bourgeois sees man's instincts—his "heart", source of
his desires and aims—as the source of his freedom. This is
false inasmuch as the instincts *unadapted* are blind and unfree.
But when adapted by the relations of society they give rise to
emotions, and these adaptations, of which the emotions are
the expression and mirror, are the means whereby the instinctive energy of man is diverted to drive the machine of
society: the machine of society, revolving, enables man to face
Nature and struggle with her, not as individual, instinctive
man but as associated, adapted men. Thus the instincts drive
on the movement which secures man's freedom. This illusion
and this truth about the relation of the instincts to freedom and
society work themselves out in bourgeois poetry and constitute
its secret energy and constant life. Thus, knowing the essence
of this bourgeois illusion to be a special belief concerning
"individualism" or the "natural man", which in turn derives
from the conditions of bourgeois economy, we cannot be
surprised that the bourgeois poet is the lonely man who,
apparently turning away from society into himself, by so doing
expresses the more strongly the essential relations of contemporary society. Bourgeois poetry is individualistic because
it expresses the collective emotion of its era.

We saw that all literary art—originally generated by the
passage of mythology into religion, so that poetry separated
itself from mythology—is rooted in freedom, and is the
expression of the spontaneity of society, which in turn is based
on the material products of society and is a kind of mould of
the emotional relations these material products demand of
associated man. It is because art is the expression of freedom
that, in a developed class-society, art is an expression of the
illusion, not of all society but only of the ruling class. In the
course of the development of the bourgeois illusion, literary
art in turn separates the story from poetry. Poetry, younger,
more primitive, more emotionally direct, is therefore in
capitalist culture concerned with the emotions struck from

the instincts—like sparks from flint—in the conditioning of instinctive responses by the relations of society. It expresses that part of the bourgeois illusion which sees the heart and the feelings of the individual man as the source of freedom, life and reality, because the freedom of society as a whole rests ultimately on the drive of those instincts whose struggle with Nature has created society. Because it must use the collective world of language it focuses all the emotional life of society in one giant "I" which is common to all, and gives to all men one breathless experience.

The story takes the reverse of the tapestry, and expresses the instincts as they emerge in society in one adapted individual. In this case the individualism of bourgeois society is expressed as an interest in men not as abstracted into one common experience, but as *characters*, as social types living in a real world.

We shall understand the way in which the bourgeois illusion gives rise to poetry, how this self-contradiction works itself out in actual poems, when we have studied (a) the development of English poetry in the persons of representative poets, schools and trends, (b) the technique of poetry, (c) its relation to language as a whole, (d) the nature of the impact of the poet's life on his environment, and (e) the particular way in which this impact gives rise to poems.

IV

ENGLISH POETS

(I. THE PERIOD OF PRIMITIVE ACCUMULATION)

I

CAPITALISM requires two conditions for its existence—masses of capital and "free"—*i.e.* expropriated—wage, labourers. Once the movement has started, capitalism generates its own conditions for further development. The sum of constant capital grows by accumulation and aggregates by amalgamation, and this amalgamation, by continually expropriating artisans and other petty bourgeoisie, produces the necessary supply of wage-labourers.

A period of primitive accumulation is therefore necessary before these conditions can be realised. This primitive accumulation must necessarily be violent and forcible, for the bourgeoisie, not yet a ruling class, has not yet created the political conditions for its own expansion: the State is not yet a bourgeois state.

In England during this period the bourgeoisie and that section of the nobility which had gone over to the bourgeoisie, seized the Church lands and treasure and created a horde of dispossessed vagrants by the enclosure of common lands, the closing of the monasteries, the extension of sheep-farming, and the final extinction of the feudal lords with their retainers. The seizure of gold and silver from the New World also played an important part in providing a base for capitalism. This movement was possible because the monarchy, in its fight with the feudal nobility, leant on the bourgeois class and in turn rewarded them for their support. The Tudor monarchs were autocrats in alliance with the bourgeoisie and bourgeoisified nobility.

In this period of primitive accumulation the conditions for

the growth of the bourgeois class are created lawlessly. To every bourgeois it seems as if his instincts—his "freedom"— are intolerably restricted by laws, rights and restraints, and that beauty and life can only be obtained by the violent expansion of his desires.

Intemperate will, "bloody, bold and resolute", without norm or measure, is the spirit of this era of primitive accumulation. The absolute-individual will overriding all other wills is therefore the principle of life for the Elizabethan age. Marlowe's Faust and Tamburlaine express this principle in its naïvest form.

This life-principle reaches its highest embodiment in the Renaissance "prince". In Italy and England—at this time leaders in primitive accumulation—life reaches its most poignant issue in the absolute will of the prince—this figure of the prince expresses most clearly the bourgeois illusion, just as in real society the prince is the necessary means of realising the conditions for bourgeois expansion. To break the moulds of feudalism and wrench from them capital requires the strength and remorselessness of an absolute monarch. Any established bound or let to the divine right of his will would be wrong, for such bounds or lets, being established and traditional, could only be feudal, and would therefore hold back the development of the bourgeois class.

Elizabethan poetry in all its grandeur and insurgence is the voice of this princely will, the absolute bourgeois will whose very virtue consists in breaking all current conventions and realising itself. That is why all Shakespeare's heroes are princely; why kingliness is the ideal type of human behaviour at this time.

Marlowe, Chapman, Greene, but above all Shakespeare, born of bourgeois parents, exactly express the cyclonic force of the princely bourgeois will in this era, in all its vigour and recklessness. Lear, Hamlet, Macbeth, Antony, Troilus, Othello, Romeo and Coriolanus, each in his different way knows no other obligation than to be the thing he is, to realise himself to the last drop, to give out in its purest and most exquisite form the aroma of self. The age of chivalry appears, not as it sees itself, but discredited and insulted, as the bourgeois class sees it, in the person of Hotspur, Falstaff and Armado, English cousins of Don Quixote.

Even the meanest creature, the empty, discredited, braggart Parolles, realises this unbounded self-realisation to be the law of his stage existence and in some sort the justification of his character:

> Simply to be the thing I am
> Shall make me live.

In this intemperate self-expression, by which they seem to expand and fill the whole world with their internal phantasmogoria, lies the significance of Shakespeare's heroes. That even death does not end their self-realisation, that they are most essentially themselves in death—Lear, Hamlet, Cleopatra and Macbeth—in this too is both the secret of their death and the solution of the tragedy.

The depth with which Shakespeare moved in the bourgeois illusion, the greatness of his grasp of human society, is shown by the fact that he is ultimately a tragedian. This unfettered realisation of human individualities involves for him the equally unfettered play of Necessity. The contradiction which is the driving force of capitalism finds its expression again and again in Shakespeare's tragedies. In *Macbeth* the hero's ambitions are realised—inverted. In *King Lear* the hero wrecks himself against the equally untempered expression of his daughters' will and also against Nature, whose necessity is expressed in a storm. The power of the storm symbolism lies in the fact that in a thunderstorm Nature seems to conduct herself, not as an inexorable machine but like a human being in an ungovernable passion. In *Othello* man's love realises the best in himself, yet by the free play of that realisation 'kills the thing it loves". In *Hamlet* the problem of a conflict of unmeasured wills is posed in yet another form—here a man's will is divided against itself, and therefore even though nothing "external" can oppose or reflect it, it can yet struggle with itself and be wrecked. This "doubleness" of a single will is aptly symbolised by the poisoned swords and goblet in which the one aim is as it were two-faced, and secures opposite ends. In *Antony and Cleopatra* and in *Romeo and Juliet* the fulfilment of the simplest and most violent instinct is to love without bound or compass, and this love ensures the destruction of the lovers, who are justified simply because the love is unbounded, and scorns patriotism, family loyalty, reason and self-interest. Such deaths are tragic because at this era the intemperate realisation of the self is heroic; it is the life principle of history. We feel that the death is necessary and is what must have been: "Nothing is here for tears".

At this stage the strength and vigour of the bourgeois depends on his cohesion as a class under monarchist leadership. In many parts already a self-armed, self-acting commune, the bourgeoisie in England, has as its spear-head the court. The court is the seat of progress, and its public collective life is for the moment the source of bourgeois progress and fountain of primitive accumulation. The court itself is not bourgeois: it seeks the coercive imposition of its will like a feudal overlord, but it can only do so by allying itself with the bourgeoisie for whom the "absoluteness" of the monarch, although feudal in its essence, is bourgeois in its outcome because it is creating the conditions for their development.

Hence we find Shakespeare, although expressing the bourgeois illusion, is an official of the court or of the bourgeois nobility. Players are the "Queen's Servants". He is not a producer for the bourgeois market or "public". He has a feudal *status*. Hence his art is not in its form individualistic: it is still collective. It breathes the collective life of the court. As player and as dramatist he lived with his audience in one simultaneous public world of emotion. That is why Elizabethan poetry is, in its greatest expression, drama—real, acted drama. It can still remain social and public and yet be an expression of the aspirations of the bourgeois class because of the alliance of the monarchy with the bourgeoisie.

Elizabethan poetry tells a story. The story always deals with men's individualities as realised in economic functions—it sees them from the outside as "characters" or "types". It sites them in a real social world seen from the outside. But in the era of primitive accumulation, bourgeois economy has not differentiated to an extent where social "types" or "norms" have been stabilised. Bourgeois man believes himself to be establishing an economic rôle by simply realising his character, like a splay foot. The instinctive and the economic seem to him naturally one: it is only the feudal rôles which seem to him forced and "artificial". Hence the story and poetry are not yet antagonistic: they have not yet separated out.

In this era of primitive accumulation all is fluid and homogeneous. Bourgeois society has not created its elaborate division of labour, to which the elaborate complexity of culture corresponds. To-day psychology, biology, logic, philosophy, law, poetry, history, economics, novel-writing, the essay, are all separate spheres of thought, each requiring specialisation for their exploration and each using a specialised vocabulary. But men like Bacon and Galileo and da Vinci did not specialise, and their language reflects this lack of differentiation. Elizabethan tragedy speaks a language of great range and compass, from the colloquial to the sublime, from the technical to the narrative, because language itself is as yet undifferentiated.

Like all great language, this has been bought and paid for. Tyndale paid for it with his life; the English prose style as a simple and clear reality, fit for poetry, was written in the fear of death, by heretics for whom it was a religious but also a revolutionary activity demanding a bareness and simplicity which scorned all trifling ornament and convention. Nothing was asked of it but the truth.

These facts combined make it possible for Elizabethan poetry to be drama and story, collective and undifferentiated, and yet express with extraordinary power the vigour of the bourgeois illusion in the era of primitive accumulation.

Shakespeare could not have achieved the stature he did if he had not exposed, at the dawn of bourgeois development, the whole movement of the capitalist contradiction, from its tremendous achievement to its mean decline. His position, his feudal "perspective", enabled him to comprehend in one era all the trends which in later eras were to separate out and so be beyond the compass of one treatment.[1] It was not enough to reveal the dewy freshness of bourgeois love in *Romeo and Juliet*, its fatal empire-shattering drowsiness in

[1] In the same way More, from his feudal perspective, anticipates the development of capitalism into communism in his *Utopia*.

Antony and Cleopatra, or the pageant of individual human wills in conflict in *Macbeth*, *Hamlet*, *Lear* and *Othello*. It was necessary to taste the dregs, to anticipate the era of *surréalisme* and James Joyce and write *Timon of Athens*, to express the degradation caused by the whole movement of capitalism, which sweeps away all feudal loyalties in order to realise the human spirit, only to find this spirit the miserable prisoner of the cash-nexus —to express this not symbolically, but with burning precision:

> Gold! yellow, glittering, precious gold! No, gods,
> I am no idle votarist. Roots, you clear heavens!
> Thus much of this will make black white, foul fair,
> Wrong right, base noble, old young, coward valiant.
> Ha! you gods, why this? What this, you gods? Why this
> Will lug your priests and servants from your sides,
> Pluck stout men's pillows from below their heads:
> This yellow slave
> Will knit and break religions; bless the accurs'd;
> Make the hoar leprosy ador'd; place thieves,
> And give them title, knee, and approbation,
> With senators on the bench; this is it
> That makes the wappen'd widow wed again;
> She, whom the spital-house and ulcerous sores
> Would cast the gorge at, this embalms and spices
> To the April day again. Come, damned earth,
> Thou common whore of mankind, that putt'st odds
> Among the rout of nations, I will make thee
> Do thy right nature.

James Joyce's characters repeat the experience of Timon:

>   all is oblique,
> There's nothing level in our cursed natures
> But direct villainy. Therefore, be abhorred
> All feasts, societies, and throngs of men!
> His semblable, yea, *himself*, Timon disdains.
> Destruction, fang mankind!

From the life-thoughts of Elizabethan poetry to the death-thoughts of the age of imperialism is a tremendous period of development but all are comprehended and cloudily anticipated in Shakespeare's plays.

Before he died Shakespeare had cloudily and phantastically attempted an *un*tragic solution, a solution without death.

Away from the rottenness of bourgeois civilisation, in the island of *The Tempest*, man attempts to live quietly and nobly, alone with his thoughts. Such an existence still retains an Elizabethan reality; there is an exploited class—Caliban, the bestial serf—and a "free" spirit who serves only for a time—Ariel, apotheosis of the free wage-labourer. This heaven cannot endure. The actors return to the real world. The magic wand is broken. And yet, in its purity and childlike wisdom, there is a bewitching quality about *The Tempest* and its magic world, in which the forces of Nature are harnessed to men's service in a bizarre forecast of communism.

2

As primitive accumulation gradually generates a class of differentiated bourgeois producers, the will of the monarch, which in its absoluteness had been a creative force, now becomes anti-bourgeois and feudal. Once primitive accumulation has reached a certain point, what is urgently desired is not capital but a set of conditions in which the bourgeois can realise the development of his capital. This is the era of "manufacture"—as opposed to factory development.

The absolute monarchy, by its free granting of monopolies and privileges, becomes as irksome as the old network of feudal loyalties. It is, after all, itself feudal. A cleavage appears between the monarchy and the class of artisans, merchants, farmers and shopkeepers.

The court supports the big landowner or noble who is already parasitic. He is allied with the court to exploit the bourgeoisie and the court rewards him with monopolies, privileges or special taxes which hamper the development of the overwhelming majority of the rising bourgeois class. Thus the absolute "will" of the prince, now that the era of primitive accumulation is over, no longer expresses the life principle of the bourgeois class at this stage.

On the contrary the court appears as the source of evil. Its glittering corrupt life has a smell of decay; foulness and mean deeds are wrapped in silk. Bourgeois poetry changes into its opposite and by a unanimous movement puritanically draws its skirt's hem away from the dirt of the court life. The movement which at first was a reaction of the Reformed Church against the Catholic Church is now a reaction of the puritan against the Reformed Church.

The Church, expressing the absolute will of the monarch and the privileges of the nobility, is met by the individual "conscience" of the puritan, which knows no law but the Spirit—his own will idealised. His thrift reflects the need, now that primitive accumulation is over, to amass the capital in which freedom and virtue inheres by "saving" and not by gorgeous and extravagant robbery.

Donne expresses the transition, for he is torn by it. At first captivated by the sensuality and glittering brilliance of the court, the insolent treatment he receives produces a movement away from it, into repentance. The movement is not complete. In Donne's last years, filled as they are with death-thoughts and magniloquent hatred of life, the pride of the flesh still tears at his heart.

Poetry, drawing away from the collective life of the court, can only withdraw into the privacy of the bourgeois study, austerely furnished, shared only with a few chosen friends, surroundings so different from the sleeping and waking publicity of court life that it rapidly revolutionises poetic technique. Crashaw, Herrick, Herbert, Vaughan—all the poetry of this era seems written by shy, proud men writing alone in their studies—appealing from court life to the country or to heaven. Language reflects the change. Lyrics no longer become something that a gentleman could sing to his lady; conceits are no longer something which could be tossed in courtly conversation. Poetry is no longer something to be roared out to a mixed audience. It smells of the library where it was produced. It is a learned man's poetry: student's poetry. Poetry is read, not declaimed: it is correspondingly subtle and intricate.

But Suckling and Lovelace write court poetry, the simple, open poetry of their class. They stand in antagonism to puritan poetry, and maintain the tradition of the Elizabethan court lyric.

The collective drama, born of the collective spirit of the court, necessarily perishes. Webster and Tourneur express the final corruption, the malignantly evil and Italiante death of the first stage of the bourgeois illusion.

3

The transitional period moves towards Revolution. The bourgeoisie revolt against the monarchy and the privileged nobility in the name of Parliament, liberty and the "Spirit" which is nothing but the bourgeois will challenging the monarchical. This is the era of armed revolution, of civil war, and with it emerges England's first openly revolutionary poet, Milton.

Revolutionary in style, revolutionary in content. The bourgeois now enters a stage of the illusion where he sees himself as defiant and lonely, challenging the powers that be. With this therefore goes an artificial and *consciously* noble style, an isolated style, the first of its kind in English poetry.

Bourgeois revolutions, which are only accomplished by the help of the people as a whole, always reach a stage where it is felt that they have "gone too far". The bourgeois demand for unlimited freedom is all very well until the "have-nots" too demand unlimited freedom, which can only be obtained at the expense of the "haves". Then a Cromwell or Robespierre steps in to hold back coercively the progress of the Revolution.

Such a bourgeois halt must always lead to a reaction, for the bourgeois class thus destroys its own mass basis. A Robespierre gives place to a Directory and then a Napoleon; at an earlier stage a Cromwell gives place to a Monk and a Charles II. The wheel does not come back full circle: there is a compromise.

To those who expressed directly the interests of the petty bourgeois, the puritans, this final stage of reaction is a betrayal of the Revolution. Therefore in *Paradise Lost* Milton sees himself as Satan overwhelmed and yet still courageous: damned and yet revolutionary. In *Paradise Regained* he has already rejected power in this world in exchange for power in the next. He scorns the temples and towers of this world; his reward is in the next because he will not compromise. Hence

F

this poem is defeatist, and lacks the noble defiance of *Paradise Lost*. In *Samson Agonistes* Milton recovers his courage. He hopes for the day when he can pull the temple down on the luxury of his wanton oppressors and wipe out the Philistine court.

Did he consciously figure himself as Satan, Jesus and Samson? Only consciously perhaps as Samson. But when he came to tackle the bourgeois theme of how man, naturally good, is everywhere bad, and to give the familiar answer—because of Adam's fall from natural goodness as a result of temptation—he was led to consider the tempter, Satan and *his* fall. And Satan's struggle being plainly a revolution, he filled it with his revolutionary experience and made the defeated revolutionary a puritan, and the reactionary God a Stuart. Thus emerged the towering figure of Satan, which by its unexpected disproportion shows that Milton's theme had "run away with him".

In *Paradise Regained* Milton tries to believe that to be defeated temporally is to win spiritually, to win "in the long run". But Milton was a real active revolutionary and in his heart he finds this spiritual satisfaction emptier than real defeat—as the unsatisfactoriness of the poem shows. In *Samson Agonistes* he tries to combine defeat and victory.

Of course the choice was already made in *Comus*, where the Lady spurns the luxury of the court and allies herself with the simple virtue of the people.

Note how already the bourgeois illusion is a little self-conscious. Milton is consciously noble—Shakespeare never. The Elizabethans are heroic: the Puritans are not, and therefore have to see themselves as heroic, in an archaistic dress. The verse and vocabulary of the Latin secretary to the Provisional Government well expresses this second movement of the illusion. The theme of the poems cannot at once be noble and in any sense contemporary. Poetry is already isolating itself from the collective daily life, which makes it inevitable that the prose "story" now begins to appear as an opposite pole.

Of course the transition from the court, like all other movements of the bourgeois illusion, is foreshadowed in Shakespeare. In *The Tempest* Prospero withdraws from corrupt court life to the peace of his island study, like a Herbert or a Milton.

Shakespeare did the same in life when he retired to Stratford-on-Avon.

But he could not write there. His magic wand was a collective one. He had broken it with the breaking of his tie with the court, and the cloud-capp'd palaces of his fancy became empty air.

4

The atmosphere of a period of reaction such as that which followed the Puritan Revolution is of good-humoured cynicism. A betrayal of the extreme "ideals" for which the battle had been fought appeared prudent to the majority. Unrestrained liberty and the free following of the spirit, excellent in theory, had in practice been proved to involve awkwardnesses for the very class of whom it was the battle-cry. The bourgeois illusion went through a new stage, that of the Restoration.

Such a movement is cynical, because it is the outcome of a betrayal of "ideals" for earthly reasons. It is luxurious because the class with whom the bourgeoisie, having taught it a sharp lesson, now allies itself again—the landed nobility—has no need of thrift to acquire capital. It is collective because there is a return to the public court life and the play. It is not decadent in any real sense; true, the bourgeoisie has allied itself with the old doomed class—but it has breathed new life into that class. Webster, expressing the decadence of the court, gives way to Dryden, expressing its vigour. And Dryden, with his turn-coat life, so different from Milton's rectitude, exactly expresses the confused and rapid movement of the bourgeoisie of the time, from Cromwell to Charles II and from James II to William III. It is a real alliance—there is no question of the feudal régime returning. James II's fate in the "Glorious Revolution" clearly shows the bourgeoisie have come to rule.

The poet must return from his study to court, but it is now a more cityfied, sensible, less romantic and picturesque court. The court itself has become almost burgher. The language shows the same passage from study to London street, from conscious heroism to business-like common sense. The sectarian bourgeois revolutionary, a little inclined to pose, becomes the sensible man-of-the-world. This is the transition from Milton to Dryden. The idealisation of compromise between rival classes as "order" and "measure"—a familiar feature of reaction—leads to the conception of the Augustan age, which passes by an inevitable transition into eighteenth-century nationalism, once the Glorious Revolution has shown that the bourgeoisie are dominant in the alliance.

The self-valuation of this age as Augustan is in fact singularly fitting. Caesar played the rôle of Cromwell, and Augustus of Charles II in a similar movement in Rome, where the knightly class at first rebelled against the senatorial and, when it became dangerous to go farther, entered on a road of compromise and reaction.

Elizabethan insurgence, the voice of primitive accumulation, thus turns into its opposite, Augustan propriety, the voice of manufacture, Individualism gives place to good taste. In its early stages bourgeoisdom requires the shattering of all feudal forms, and therefore its illusion is a realisation of the instincts in freedom. In the course of this movement, first to acquire capital, and then to give capital free play, it leans first on the monarchy—Shakespeare—and then on the common people—Milton. But because it is the interests of a class it dare not go too far in its claims, for to advance the interests of all society is to deny its own. It must not only shatter the old forms which maintained the rule of the feudal class, but it must create the new forms which will ensure its own development as a ruling class. This is the epoch of manufacture and of agricultural capitalism. Land, not factories, is still the pivot.

This epoch is not only opposed to that of primitive accumulation, it is also opposed to that of free trade. Capital exists, but the proletariat is as yet barely in existence. The numerous artisans and peasants are not yet proletarianised by the very movement of capital: the State must therefore be invoked to assist the process. The expansive period of capitalism, in which the rapid expropriation of the artisan hurls thousands of free labourers on to the market, has not yet arrived. The vagrants of Elizabethan days have already been absorbed. The bourgeoisie finds that there is a shortage of wage labour which might lead to a rise in the price of labour-power over and above its value (*i.e.* its cost of reproduction in food and rent).

Hence there is need for a network of laws to keep down wages and prices and regulate labour in order to secure for the bourgeois class the conditions of its development. It now sees the "impracticable idealism" of its revolutionary demands for liberty. Order, measure, law, good taste and other imposed forms are necessary. Tradition and convention are valuable. Now that the feudal State has perished, these restraints ensure the development of bourgeois economy. Free trade seems the very opposite of desirable to the economists of this era. The bourgeois illusion betrays itself.

5

Therefore, during the eighteenth century, bourgeois poetry expresses the spirit of manufacture, of the petty manufacturing bourgeoisie, beneath the wings of the big landowning capital-ists, giving birth to industrial capitalism. The shattering expansion of capitalism has not yet begun. Capitalism still approximates to those economies where "conservation is the first condition of existence" and has not yet fully entered into the state where it "cannot exist without constantly revolution-ising the means of production". Capitalism is revolutionising itself, but like a slowly-growing plant that needs protection, instead of like an explosion in which the ignition of one part detonates the rest. By the compromise of the Glorious Revolu-tion, the Whig landed-aristocracy were prepared to give that protection because they had themselves become bourgeoisified.

It was only when the separation between agricultural and industrial capitalism took place as a result of the rise of the factory that the cleavage between the aristocracy and the bourgeoisie began to have a determining effect on the bourgeois illusion. While the woollen-mill was still no more than a hand-loom and an appendage of the agricultural capitalist's sheep-farm there was no direct antagonism between the classes: it was only as the woollen-mill became a cotton-mill, depending for its raw material on outside sources, and when sheep-farming developed in Australia and provided wool for English mills, that there arose a direct antagonism between agricultural and industrial capitalism which expressed itself ultimately on the side of the industrialists as a demand for Free Trade and the repeal of the Corn Laws.

Pope's poetry, and its "reason"—a reason moving within singularly simple and shallow categories but moving accurately —with its polished language and metre and curt antitheses, is a reflection of that stage of the bourgeois illusion where freedom for the bourgeoisie can only be "limited"—man must be prudent in his demands, and yet there is no reason for despair, all goes well. Life is on the up-grade, but it is impossible to hurry. The imposition of outward forms on the heart is necessary and accepted. Hence the contrast between the elegant corset of the eighteenth-century heroic couplet and the natural luxuriance of Elizabethan blank verse, whose sprawl almost conceals the bony structure of the iambic rhythm inside it.

Pope perfectly expresses the ideals of the bourgeois class in alliance with a bourgeoisified aristocracy in the epoch of manufacture.

It is important to note that even now the poet himself has not been bourgeoisified as a producer. He does not produce as yet for the free market. Almost a court or aristocratic official in the time of Shakespeare, poet is a parson's or scholar's occupation in the ensuing period, and even as late as Pope he is dependent on being patronised, *i.e.* he has a "patriarchal" or "idyllic" relation to the class of whom he is the spokesman in the time of Pope.

Such an "idyllic" relation means that the poet writes non-idyllic poetry. He still sees himself as a man playing a social rôle. This was the case with the primitive poet; it remains true of Pope. It imposes on him the obligation to speak the language of his paymasters or co-poets—in the primitive tribe these constitute the whole tribe, in Augustan society these are the men who form his patron's circle—the ruling class. Johnson—dependent on subscribers—bridges the gap between the poet by status and the poet as producer. Thus poetry remains in this sense collective. It talks a more or less current language, and the poet writes for an audience he has directly in mind, to whom perhaps he will presently read his poems and so be able to watch their effect. Poetry is still for him not so much a poem—a self-subsisting work of art—as a movement from writer to reader, like the movement of emotion in a publicly-acted drama or the movement of a Muse in the minds of men. Hence he realises himself as playing a social rôle: inspirer of humanity or redresser of the follies of mankind. He has not yet become a self-conscious artist.

V

ENGLISH POETS

(II. THE INDUSTRIAL REVOLUTION)

I

THE bourgeois illusion now passes to another stage, that of the Industrial Revolution, the "explosive" stage of capitalism. Now the growth of capitalism transforms all idyllic patriarchal relations—including that of the poet to the class whose aspirations he voices—into "callous" cash-nexus.

Of course this does not make the poet regard himself as a shopkeeper and his poems as cheeses. To suppose this is to overlook the compensatory and dynamic nature of the connection between illusion and reality. In fact it has the opposite effect. It has the effect of making the poet increasingly regard himself as a man removed from society, as an individualist realising only the instincts of his heart and not responsible to society's demands—whether expressed in the duties of a citizen, a fearer of God or a faithful servant of Mammon. At the same time his poems come increasingly to seem worthy ends-in-themselves.

This is the final explosive movement of the bourgeois contradiction. The bourgeois illusion has already swayed from antithesis to antithesis, but as a result of this last final movement it can only pass, like a whirling piece of metal thrown off by an exploding flywheel, out of the orbit of the bourgeois categories of thought altogether.

As a result of the compromise of the eighteenth century, beneath the network of safeguards and protections which was characteristic of the era of manufacture, bourgeois economy developed to the stage where by the use of the machine, the steam-engine and the power-loom it acquired an enormous power of self-expansion. At the same time the "factory" broke away from the farm of which it was the handicraft adjunct and challenged it as a mightier and opposed force.

On the one hand organised labour inside the factory progressively increased, on the other hand the individual anarchy of the external market also increased. On the one hand there was an increasingly public form of production, on the other hand an increasingly private form of appropriation. At the one pole was an increasingly landless and toolless proletariat, at the other an increasingly wealthy bourgeoisie. This self-contradiction in capitalist economy provided the terrific momentum of the Industrial Revolution.

The bourgeoisie, who had found its own revolutionary-puritan ideals of liberty "extreme", and returned to the compromise of mercantilist good taste that seemed eternal reason, now again found its heart had been right, and reason wrong.

This revealed itself first of all as a cleavage between the former landed-aristocracy and the industrial bourgeoisie, expressing the rise of the factory to predominance over the farm. The landed aristocracy, and the restrictions it demanded for its growth, was now confronted by industrial capital and its demands. Capital had found an inexhaustible self-expansive power in machinery and outside sources of raw material. So far from any of the earlier forms being of value to it, they were so many restraints. The cost of labour-power could safely be left to fall to its real value, for the machine by its competition creates the proletariat it requires to serve it. The real value of labour-power in turn depends on the real value of wheat, which is less in the colonies and America than in England because there it embodies less socially-necessary labour. The Corn Laws, which safeguard the agricultural capitalist, therefore hamper the industrialist. Their interests—reconciled during the period of wage-labour shortage—are now opposed. All the forms and restraints that oppose this free expansion of the industrial bourgeoisie must be shattered. To accomplish this shattering, the bourgeoisie called to its standard all other classes, precisely as in the time of the Puritan Revolution. It claimed to speak for the people as against the oppressors. It demanded Reform and the Repeal of the Corn Laws. It attacked the Church, either as Puritan (Methodist) or as open sceptic. It attacked all laws as restrictive of equality. It advanced the conception of the naturally good man, born free but everywhere in chains. Such revolts against existing systems of laws, canons, forms and traditions always appear as a revolt of the heart against reason, a revolt of feeling and the sentiments against sterile formalism and the tyranny of the past. Marlowe, Shelley, Lawrence and Dali have a certain parallelism here; each expresses this revolt in a manner appropriate to the period.

We cannot understand this final movement of poetry unless we understand that at every step the bourgeois is revolutionary in that he is revolutionising his own basis. But he revolutionises it only to make it consistently more bourgeois. In the same way each important bourgeois poet is revolutionary, but he expresses the very movement which brings more violently into the open the contradiction against which his revolutionary poetry is a protest. They are "mirror revolutionaries". They attempt to reach an object in a mirror, only to move farther away from the real object. And what can that object be but the common object of man as producer and as poet—freedom? The poignancy of their tragedy and pessimism derives its bite from this perpetual recession of the desired object as they advance to grasp it. "La Belle Dame Sans Merci" has them all in thrall. They wake up on the cold hillside.

2

Blake, Byron, Keats, Wordsworth and Shelley express this ideological revolution, each in their different ways, as a Romantic Revolution.

Byron is an aristocrat—but he is one who is conscious of the break-up of his class as a force, and the necessity to go over to the bourgeoisie. Hence his mixture of cynicism and romanticism.

These deserters are in moments of revolution always useful and always dangerous allies. Too often their desertion of their class and their attachment to another, is not so much a "comprehension of the historical movement as a whole" as a revolt against the cramping circumstances imposed on them by their own class's dissolution, and in a mood of egoistic anarchy they seize upon the aspirations of the other class as a weapon in their private battle. They are always individualistic, romantic figures with a strong element of the *poseur*. They will the destruction of their own class but not the rise of the other, and this rise, when it becomes evident and demands that they change their merely destructive enmity to the dying class to a constructive loyalty to the new, may, in act if not in word, throw them back into the arms of the enemy. They become counter-revolutionaries. Danton and Trotsky are examples of this type. Byron's death at Missolonghi occurred before any such complete development, but it is significant that he was prepared to fight for liberty in Greece rather than England. In him the revolt of the heart against the reason appears as the revolt of the hero against circumstances, against morals, against all "pettiness" and convention. This Byronism is very symptomatic, and it is also symptomatic that in Byron it goes with a complete selfishness and carelessness for the sensibilities of others. Milton's Satan has taken on a new guise, one far less noble, petulant even.

Byron is most successful as a mocker—as a Don Juan. On the one hand to be cynical, to mock at the farce of human existence, on the other hand to be sentimental, and complain of the way in which the existing society has tortured one's magnificent capabilities—that is the essence of Byronism. It represents the demoralisation in the ranks of the aristocracy as much as a rebellion against the aristocracy. These men are therefore always full of death-thoughts: the death-thoughts of Fascism fighting in the last ditch, the death-thoughts of Jacobites; the glorification of a heroic death justifying a more dubious life. The same secret death-wishes are shown by these aristocrats if they turn revolutionary, performing deeds of outstanding individual heroism—sometimes unnecessary, sometimes useful, but always romantic and single-handed. They cannot rise beyond the conception of the desperate hero of revolution.

Shelley, however, expresses a far more genuinely dynamic force. He speaks for the bourgeoisie who, at this stage of history, feel themselves the dynamic force of society and therefore voice demands not merely for themselves but for the whole of suffering humanity. It seems to them that if only *they* could realise themselves, that is, bring into being the conditions necessary for their own freedom, this would of itself ensure the freedom of all. Shelley believes that he speaks for all men, for all sufferers, calls them all to a brighter future. The bourgeois trammelled by the restraints of the era of mercantilism is Prometheus, bringer of fire, fit symbol of the machine-wielding capitalist. Free him and the world is free. A Godwinist, Shelley believed that man is naturally good—institutions debase him. Shelley is the most revolutionary of the bourgeois poets of this era because *Prometheus Unbound* is not an excursion into the past, but a revolutionary programme for the present. It tallies with Shelley's own intimate participation in the bourgeois-democratic revolutionary movement of his day.

Although Shelley is an atheist, he is not a materialist. He is an idealist. His vocabulary is, for the first time, consciously idealist—that is, full of words like "brightness", "truth", "beauty", "soul", "aether", "wings", "fainting", "panting", which stir a whole world of indistinct emotions. Such complexes, because of their numerous emotional associations, appear to make the word indicate one distinct concrete entity, although in fact no such entity exists, but each word denotes a variety of different concepts.

This idealism is a reflection of the revolutionary bourgeois belief that, once the existing social relations that hamper a human being are shattered, the "natural man will be realised" –his feelings, his emotions, his aspirations, will all be immediately bodied forth as material realities. Shelley does not see that these shattered social relations can only give place to the social relations of the class strong enough to shatter them and that in any case these feelings, aspirations and emotions are the product of the social relations in which he exists and that to realise them a social act is necessary, which in turn has its effect upon a man's feelings, aspirations and emotions.

The bourgeois illusion is, in the sphere of poetry, a revolt. In Wordsworth the revolt takes the form of a return to the natural man, just as it does in Shelley. Wordsworth, like Shelley profoundly influenced by French Rousseauism, seeks freedom, beauty—all that is not now in man because of his social relations—in "Nature". The French Revolution now intervenes. The bourgeois demand for freedom has now a regressive tinge. It no longer looks forward to freedom by revolt but by return to the natural man.

Wordsworth's "Nature" is of course a Nature freed of wild beasts and danger by aeons of human work, a Nature in which the poet, enjoying a comfortable income, lives on the products of industrialism even while he enjoys the natural scene "unspoilt" by industrialism. The very division of industrial capitalism from agricultural capitalism has now separated the country from the town. The division of labour involved in industrialism has made it possible for sufficient surplus produce to exist to maintain a poet in austere idleness in Cumberland. But to see the relation between the two, to see that the culture, gift of language and leisure which distinguish a Nature poet from a dumb sub-human are the product of economic activity —to see this would be to pierce the bourgeois illusion and expose the artificiality of "Nature" poetry. Such poetry can only arise at a time when man by industrialism has mastered Nature—but not himself.

Wordsworth therefore is a pessimist. Unlike Shelley, he revolts regressively—but still in a bourgeois way—by demanding freedom from social relations, the specific social relations of industrialism, while still retaining the products, the freedom, which these relations alone make possible.

With this goes a theory that "natural", *i.e. conversational* language is better, and therefore more poetic than "artificial", *i.e. literary* language. He does not see that both are equally artificial—*i.e.* directed to a social end—and equally natural, *i.e.* products of man's struggle with Nature. They merely represent different spheres and stages of that struggle and are good or bad not in themselves, but in relation to this struggle. Under the spell of this theory some of Wordsworth's worst poetry is written.

Wordsworth's form of the bourgeois illusion has some kinship with Milton's. Both exalt the natural man, one in the form of Puritan "Spirit", the other in the more sophisticated form of pantheistic "Nature". One appeals to the primal Adam as proof of man's natural innocence, the other to the primal child. In the one case original sin, in the other social relations, account for the fall from grace. Both therefore are at their best when consciously noble and elevated. Milton, reacting against primitive accumulation and its deification of naïve princely desire and will, does not, however—as Wordsworth does—glorify the wild element in man, the natural primitive. Hence he is saved from a technical theory that conduces to "sinking" in poetry.

Keats is the first great poet to feel the strain of the poet's position in this stage of the bourgeois illusion, as producer for the free market. Wordsworth has a small income; Shelley, although always in want, belongs to a rich family and his want is due simply to carelessness, generosity and the impracticability which is often the reaction of certain temperaments to a wealthy home. But Keats comes of a small bourgeois family and is always pestered by money problems. The sale of his poems is an important consideration to him.

For Keats therefore freedom does not lie, like Wordsworth, in a return to Nature; his returns to Nature were always accompanied by the uncomfortable worry, where was the money coming from? It could not lie, as with Shelley, in a release from the social relations of this world, for mere formal liberty would still leave the individual with the problem of earning a living. Keats' greater knowledge of bourgeois reality therefore led him to a position which was to set the keynote for future bourgeois poetry: "revolution" as a flight *from* reality. Keats is the bannerbearer of the Romantic Revival. The poet now escapes upon the "rapid wings of poesy" to a world of romance, beauty and sensuous life separate from the poor, harsh, real world of everyday life, which it sweetens and by its own loveliness silently condemns.

This world is the shadowy enchanted world built by Lamia for her lover or by the Moon for Endymion. It is the golden-gated upper world of Hyperion, the word-painted lands of the nightingale, of the Grecian urn, of Baiae's isle. This other world is defiantly counterposed to the real world.

> "Beauty is truth, truth beauty"—that is all
> Ye know on earth, and all ye need to know.

And always it is threatened by stern reality in the shape of sages, rival powers or the drab forces of everyday. Isabella's

world of love is shattered by the two money-grubbing brothers.
Even the wild loveliness of *The Eve of St. Agnes* is a mere
interlude between storm and storm, a coloured dream snatched
from the heart of cold and darkness—the last stanzas proclaim
the triumph of decay. "La Belle Dame Sans Merci" gives her
knight only a brief delight before he wakes. The flowering
basil sprouts from the rotting head of Isabella's lover, and is
watered with her tears.

> The fancy cannot cheat so well
> As she is famed to do, deceiving elf! . . .
> Was it a vision or a waking dream?
> Fled is that music—do I wake or sleep?

Like Cortez, Keats gazes entranced at the New World of
poetry, Chapman's realms of gold, summoned into being to
redress the balance of the old, but however much voyaged in,
it is still only a world of fancy.

A new vocabulary emerges with Keats, the dominating
vocabulary of future poetry. Not Wordsworth's—because
the appeal is not to the unspoilt simplicity of the country.
Not Shelley's—because the appeal is not to the "ideas" that
float on the surface of real material life and can be skimmed
off like froth. The country is a part of the real material world,
and the froth of these metaphysical worlds is too unsubstantial
and therefore is always a reminder of the real world which
generated it. A world must be constructed which is more real
precisely because it is more unreal and has sufficient inner
stiffness to confront the real world with the self-confidence
of a successful conjuring trick.

Instead of taking, like Wordsworth and Shelley, what is
regarded as the most natural, spiritual or beautiful part of
the real world, a new world is built up out of words, as by
a mosaic artist, and these words therefore must have solidity
and reality. The Keatsian vocabulary is full of words with
a hard material texture, like tesserae, but it is an "artificial"
texture—all crimson, scented, archaic, stiff, jewelled and anti-
contemporary. It is as vivid as missal painting. Increasingly
this world is set in the world of feudalism, but it is not a feudal

world. It is a bourgeois world—the world of the Gothic
cathedrals and all the growing life and vigour of the bourgeois
class under late feudalism. Here too poetic revolution has a
strong regressive character, just as it had with Wordsworth,
but had not with the most genuinely revolutionary poet,
Shelley.

The bourgeois, with each fresh demand he makes for
individualism, free competition, absence of social relations
and more equality, only brings to birth greater organisation,
more complex social relations, higher degrees of trustification
and combination, more inequality. Yet each of these contradictory movements revolutionises his basis and creates new
productive forces. In the same way the bourgeois revolution,
expressed in the poetry of Shelley, Wordsworth and Keats,
although it is contradictory in its movement, yet brings into
being vast new technical resources for poetry and revolutionises
the whole apparatus of the art.

The basic movement is in many ways parallel to the movement of primitive accumulation which gave rise to Elizabethan
poetry. Hence there was at this era among poets a revival of
interest in Shakespeare and the Elizabethans. The insurgent
outburst of the genetic individuality which is expressed in
Elizabethan poetry had a collective guise, because it was
focused on that collective figure, the prince. In romantic
poetry it has a more artificial air as an expression of the
sentiments and the emotions of the individual figure, the
"independent" bourgeois. Poetry has separated itself from the
story, the heart from the intellect, the individual from society;
all is more artificial, differentiated and complex.

The poet now begins to show the marks of commodity-
production. We shall analyse this still further when, as in a
later date, it sets the whole key for poetry. At present the
most important sign is Keats' statement, that he could write
for ever, burning his poems afterwards. The poem has become
already an end in itself.

But it is more important to note the air of tragedy that from
now on looms over all bourgeois poetry that is worth the
adjective "great". Poetry has become pessimistic and self-
lacerating. Byron, Keats and Shelley die young. And though it

is usual to regret that they died with their best works unwritten, the examples of Wordsworth, Swinburne and Tennyson make fairly clear that this is not the case, that the personal
tragedy of their deaths, which in the case of Shelley and Byron
at least seemed sought, prevented the tragedy of the bourgeois
illusion working itself out impersonally in their poetry. For
the contradiction which secures the movement of capitalism
was now unfolding so rapidly that it exposed itself in the life-
time of a poet and always in the same way. The ardent hopes,
the aspirations, the faiths of the poet's youth melted or else
were repeated in the face of a changed reality with a stiffness
and sterility that betrayed the lack of conviction and made
them a mocking caricature of their youthful sincerity. True,
all men grow old and lose their youthful hopes—but not in
this way. A middle-aged Sophocles can speak with searching
maturity of the tragedy of his life, and at eighty he writes a
drama that reflects the open-eyed serenity of wisdom's child
grown aged. But mature bourgeois poets are not capable of
tragedy or resignation, only of a dull repetition of the faiths
of youth—or silence. The movement of history betrays the
contradiction for what it is, and yet forces the bourgeois to
cling to it. From that moment the lie has entered his soul, and
by shutting his eyes to the consciousness of necessity, he has
delivered his soul to slavery.

In the French Revolution the bourgeoisie, in the name of
liberty, equality and fraternity, revolted against obsolete
social relations. They claimed, like Shelley, to speak in the
name of all mankind; but then arose, at first indistinctly, later
with continually increasing clarity, the claim of the proletariat
also demanding liberty, equality and fraternity. But to grant
these to the proletariat means the abolition of the very
conditions which secure the existence of the bourgeois class
and the exploitation of the proletariat. Therefore the movement for freedom, which at first speaks largely in the voice of
mankind, is always halted at a state where the bourgeoisie
must betray its ideal structure expressed in poetry, forget that
it claimed to speak for humanity, and crush the class whose
like demands are irreconcilable with its own existence. Once
robbed of its mass support, the revolting bourgeoisie can

G

always be beaten back a stage by the forces of reaction. True, these forces have learned "a sharp lesson" and do not proceed too far against the bourgeoisie who have shown their power. Both ally themselves against the proletariat. Ensues an equilibrium when the bourgeoisie have betrayed their talk of freedom, and compromised their ideal structure, only themselves to have lost part of the ideal fruit of their struggle to the more reactionary forces—feudal forces, if the struggle is against feudalism, landowning and big financial forces, if the struggle is between agricultural and industrial capitalism.

Such a movement was that from Robespierre to the Directory and the anti-Jacobin movement which as a result of the French Revolution swept Europe everywhere. The whole of the nineteenth century is a record of the same betrayal, which in the life of the poets expresses itself as a betrayal of youthful idealism. 1830, 1848 and, finally, 1871 are the dates which make all bourgeois poets now tread the path of Wordsworth, whose revolutionary fire, as the result of the proletarian content of the final stage of the French Revolution, was suddenly chilled and gave place to common sense, respectability and piety.

It was Keats who wrote:

> "None can usurp this height", the shade returned,
> "Save those to whom the misery of the world
> Is misery and will not let them rest."

The doom of bourgeois poets in this epoch is precisely that the misery of the world, including their own special misery, will not let them rest, and yet the temper of the time forces them to support the class which causes it. The proletarian revolution has not yet advanced to a stage where "some bourgeois ideologists, comprehending the historical movement as a whole", can ally themselves with it and really speak for suffering humanity and for a class which is the majority now and the whole world of men to-morrow. They speak only for a class that is creating the world of to-morrow willy-nilly, and at each step draws back and betrays its instinctive aspirations because of its conscious knowledge that this world of to-morrow it is creating, *cannot include itself.*

ENGLISH POETS

(III. The Decline of Capitalism)

I

ARNOLD, Swinburne, Tennyson and Browning, each in his own way, illustrate the movement of the bourgeois illusion in this "tragic" stage of its history.

Tennyson's Keatsian world is shattered as soon as he attempts to compromise between the world of beauty and the real world of misery which will not let him rest. Only the elegiac *In Memoriam*, with its profound pessimism, the most genuinely pessimistic poem in English up to this date, in any way successfully mirrors contemporary problems in contemporary terms.

Like Darwin, and even more Darwin's followers, he projects the conditions of capitalist production into Nature (individual struggle for existence) and then reflects this struggle, intensified by its instinctive and therefore unalterable blindness, back into society, so that God—symbol of the internal forces of society—seems captive to Nature—symbol of the external environment of society:

> Are God and Nature then at strife,
>   That Nature lends such evil dreams?
>   So careful of the type she seems,
> So careless of the single life;
>
> That I, considering everywhere
>   Her secret meaning in her deeds,
>   And finding that of fifty seeds
> She often brings but one to bear,
>
> I falter where I firmly trod. . . .

The unconscious ruthlessness of Tennyson's "Nature"
in fact only reflects the ruthlessness of a society in which
capitalist is continually hurling down fellow-capitalist into
the proletarian abyss:

> "So careful of the type?" but no.
> From scarped cliff and quarried stone
> She cries: "A thousand types are gone:
> I care for nothing, all shall go."
>
> . . . No more! A monster then, a dream,
> A discord. Dragons of the prime
> Which tear each other in the slime
> Were mellow music matched with him.
>
> O life as futile, then, as frail!
> O for thy voice to soothe and bless!
> What hope of answer, or redress
> Behind the veil, behind the veil?

Browning revolts from the drab present not to the future
but to the glories of the virile Italian springtime of the bourgeoisie. Never before had that vigour been given in English
poetry so deep a colouring. But his vocabulary has a foggy
verbalism which is a reflection of his intellectual dishonesty
in dealing with real contemporary problems. To Tennyson
the Keatsian world of romance, to Browning the Italian
springtime; both are revolting backwards, trying to escape
from the contradiction of the class for whom they speak.
Browning dealing with contemporary problems, can produce
no higher poetry than that of Mr. Sludge or Bishop Blougram.
Yet he too in his eager youth could reproach an older bourgeois
poet for following the familiar round of reaction:

> Shakespeare was of us, Milton was for us,
> Burns, Shelley was with us—They watch from their graves!
> He alone breaks from the van and the freemen,
> He alone sinks to the rear and the slaves!

Swinburne's poetry is Shelley's world of immanent light
and beauty made more separate by being stiffened with
something of the materiality and hypnotic heaviness of Keats'
world. Fate, whether as Hertha or the Nemesis of *Atalanta in*

Calydon, is no longer tragic, but sad, sad as the death of Baudelaire. Swinburne is profoundly moved by the appeal of the contemporary bourgeois-democratic revolutions taking place all over Europe (1848–1871), but the purely verbal and shallow character of his response reflects the essential shallowness of all such movements in this late era when, owing to the development of the proletariat, they almost instantly negate themselves.

Arnold's poems breathe the now characteristic "pessimism" of the bourgeois illusion, which is now working out its final and (to itself) tragic stages. Arnold battles against the Philistine, but he has an uneasy suspicion that he is doomed to lose. And in fact he is, for he fights his mirror reflection. As long as he moves within the categories of bourgeois society his own movement produces the Philistine; he drives on the movement which generates Philistine and poet, by separating the poet from society.

2

The next phase of bourgeois poetry is therefore that of "commodity-fetishism"—or "art for art's sake"—and is given in the false position of the bourgeois poet as producer for the market, a position forced on him by the development of bourgeois economy. As soon as the pessimism of Arnold and the young Tennyson, and the even sadder optimism of Browning and Swinburne and the old Tennyson when dealing with the contemporary scene, made it inevitable that the poet quit the contemporary scene, it was equally inevitable that the poet should fall a victim to commodity-fetishism. This meant a movement which would completely separate the world of art from the world of reality and, in doing so, separate it from the source of art itself so that the work would burst like a bubble just when it seemed most self-secure.

Engels in *Anti-Dühring* very clearly explains the characteristic of every society based on commodity-production:

[It] has the peculiarity that in it the producers have lost control of their own social relationships. Each produces for himself, with the means of production which happen to be at his disposal and in order to satisfy his individual needs through the medium of exchange. No one knows how much of the article he produces is coming on the market, or how much demand there is for it; no one knows whether his individual product will meet a real need, whether he will cover his costs or even be able to sell at all. Anarchy reigns in social production. But commodity production, like all other forms of production, has its own laws, which are inherent and inseparable from it; and these laws assert themselves in spite of anarchy, in and through anarchy. . . . They assert themselves, therefore, apart from the producers and against the producers, as the natural laws of their form of production, working blindly. *The product dominates the producers.*

Engels contrasts this with the older and more universal method of production for use instead of exchange. Here the origin and end of production are clearly seen. All are part of the one social act, and the product is only valued in so far as it is of use to the society which produces it. In such a society the poem as such derives its value from its collective appearance, from the effect it has on the hearts of its hearers and the impact, direct and evident, on the life of the tribe.

In capitalist production, which is commodity production *in excelsis*, all this is altered. Everyone produces blindly for a market whose laws are unfathomable, although they assert themselves with iron rigidity. The impact of the commodity upon the life of society cannot be measured or seen. "Man has lost control of his social relationships." The whole elaborate warp and woof of capitalism, a complex web spun in anarchy, makes this helplessness inevitable.

To the poet the bourgeois market appears as the "public". The invention and development of printing and publishing was part of the development of the universal bourgeois free market. Just as the development of this market (by the extension of colonisation and transport and exchange facilities) made it possible for a man to produce for places whose very names he did not know, much less their location, so the poet now writes for men of whose existence he is ignorant, whose social life, whose whole mode of being is strange to him. The market is for him "The Public"—blind, strange, passive.

This leads to what Marx called "commodity-fetishism". The social character of the art-process, so evident in the collective festival, now disappears. "A commodity is therefore a mysterious thing, simply because in it the social character

of men's labour appears to them as an objective character
stamped upon the product of that labour. . . . In the same
way the light from an object is perceived by us not as the
subjective excitation of our optic nerve, but as the objective
form of something outside the eye itself." In the same way the
art work, once its social realisation in the hearts of society is
veiled by the "market" or the "public", appears to the poet
as something objective. This is helped by the swing-over of
art from forms visibly dependent on men in association—the
dance, the song, music, the spontaneous drama and *commedia
dell' arte*—to crystallised records of the art process not therefore
visibly dependent on society—the written poem, the musical
score, the written play, the picture or sculpture. The art
stimulus becomes objective—a commodity.

Capitalist production requires for its movement—capital.
Constant capital is a continually increasing part of the sum
of capital. This constant capital takes the visible form of
elaborate factory plant and indirectly the more highly-developed technique and organisation necessary to use this plant.
This growth of constant capital and therefore of social organisation due to increasing productivity of labour contrasts with the
growth of individualism in ownership and appropriation due
to the increasing wealth of private capitalists. In the same way
bourgeois poetry is marked by a continually increasing sum of
tradition and technique, of which the poet feels the pressure,
so that there is a continual contradiction between the tremendous social experience embodied in the poem and the individualistic and anti-social attitude of the poet. "Tradition"
towers up before the poet as something formidable and
tremendous, with which he must settle accounts as an ego.

But the poet is not a capitalist. He does not exploit labour.
To the capitalist commodity-fetishism takes the form of
sacralisation of the common market-denominator of all
commodities—money. Money acquires for him a high, mystic,
spiritual value. But the writer is himself exploited.

In so far as he "writes for money" of course he acquires
a purely capitalist mentality. He may even himself exploit
labour by means of secretaries and hacks who do his "donkey-
work" for him. But the man who writes for money is not an

artist, for it is the characteristic of the artist that his products
are adaptative, that the artistic illusion is begotten of the
tension between instinct and consciousness, between productive
forces and productive relations, the very tension which drives
on all society to future reality. In bourgeois society this
tension is that between the productive forces (the socially
organised power of capitalist technique in the factories) and
the social relations (production for private profit and the
resulting anarchy in the market as a whole indicated by the
universality of the money or "exchange" relation instead of
the direct or "use" relation). Because this is the fundamental
contradiction, the poet "revolts" against the system of profit-
making or production for exchange-value as crippling the
meaning and significance of art. But as long as he revolts
within the categories of bourgeois thought—that is, as long
as he cannot cast off the basic bourgeois illusion—his revolt
takes a form made necessary by the system of commodity
production.

3

The exploited—of which the poet thus becomes one—are
of two kinds in capitalist production: These two kinds, the
labourer and the craftsman, may be regarded as descendants
of the serfs and artisans of medieval days. However, the
lineage is not direct. Serfs became capitalists and artisans were
hurled down into the proletariat during the capitalist revolution. The exploited may be regarded as descendants of the
one class of artisans. The *labourer* has been thoroughly proletarianised; the *craftsman*, for special reasons, has still retained
a measure of privilege in capitalist production which gives
him the illusion of belonging to the "middle class", a class
immune from and superior to the class struggle as a whole.
None the less, the proletarian abyss yawns always beneath his
feet. His privilege is an accident of a particular stage of
capitalist production and is always being torn from his grasp.
However, the historical change of capitalist production produces always new members of this class, which therefore
appears always to have a certain stability and separate existence,
although its actual composition is in a state of wild flux.

The final stages of capitalism reveal the fallacy of even this phantom separation, and the petty bourgeoisie finds its privileges being torn from its hands.

Let us examine the main history of these two divisions in England.

(i) *The Labourer.*—He is the man who works drably, monotonously and at the most-sweated wages, a mere cog in the machine. He is the proletarian proper, the unique creation of capitalism. His fight against the capitalist is most bitter and uncompromising because his work, by its very nature, is of a kind it is impossible to like, and therefore his revolt is expressed as a fight for leisure, an attempt to snatch from his employers' reluctant hands every extra hour of decent human existence outside the factory. This fight goes with a struggle for higher wages, to make those short hours of leisure as full and free as possible.

This is the only form his struggle for freedom can take within the categories of capitalist production, for in his dull task freedom expresses itself as the opposite to social activity or "work". Because he constitutes the majority of those from the surplus value of whose labour-power the capitalist derives his profit, the antagonism between the two classes is naked and direct. This antagonism is the real core of the class struggle in capitalist society. Each minute of his leisure or penny of his wages is so much from the capitalist's profit. His freedom is precisely the capitalist's unfreedom, and *vice versa.*

(ii) *The Craftsman.*—This class, as foreman, overseer, or mechanic, or in a profession as barrister, doctor, engineer or architect, occupies a special position in capitalist production because of his personal skill, technique or "key" job. Because of his favoured position, his delight in his skill, and his higher wages, the craftsman finds himself often in opposition to the genuine proletariat. Work for him does not stand in such sharp opposition to leisure, or his freedom to the capitalist's freedom, as in the case of the labourer. Sometimes he is even in business "in a small way" himself, not as a capitalist, but employing two or three apprentice-assistants and selling to large capitalists. This apparent cleavage of interests is expressed in these workers' organisations. The great general labouring

unions—the T. & G.W., N.U.G. & M.W., and such similar
unions—in their early days, led by Ben Tillett, Tom Mann
and John Burns, found themselves opposed by and contending
with the "amalgamated" craft unions such as the old A.S.E.,
which inherited the Liberal traditions of the "Junta" that
had, at an earlier date, ousted the original militant but badly
organised lodges.

None the less, the development of capitalist production
remorselessly turns the craftsman into a labourer. The machine
competes with and ousts the product of his skilled hands in
all departments and forces him into the "industrial reserve
army" of the unemployed.

The effect is at first to make him revolt against the demands
of a "commercialised" market by setting up his skill as a good
in itself, detached from social uses. You will hear such a
craftsman admire an old Napier car, for example, as a superb
production of skilled *craftsmen*, and compare it with a modern
mass-production Ford, which fulfils the same social rôle and is
cheaper. The old skill, although more wasteful of human
labour, has acquired a special value to the craftsman because
it is the condition for his existence as a class distinct from the
proletariat, and is set over and against the market with its
criterion of profit, which is the cause of the outdating of his
skill. Eventually, employed as a factory hand, he may still
cherish his outdated skill by making models, by indulging in
little private "hobbies" and other socially meaningless activities
that exercise his craft.

In this his attitude is fundamentally akin to that of the
writer. The writer's relation to capitalism is also privileged
and craft, although its "ideal" content gives it a still higher
privilege than manual craftsmanship in an age where the class
division has separated thinking from doing. The writer is a
part of upper bourgeois society, like the doctor, barrister,
architect, teacher or scientist whose work has a similar
theoretical content—the manual craftsman is never more than
"lower middle class". None the less, both find themselves
expressing the special aspirations and delusions of the petty
bourgeoisie.

Just as the growth of capitalism tends more and more to

whelm all industrial production in mass production, expropriate artisans in thousands, and proletarianise the craftsman to the level of a labourer or machine-minder, so it has the same effect in the realm of art. Mass-production art enforces a dead level of mediocrity. Good art becomes less saleable. Because art's rôle is now that of adapting the multitude to the dead mechanical existence of capitalist production, in which work sucks them of their vital energies without awakening their instincts, where leisure becomes a time to deaden the mind with the easy phantasy of films, simple wish-fulfilment writing, or music that is mere emotional massage—because of this the paid craft of writer becomes as tedious and wearisome as that of machine-minder. Journalism becomes the characteristic product of the age. Films, the novel and painting all share in the degradation. Immense technical resources and steady debasement and stereotyping of the human psyche are characteristics alike of factory production and factory art in this stage of capitalism. Let any artist who has had to earn a living by journalism or writing "thrillers" testify to the inexorable proletarianisation of his art. The modern thriller, love story, cowboy romance, cheap film, jazz music or yellow Sunday paper form the real *proletarian* literature of to-day—that is, literature which is the characteristic accompaniment of the misery and instinctual poverty produced in the majority of people by modern capitalist production. It is literature which proletarianises the writer. It is at once an expression of real misery and a protest against that real misery. This art, universal, constant, fabulous, full of the easy gratifications of instincts starved by modern capitalism, peopled by passionate lovers and heroic cowboys and amazing detectives, is the religion of to-day, as characteristic an expression of proletarian exploitation as Catholicism is of feudal exploitation. It is the opium of the people; it pictures an inverted world because the world of society *is* inverted. It is the real characteristic art of bourgeois civilisation, expressing the real and not the self-appraised content of the bourgeois illusion. "High-brow" bourgeois art grows on the bourgeois class's freedom. "Low-brow" proletarian art grows on the proletariat's unfreedom and helps, by its massage of the starved revolting instincts, to maintain that unfreedom in being. Because it is mere massage, because it helps to maintain man in unfreedom and not to express his spontaneous creation, because of that, it is bad art. Yet it is an art which is far more really characteristic, which plays a far more important and all-pervasive rôle in bourgeois society than, for example, the art of James Joyce.

The poet is the most craft of writers. His art requires the highest degree of technical skill of any artist; and it is precisely this technical skill which is not wanted by the vast majority of people in a developed capitalism. He is as out of date as a medieval stone-carver in an era of plaster casts. As the virtual proletarianisation of society increases, the conditions of men's work, robbed of spontaneity, more and more make them demand a mass-produced "low-brow" art, whose flatness and shallowness serve to adapt them to their unfreedom. The poet becomes a "high-brow", a man whose skill is not wanted. It becomes too much trouble for the average man to read poetry.

Because of the conditions of his life, the poet's reaction is similar to that of the craftsman. He begins to set craft skill in *opposition* to social function, "art" in opposition to "life". The craftsman's particular version of commodity-fetishism is *skill-fetishism*. Skill now seems an objective thing, opposed to social value. The art work therefore becomes valued in and for itself.

But the art work lives in a world of society. Art works are always composed of objects that have a social reference. Not mere noises but words from a vocabulary, not chance sounds but notes from a socially-recognised scale, not mere blobs but forms with a *meaning*, are what constitutes the material of art. All these things have emotional associations which are social.

Yet if an art work is valued for *its own sake* in defiant and rebellious opposition to the sake of a society which now has no use for skill, it is in fact valued *for the artist's sake*. One cannot simply construct random poems. If their associations are not social they are personal, and the more the art work is opposed to society, the more are personal associations defiantly selected which are exclusive of social—bizarre, strange, phantastic. In this stage of the bourgeois illusion therefore poetry exhibits a rapid movement from the social world of art to the personal world of private phantasy. This leads to individualism. In revolting against capitalism the poet, because he remains within the sphere of bourgeois categories, simply moves on to an extreme individualism, utter "loss of control of his social relationships", and absolute commodity-production—to the essence, in fact, of the capitalism he condemns. He is the complete mirror-revolutionary.

And his too triumphant proclamation of liberty at last achieved in full, marks the very moment when liberty completely slips out of his hands.

4

This movement into the world of "art for art's sake"—*i.e.* "art for my sake"—of course is well marked in England with Rossetti, Morris before he became a socialist, Wilde and to a certain extent Hopkins. But in this epoch of the final stage of capitalism the movement becomes most rapid in other countries. England, the quickest to develop methods of capitalist production, is slowest to decline. The final movement in bourgeois art is accomplished most fully in other countries.

The movement is seen in its purity in France. Baudelaire begins it: "Il ne peut être du progrès (vrai, c'est à dire moral) que dans l'individu et par l'individu lui-même". Verlaine and Rimbaud continue it, though Rimbaud, allying himself with the Commune, passes from poetry with the collapse of the first proletarian dictatorship.

From then on the movement develops *via* the Parnassians, through the symbolists, to its climax in the *surréalistes*. With the Parnassians the word is valued for its marmoreal craft qualities; with the symbolists for the vague penumbra of emotional associations lying beyond the word—that is, for its extra-social associations—; with the *surréalistes* directly for its private unconscious significance. The transition from Heredia *via* Laforgue to Apollinaire is surprisingly rapid and clear.

In England poetry at first seems exhausted. The universal movement of the bourgeois economy which is debasing all art, or making it move to *surréalisme,* is halted in England by little "pockets" or sheltered occupations, representing the reserves of England's long bourgeois summer. The country—preserved and protected by the rich industrial capitalist who finds it better to exploit ruthlessly the colonial "country" for raw material and keep some vestige of idyllic relations around him —is one such pocket; it gives us Hardy and a succession of less gnarled country poets such as Thomas and Davies. Oxford and Cambridge are other such pockets; they give us Housman, Flecker, Brooke and various other "Georgian" poets. The war closes this period. In 1929 the final economic crisis of capitalism affects even England, and English poetry too moves rapidly towards symbolism and the most logically consistent expression of poetic craft revolt—*surréalisme*.

The *surréaliste* is somewhat equivalent to the craftsman who makes trifling models and toys in his spare time to exercise his skill. This is the way he expresses his revolt and secures some free outlet for his craft, by deliberately making something of its nature useless and therefore opposed to the sordid craftlessness of mass-production. We will deal later with the aesthetic theory of *surréalisme* and the importance it attaches to the Unconscious, when we have had time to consider the real function of the instincts and of the Unconscious in art. At the moment we need only point out that, so far from the free association which is the basis of surrealistic technique being really free, it is far more compulsive than ordinary rational association, as Freud, Jung and MacCurdy have clearly shown. In rational association images are controlled by a social experience of reality—the consciousness of necessity. In free association the images are controlled by the iron hand of the unconscious instincts—and it is therefore no more free than the "thinking" of the ant. Man becomes free not by realising himself in opposition to society but by realising himself through society, and the character of the association in itself imposes certain common forms and conventions which are the badge of his freedom. But because the *surréaliste* is a bourgeois and has lost control of his social relationships, he believes freedom to consist in revolting against these forms whereby freedom has been realised in the past. Social activity, the means of freedom, is—because its products are appropriated more completely by individuals the more social the activity becomes —opposed by a resolutely non-social activity which is felt to constitute freedom because its products are useless to society and therefore cannot be appropriated by individuals. Of course this is an outside view of the process. Subjectively the artist believes himself to be realising an ideal freedom derived from the "magic" qualities of art works and the unique features of the artist's mind.

At each stage the bourgeois contradiction by unfolding itself revolutionises its own base and secures a fresh development of technical resources. Hence the movement from "art for art's sake" to *surréalisme* secures a development of the technique of poetry, of which in England Eliot is the best example owing to the already-mentioned lag. But it cannot continue indefinitely. The conflict between technical resources and content reaches a limit where it explodes and begins to turn into its opposite. A revolution of content, as opposed to a mere movement of technique, now begins, corresponding in the social sphere to a change in productive relations as opposed to a mere improvement in productive forces. As a result the social associations of words will all be re-cast, and the whole subject-matter of poetry will become different, because language itself is now generated in a different society. There will be a really revolutionary movement from the categories of bourgeois poetry to the categories of communist poetry.

The *surréaliste* therefore is the last bourgeois revolutionary. To pass beyond him—beyond Milton, beyond Godwin, beyond Pater, beyond finally Dada and Dali, is to pass beyond the categories of bourgeois thought. What politically is this final bourgeois revolutionary? He is an anarchist.

The anarchist is a bourgeois so disgusted with the development of bourgeois society that he asserts the bourgeois creed in the most essential way: complete "personal" freedom, complete destruction of all social relations. The anarchist is yet revolutionary because he represents the destructive element and the complete negation of all bourgeois society. But he cannot really pass beyond bourgeois society, because he remains caught in its toils. In the anarchic organisation of bourgeois economy certain laws of organisation still assert themselves, and therefore can only be shattered by a higher organisation, that of a new ruling-class.

The anarchist is the typical revolutionary product of the country where industrial capitalism has developed late under "hot-house" conditions and has resulted in the rapid proletarianisation of a large number of artisans or petty bourgeois craftsmen. It is a petty bourgeois creed. Hence its strength in "late" capitalist countries like Italy, Spain, Russia and France —precisely the countries where the surrealistic tendency in art is also most marked.

But it is also the character of *surréalisme,* as it is the character of anarchy as a political philosophy, that it *negates itself in practice.* The difference between communism and anarchy as a political philosophy is that communism believes that bourgois rule can only be successfully overthrown by an organised movement. This organisation, expressed in soviets and trade unions, is a direct outcome of the organisation forced on the proletariat by the general conditions of capitalist economy. The anarchist, however, has recently been a petty bourgeois, a peasant or an artisan. He has not been organised for long in an industrial and political struggle against the capitalist class. He therefore sees revolution as an individual destruction of authority which would suffice to restore the conditions in which he enjoyed the fruit of his own small-scale labour.

But in practice the anarchist discovers that the mere destruction of an outworn society, let alone the building of a new, requires organisation. The mere necessities of the task drive him first into trade unions and then into the creation of soviets. This was seen in the Russian Revolution, when the sincere Social Revolutionaries were mostly forced, by the logic of events, to the Bolshevik standpoint, and again in Spain, where in Barcelona the anarchists have had to support a strong Central Government, help in the organisation of militia, defence and supplies, and in every way negate their own creed. Hence the truth of the old joke as to the anarchist's code:

"Para. 1. There shall be no order at all.
"Para. 2. No one shall be obliged to comply with the
           preceding paragraph",

and the significance of the newspaper report after the Fascist revolt in Spain: "The anarchists are keeping order in Barcelona".

In the same way, as a revolutionary situation develops, the *surréaliste* poets either retreat to reaction and Fascism (as many in Italy) or are thrown into the ranks of the proletariat, like Aragon in France.

In a country such as England, the final revolt of the crafts-man usually takes a different form. The craftsman is not there an independent artisan or petty bourgeois whose first taste of proletarianisation gives him a hatred of "organisation". The proletarianisation of the artisan took place in the late eighteenth century in England, and because the possibilities of revolution were more hopeless, his rebellion took the form of Ludditism —the smashing of the machines which expropriated them. The next great proletarianisation of the craftsman was marked by the rise of the general labourers' unions in the face of the opposition of the craft unions, and the struggle then was a struggle between a developing proletariat and the capitalists, with the craft unions standing aside.

Thus the final crisis in England found the craftsman a man who, as the result of the long springtime of English capitalist development, occupied a privileged position in production. He formed the famous labour aristocracy who made it seem as if England, not content with a bourgeois aristocracy and a bour-geois monarchy, aimed also at a bourgeois proletariat. In the final crisis it soon became apparent that this favoured position was only the expression of the temporary supremacy of England in world capitalism and vanished with the growth of competi-tion and tariffs. Unemployment, insecurity, wage-cuts and dis-missals as the result of rationalisation, from 1929 to 1936, ravaged all the ranks of the "craft" and "professional" elements of England just as, at a somewhat earlier date, they had those of Germany. So far, however, from proletarianisation in all cases producing an anarchic frame of mind in these types, it has an opposite effect in those who are "key" men rooted in the heart of industry everywhere—in the tool-room of the factory, as supervisors, foremen, technicians, specialists, managers and consultants. In these positions they find that their skill is wasted, not by the organisation of men into factories, but because the progress of this organisation—its logical conclusion

H

in an immensely increased human productivity—is defeated by the characteristic anarchy of capitalist production—the individual ownership and mutual competition of the various factories.

Hence their revolution against the system which is crippling them is not reactionary in content, like the artisan's, but genuinely progressive, in that it demands greater organisation —the extension of the organisation already obtaining in the factories to production as a whole.

But though progressive in content, it by no means follows that this demand will find an outcome in a progressive act. Even at this revolutionary stage the craftsman halts at two paths. One leads up to the bourgeoisie, with whom his responsible position and higher salary have always associated him— indeed the doctor, architect, and artist, owing to the "ideal" content of their work, have actually been a genuine part of the bourgeoisie. The other path leads downward to the proletariat, from whom his privileged position has always sundered him— for proletarianisation, because it has involved worsened living conditions, has been something to be avoided at all costs. Hence he has an ingrained repulsion from alliance with the proletariat. In the past he has measured his success and freedom by the distance he has climbed up from the proletariat to the bourgeoisie —the famous petty bourgeois snobbery and exclusiveness which is only the cold reflection of man's constant desire for freedom.

If he chooses the upward path, he chooses organisation imposed from above by the bourgeoisie—in other words, Fascism. Of course this organisation is a mere sham—it is a cloak for further rationalisation, and the consolidating of the power of the most reactionary section of the capitalist class. It results, not in the increased organisation of production but in greater anarchy and more bitter competition. Rationalisation is in fact irrationalisation. It leads to an increase in anarchy outside and inside—internally by a profound disturbance in economy resulting from the growth of armament and luxury industry at the expense of necessities and a general lowering of wages, and externally by an increase in tariffs and imperialism and a general drive towards war. The only real organisation consists in the counter-revolutionary regimentation of the proletariat and petty bourgeois classes and the smashing of working-class organisations.

But equally the craftsman may choose the downward path, and he is the more likely to do so as the development of the industrial crisis and the objective examples of Fascism abroad reveal the inevitability of this move. This path consists of allying himself with the proletariat and extending the organisation of the workers within the factories to the organisation of production as a whole by liquidating those rights which stand in the way—individual ownership of the means of production. Since this right is the real power of existing society, this means the substitution of workers' power for capitalists' power. When he makes this choice, the craftsman, because of his key position in production, his privileged income (giving him more leisure and cultural opportunities), and his experience of responsibility, becomes a natural leader of the proletariat, instead of their most treacherous enemy, as he is when he is allied with the bourgeoisie.

It is for this reason that the last three years in England have been marked by the development of a revolutionary outlook among those very craft and petty bourgeois types—the "labour aristocracy"—who formerly displayed all the reactionary qualities that made a craft union notorious in this country and made many of their spokesmen in Germany actual supporters of the Fascist régime. Anyone familiar with trade union affairs is aware that just as the craft unions and those industrial unions with a strong craft composition formerly opposed the general labourer's unions as being too militant and "socialist", it is now the craft and semi-professional unions like the A.E.U., E.T.U., A.S.L.E. & F., N.A.U.S.W. & C. and N.U.C. who at the Trades Union Congress and through their branches and Metropolitan Councils or District Committees press for militant action and are reproached by the general unions for being too extreme and communist. In the same way those craftsmen whose ideal theoretical content has given them a special position among the bourgeoisie itself—doctors, scientists, architects and teachers—are now moving Left and entering the Communist Party in considerable numbers, passing straight from Liberalism without an intermediate sojourn in the Labour Party.

The same final movement of the bourgeois illusion is reflected in the growth of the People's Front, where all the liberal elements, representing the craft content of modern society, put themselves under the leadership of the proletariat in a formal written alliance limiting the scope of that leadership.

In English poetry this is reflected in the fact that English poets, without ever moving completely into *surréaliste* anarchy, change from a position near *surréalisme* into its opposite—a communist revolutionary position, such as that adopted by Auden, Lewis, Spender and Lehmann. How far this is genuinely communist and what level of art it represents, is a consideration which will be deferred to our final chapter, for with this movement the bourgeois contradiction passes into its synthesis. It now starts to revolutionise, not merely its productive forces but its own categories, which now impossibly restrict those productive forces which its tension has generated. This movement is farther advanced in France, with Gide, Rolland, Malraux and Aragon wearing the uniform at which all once sneered. Here it has only begun.

We have surveyed briefly the most important general determining forces influencing bourgeois English poetry. It is now necessary to change from a consideration of the social and historical movement which determines the poet's attitude and produces that very tension which can only be resolved by poetry, to a consideration of the movement of individual creation—the specific way in which the individual responds to this outward pressure and by a dialectic process imparts to it an impulsion from his own instinctive energy. Before we can do so, we must survey the general technical characteristics of poetry which condition his task.

THE MOVEMENT OF BOURGEOIS POETRY

	General Characteristics	Technical Characteristics
Primitive Accumulation, 1550–1600.	*The Elizabethan Age.*—Marlowe, Shakespeare. The dynamic force of individuality, realising itself by smashing all outward forms, is expressed in poetry. Its characteristic hero is the absolute prince, with his splendid public life, which is collective and through which other individualities can therefore realise themselves without negating his.	(*a*) The iambic rhythm, expressing the heroic nature of the bourgeois illusion in terms of the ancient world, is allowed to flower luxuriantly and naturally; it indicates the free and boundless development of the personal will. It is collective—adapted for declamation; noble—suitable to princely diction: flexible—because the whole life of the prince, even to its intimacies, is lived in easy openness. (*b*) The lyrics are suitable for group singing (simple metres) but courtly (ornamental stanzas) and polished (bright conceits).
The Transition, 1600–1625	*The Jacobean Age.*—Donne, Herrick, Vaughan, Herbert, Crashaw. The absolute monarch now becomes a force producing corruption and there is a withdrawal from the brilliant public life of the court to the private study and the country.	The Puritan takes the lyric stanzas and makes them elaborate and scholarly. Court poetry becomes learned poetry with a study vocabulary. Blank verse (Webster) portrays the decline of princeliness and loses its noble undertone. The lyric is no longer singable and the conceits become knotted and thoughtful.

THE MOVEMENT OF BOURGEOIS POETRY—*continued*

General Characteristics	*Technical Characteristics*
The Bourgeois Revolt, 1625–1650.	*The Puritan Revolution.*—Milton. The bourgeoisie feels itself strong enough to revolt against the monarchy, and with the help of "the people", overthrows the Stuarts. But this realisation of bourgeois freedom proves dangerous: the people demand it too, and there is a dictatorship which isolates the bourgeoisie, followed by a reaction. The noble simplicity of the self-idealised revolutionary (Satan, Samson Agonistes, Christ in the desert) then vanishes in an atmosphere of defeat.	The heroic bourgeois illusion returns in terms of the ancient world but is more self-conscious and not projected into the figure of the prince. It is personal instead of dramatic. The Puritan revolt against the court gives it a bare and learned vocabulary; and this conscious restraint is reflected in a stricter rhythm.
The Counter-Puritan Reaction, 1650–1688.	*The Restoration.*—Dryden, Suckling, Lovelace. Poetry forgets its noble sentiments and becomes cynical, measured or rational. There is an alliance of the bourgeoisie with the aristocracy instead of the people; and the court returns, but no longer in the form of the absolute prince. The prince is now subject to "reason".	Formal rules are imposed to restrain the "spirit" whose violence has proved dangerous. Poetry indicates its readiness to compromise by moving within the bounds of the heroic couplet. Court poetry reappears for the bourgeoisie is allied with the aristocracy, and therefore the simple metres and courtly elegance of Elizabethan lyrics drive out the crabbed scholar's poems. The vocabulary becomes more conversational and social.

| The Era of Mercantilism and Manufacture, 1688–1750. | *The Eighteenth Century.*—Pope. The shortage of labour makes the bourgeoisie continue to ally itself with the agricultural capitalist (the Whig "aristocrat") in order to maintain the laws and restrictions which will keep down the price of labour and enable it to develop through the stage of manufacture. Poetry reflects a belief in the rightness and permanence of forms and restrictions, good taste and an upper-class "tone". | The outward "rules" are now accepted, not as a compromise but as obvious and rational ingredients of style. Poetry becomes Augustan, idealises style, measure, polish and the antithesis which restrains natural luxuriance. Vocabulary becomes formalised and elegantly fashionable. |
| The Industrial Revolution and the "Anti-Jacobin" Reaction, 1750–1825. | *The Romantic Revival.*—Byron, Keats, Shelley and Wordsworth. The development from manufacture to machine power proletarianises the artisan class and makes the restrictions of mercantilism no longer necessary. The alliance between the landed capitalist and the petty bourgeois ends now that the expansion of the market and the development of machinery causes manufacture to fling off its subjection to the country and emerge as industry, the predominant force in the State. Small capitals now acquire huge expansive powers and the bour- | Poetry revolts against the old "forms" by an appeal to the heart and the sentiments. Poetry demands simultaneously the inclusion of natural speech and the romanticising of speech by a return to Elizabethan and Jacobean metres and vocabularies. There is a strong injection of words expressing "abstract" ideas at the same time as sensuous and materially "rich" words come into vogue. Both combine to separate the poetic vocabulary from real life. Rhythm—with Elizabethan poetry declamatory, with Jacobean contemplative, with Puritan ele- |

THE MOVEMENT OF BOURGEOIS POETRY—*continued*

	General Characteristics	*Technical Characteristics*
The Industrial Revolution and the "Anti-Jacobin" Reaction, 1750–1825—*continued*.	geoisie grow light-headed with power. The forms of the era of manufacture are a check on industry. The "Liberal" capitalist leads the people in a crusade against privilege in the name of freedom. Poetry becomes ardent and full of feeling. It sees in itself a kinship to the Elizabethan era of individualism. It revolts against tradition and yearns for a fuller, freer life. But the alliance of the people with the bourgeoisie in the French Revolution leads to a revolutionary demand for proletarian freedom. The bourgeoisie becomes frightened, retracts its demands, loses its mass basis and enters on a reaction in alliance with the landed aristocracy. Poetry, disillusioned, more and more withdraws into the private world of romance. It is too compromised to make much of social reality except by extreme hypocrisy or empty pompousness. All poets now betray their youth as they mature.	vated, with Augustan elegant—becomes with Romantic poetry hypnotic. There is a great advance in the development of poetic technique.

The Decline of British Capitalism, 1825–1900.

The Victorians.—Tennyson, Browning, Arnold, Swinburne, Rossetti, Patmore, Morris. The first capitalist crisis occurs in 1825. The poet becomes pessimistic or withdraws more and more into a private world, as the poet becomes isolated from society by the conditions of capitalist production.

A general intensification of the technical resources already discovered in the preceding era.

The Epoch of Imperialism, 1900–1930.

"Art for Art's Sake"; the Parnassians; Symbolism; Futurism; Surréalisme.—The poet revolts by extreme individualism, commodity-fetishism and loss of control of social relations. The poem passes, by a series of stages, from the social world to the completely private world. This revolt against bourgeois conditions finally expresses in extreme purity the categories of bourgeois production. It thus negates itself in anarchy, and must necessarily move outside the bourgeois illusion. English poetry now follows behind the rest of Europe in its development, owing to the sheltered conditions of English capitalism. The classic example for development becomes French poetry and

The attempt entirely to separate the world of art from that of society. The rejection of all the specifically social features in poetry as a revolt against *convention.* Words increasingly used for personal associations. Either the rejection of its social genesis or its use hypnotically to release associations which will be personal in proportion to their depth and therefore their unconsciousness. Finally, the "completely free" word of *surréalisme.*

THE MOVEMENT OF BOURGEOIS POETRY—*continued*

	General Characteristics	Technical Characteristics
The Epoch of Imperialism, 1900–1930—*continued*.	(secondarily) Italian, Spanish and Russian. Wilde, Eliot, Flecker and Pound may perhaps be mentioned. Victorian poetry persists in sheltered areas: the Country (Hardy, Thomas and Davies), Oxford and Cambridge (Housman, Brooke, Squire, etc.). The Great War expresses the insoluble antagonisms of developed capitalism, and the general economic crisis which follows it, 100 years after the first capitalistic crisis, closes this period.	
The Final Capitalistic Crisis, 1930–?	*The People's Front.*—Poetry now expresses a real revolt against bourgeois conditions by an alliance of the bourgeois ideologist or "craftsman" with the proletariat against the bourgeoisie. France still leads: Aragon, Gide, etc. In England: Lewis, Auden and Spender.	An attempt once again to give a social value to all the technical resources, developed by the movement of the preceding stages. This period sees the beginning of a complete change of the whole content of poetry, which by the end of the preceding movement had become contentless and formal. The question of form now tends to take a second place until the problem of social relations has been solved poetically.

THE CHARACTERISTICS OF POETRY

By poetry we mean modern poetry, because not only have we a special and intimate understanding of the poetry of our age and time, but we look at the poetry of all ages through the mist of our own. Modern poetry is poetry which is already separate from story and has played a special part in the relation of the consciousness of the developing bourgeois class to its surroundings.

What are the specific characteristics of this modern poetry—not of good modern poetry, but of any modern poetry? *Mimesis*, the characteristic of Greek poetry, is not a specific characteristic of bourgeois poetry but is common to the bourgeois story and play.

The characteristics which would make a given piece of literature poetry for the sophisticated modern are as follows:

(a) *Poetry is rhythmic*

The marked rhythm of poetry, superimposed upon the "natural" rhythm of any language, seems to have taken its root from two sources—

(1) It makes easier declamation in common and therefore emphasises the collective nature of poetry. It is the impress of the social mould in which poetry is generated. As a result the nature of the rhythm expresses in a subtle and sensitive way the precise balance between the instinctive or emotional content of the poem and the social relations through which emotion realises itself collectively. Thus any change in man's self-valuation of the relation of his instincts to society is reflected in his attitude to the metre and rhythmical conventions into which he is born, and which he therefore as poet changes in one direction or another. We have already studied in outline these changes in attitude toward metrical technique during the movement of bourgeois English poetry, and it is

obvious that the final movement towards "free verse" reflects the final anarchic bourgeois attempt to abandon all social relations in a blind negation of them, because man has completely lost control of his social relationships.

(2) But this brings us to a special feature of the bourgeois contradiction in poetry—the specific way in which rhythm facilitates collective declamation and emotion. The body has certain natural periodicities (pulse-beat, breath, etc.) which form a dividing line between the casual character of outside events and the ego, and make it appear as if we experience time subjectively in a special and direct manner. Any rhythmical movement or action therefore exalts the physiological component of our conscious field at the expense of the environmental. It tends to produce introversion of a special kind, which I will call *emotional* introversion and contrast with *rational* introversion, such as takes place when we concentrate on a mathematical problem. *There* rhythm would be out of place.

Rhythm puts people at a collective festival in touch with each other in a particular way—physiologically and emotionally. They already *see* each other, but this is not the kind of communion that is desired. On the contrary, when they cease to see each other so clearly, when each retires darkly into his body and shares the same physiological and elemental beat, then they have a special herd commonness that is distinct from the commonness of seeing each other in the same real world of perceptual experience. It is instinctive commonness as opposed to conscious commonness; subjective unity as opposed to objective unity. In emotional introversion men return to the genotype, to the more or less common set of instincts in each man which is changed and adapted by outer reality in the course of living.

This emotional introversion is in itself a social act. Society hangs together as a coherent working whole because men all have the same equipment of instincts. The productive relations into which a man is born, the environment he enters into, mould his consciousness in a social way and also secure the cohesion of any one society. It is true that the same two genotypes, one born into primitive Australian culture and the other into modern European culture, would be different and if brought together later could not form one social complex. But a monkey and a man born into the same culture would be different too, in spite of their like surroundings, and could not form the same complex either. This contradiction between instinct and cultural environment is absolutely primary to society. Just as the specific form of it we have been analysing drives on the development of *capitalist* society, so this general contradiction drives on the development of *all* society. In language this contradiction is represented by the opposition between the rational content or objective existence expressed by words and the emotional content or subjective attitude expressed by the same words. It is impossible to separate the two completely, because they are given in the way language is generated—in man's struggle with Nature. But science (or reality) is the special field of the former, and poetry (or illusion) the domain of the latter. Hence poetry in some form is as eternal to society as man's struggle with Nature, a struggle of which association in economic production is the outcome.

In poetry itself this takes the form of man entering into emotional communion with his fellow men by retiring into himself. Hence when the bourgeois poet supposes that he expresses his individuality and flies from reality by entering into a world of art in his inmost soul, he is in fact merely passing from the social world of rational reality to the social world of emotional commonness. When the bourgeois poet becomes (as he thinks) anti-social and completely vowed to the world of "art for art's sake", his rhythm becomes increasingly marked and hypnotically drowsy, as in Mallarmé's *L'Après-midi d'un Faune* and Apollinaire's *Alcools*. Only when the bourgeois passes to the anarchistic stage where he negates all bourgeois society and deliberately chooses words with only personal associations, can rhythm vanish, for the poet now dreads even the social bond of having instincts common with other men, and therefore chooses just those words which will have a *cerebral* peculiarity. If he chooses words with too strong an emotional association, this, coupled with the hypnosis of a strong rhythm, will sink him into the common lair of the human instincts. Hence the *surréaliste* technique of selecting word combinations whose bizarre associations, though personal, are not emotional but rational. Ultimately this is only possible by departing from language and significance altogether, because all the contents of consciousness are both genetically and environmentally social in basis.

Thus, though rhythm is fundamental to poetry, it cannot be dismissed with some simple formula such as "Rhythm is hypnotic and produces hyperæsthesia" or "Metrical patterns express social norms". The significance of rhythm is *historical* and at any given time depends upon the unfolding of society's basic contradiction in language.

(b) *Poetry is difficult to translate*

It is recognised as one of the characteristics of poetry that translations convey little of the specific emotion aroused by that poetry in the original. This can be confirmed by anyone who, after reading a translation, has learned the language of the original. The metre may be reproduced. What is called the "sense" may be exactly translated. But the specific poetic emotion evaporates. Where translations are good poetry, like FitzGerald's *Rubáiyát* or Pope's *Iliad*, they are virtually re-creations. The poetic emotion they re-create rarely has much resemblance to that aroused by the original.

We have no right to attribute this to any mysterious transcendent quality in poetry. It may be so, or it may not. It is a special characteristic of puns. It is a special characteristic of poetry. No one certainly would claim that the translations of great novels like *War and Peace* or *The Idiot* give to the English reader all that is in the original. But the extraordinary power of these works even in translation, when compared to translations of, say, the *Inferno* or the *Odyssey*, warrants us in claiming that the important aesthetic qualities of the novel do survive translation in a way that those of poetry cannot. This is certainly not due to the difficulty of transferring the formal metrical pattern. On the contrary—a point often overlooked— much more of the formal metrical pattern of French poetry can be carried over into an English translation in verse than can be salvaged of the unstressed spoken rhythm of French prose in an English prose translation. Yet critics, anxious to get some faint flavour of a foreign poet, would far prefer a literal prose translation to a metrical translation.

(c) *Poetry is irrational*

That is not to say that poetry is incoherent or meaningless. Poetry obeys the rules of grammar, and is generally capable of paraphrase, *i.e.* the series of propositions of which it consists can be stated in different prose forms in the same or other languages. But whereas the philosophy of Spinoza remains the philosophy of Spinoza when explained by a disciple, and a novel of Tolstoi remains a novel of Tolstoi when translated, and a fairy tale is the same fairy tale by whomsoever it is told, a paraphrase of a poem, though still making the same statements as the original, is no longer the same poem—is probably not a poem at all. By "rational" we mean conforming with the orderings men agree upon seeing in the environment. Scientific argument is rational in this sense, poetry is not. We have already seen, however, that there is another commonness or social congruence in language distinguishable from environmental congruence. This is *emotional*, or subjective congruence. Let us call it "congruence with inner reality". We have also seen that this characteristic of poetry is linked with its rhythmical form. Evidently, therefore, poetry is irrational as regards its environmental congruity, because it is rational as regards its emotional congruity and there is a contradiction between these two forms of congruity. This contradiction is not exclusive: they interpenetrate in language because they interpenetrate in life. Poetry is in fact just the expression of one aspect of the contradiction between man's emotions and his environment, which takes the very real and concrete form of man's struggle with Nature. Because it is a product of this struggle, poetry at every stage of its historical development reflects in its own province man's active relation to his environment.

Plato referred to this special irrationality of poetry in the quotation already made from *Ion*. This was what Shelley meant when he said: "Poetry is something not subject to the active powers of the mind".

(d) *Poetry is composed of words*

This may seem a commonplace, but nothing is commonplace if it is, at almost all times and occasions, forgotten by those who should know it. For instance we have Matthew Arnold: "For poetry the idea is everything; the rest is a world of illusion, of divine illusion. Poetry attaches its emotion to the idea; the idea *is* the fact. The strongest part of our religion to-day is its unconscious poetry."

We know that the last sentence distorts a real truth. But the first two are so muddled that it is difficult to pick out the actual meaning, although subsequent chapters will show that Arnold, as a good craftsman, was indicating an important aspect of poetry.

Shelley uses the same loose speech: "Language, colour, form and religious and civil habits of actions, are all the instruments and materials of poetry; they may be called poetry by that figure of speech which considers the effect as a synonym of the cause."

Beneath the looseness is the truth that poetry is produced by man's real existence in society.

He also says: "The distinction between poets and prose writers is a vulgar error. . . . Plato was essentially a poet. Lord Bacon was a poet. . . . A poem is the very image of life expressed in its external truth. . . ."

Here he talks with a looseness which conceals nothing. Bacon was not a poet. These overstatements are attempts to justify poetry at the time when the sweeping away of "idyllic relations" by the development of bourgeois economy has started to give the poet an inferiority complex.

Mallarmé's advice to his painter friend is well known: "Poetry is written with words, not ideas". This adds to our own positive characteristic a negative one that we cannot endorse. Poetry certainly evokes *ideas*, *i.e.* memory images, or it would be mere sound. We confine ourselves here therefore to the proposition: "Poetry is composed of words".

The reader will see that this characteristic is really generated by the preceding characteristic, "Poetry is difficult to translate". For if poetry were written only with ideas, *i.e.* with the

aim of stimulating *only* ideas in the hearer, it could be translated by choosing in the other language the words which would
stimulate the same ideas. Since it cannot, the word as word
must have some component additional to the idea it stimulates.
Hence we can say poetry is written with words in a way the
novel is not, without meaning that a special magic inheres in
the sound-symbol or black mark that objectively is the word.
In fact the word stimulates in addition to the idea an affective
"glow", of such a character that it cannot be carried over by
translation.

(e) *Poetry is non-symbolic*

Here we shall not be accused of a commonplace. On the
contrary, this is the negative of a commonplace, since the
customary idealistic conception of poetry is of something
vaguely symbolic. Yet it necessarily follows from the fact that
poetry is irrational that it is non-symbolic.

What do we mean when we say words are symbolic, that is,
symbols and nothing else? We mean that the words themselves
are nothing, we are not interested in them, but in what they
refer to[1]. Thus when a mathematician writes *eight plus nine
equals seventeen*, he is not interested in the words themselves,
but in the ordering of certain generalised classes encountered
in empirical reality. Because the words he makes use of are
symbolic, that is, emptied of personal meaning, the sentence
would have precisely the same validity whatever words were
used. For instance, in French, German or Italian the operations
of ordering referred to would be precisely the same to a
mathematician, although described in different words, because
the words themselves are regarded as an arbitrary convention
standing for real mathematical operations of ordering. If the
phrase be translated into $8+9=17$, the sentence is still just
as adequate from the mathematician's point of view. Indeed
we can go farther, and if to-morrow mathematicians agreed
on a convention whereby 8 was replaced by 9, 9 by 8, and 17
by 23, the *plus* sign by the *minus* and the *equals* by the *is greater*

[1] There is a good discussion of this referential character of words in
Ogden and Richards, *Meaning of Meaning*.

I

than, then the sentence $9-8\angle 23$ would be the precise expression of the empirical operations symbolically expressed by $8+9=17$. But if to-morrow we decided to abolish all words and give every word in the English dictionary its own number, the poetic content of a speech of Hamlet would not be expressed by a series of numbers. We should have to translate them mentally back into the original words before attaining it.

The extreme translatability of the symbolic language of mathematics, which has made it possible to evolve a universal mathematical language, therefore stands in opposition to the untranslatability of non-symbolic poetry. This universal mathematical language is logistic or symbolic logic.[1]

In so far as some of the quality of poetry can be carried over into translation, then in so far poetry has an element of symbolism in it.

But we also saw that just as poetry, though it was deficient in rational congruence, was full of emotional congruence, so, although it lacks external symbolism—reference to external objects—it is full of internal symbolism—reference to emotional attitudes. Now every real word indicates both an external referent and a subjective attitude. Hence scientific argument contains some value-judgment; it is impossible to eliminate it. These judgments are eliminated only in logistic. And poetry contains some reference to external objects—it is impossible to eliminate them and remain poetry.

What does poetry become if all external reference is eliminated, in the way that all value-judgments are eliminated from a scientific argument to make it become logistic? Poetry becomes "meaningless" sound, but sound full of emotional reference—in other words, *music*; and music, like logistic, is translatable and universal. Thus we see that the mingling of reference and emotion, which is characteristic of poetry, is not an adulteration, but expresses a dialectic relation between the opposite poles of instinct and environment, a relation which is rooted in real concrete social life—English, French or Athenian. Poetry is clotted social history, the emotional sweat of man's struggle with Nature.

[1] Invented by Peano and developed by Russell and Whitehead. See *Principia Mathematica*. It has not fulfilled the hopes of its inventors.

(f) *Poetry is concrete*

This is a positive that matches the previous negative statement. But concreteness is not the automatic converse of symbolism. For instance, a symbolic language may approach nearer to the concrete by rejecting the general for the particular. Arithmetic is more concrete than algebra, because its symbols are less generalised. A mathematic symbolism in which the symbol *two* stood only for two bricks, and other symbols were needed for two horses, two men, etc., would plainly be more concrete than existing mathematical symbolism, but it would not be less symbolic, for it would be still as conventional and susceptible to arbitrary sign substitution. But it would be plain that as a symbolic language becomes more concrete, it becomes more and more cumbersome. Since no two men are the same, different symbols would be needed for each possible pairing of men in a perfectly concrete symbolic language.

The generality of mathematics is a generality of external reality; hence the particularity of mathematics would also be a particularity of external reality, and since the number of objects in external reality is infinite, mathematics *must* be generalised. It is the most flexible tool for dealing with outer reality because it is the most generalised. Since it is dealing with orderings only, *i.e.* with classes, it can subdue the infinite particularity of the universe. It is no accident that infinity appears so often in mathematics.

Compare poetry. Its province is subjective attitudes. Now the conscious field consists of real objects and subjective attitudes towards them. By ordering these real objects in the most general way, mathematics arrives at infinity, a single symbol which puts all external reality in its grasp. But if poetry orders all these subjective attitudes in the most generalised way, it arrives at the *ego*, a single symbol which puts all subjective reality in its grasp.

In fact it is music, not poetry, which is as abstract and generalised in regard to subjective reality as mathematics is to external reality. In music the environment sinks away, the ego inflates, and all the drama takes place within its walls. Mathematics is *externally* abstract and generalised; music *internally* so.

But poetry is like scientific argument, it is "impure". Its emotions are attached to real objects and this gives them a certain peculiarity. Reality hovers in the ego's vision. This means that poetry is concrete and particularised, just as scientific argument is concrete and particularised, although of course in each case the concretion and generality refers to different spheres of reality.

For example, when the poet says

My love is like a red, red rose,

the language is non-symbolic, for no conventional acceptation will make the paraphrase, "my fiancée is a flower of the genus *rosacea* var. red", a statement containing the poetic emotion expressed in the original statement. The line is non-symbolic. It is not therefore to be supposed that it *must* be concrete. But if it were not concrete, the statement would be in its present form quite generally true. That is to say, if it were abstract, it would not be a specific case, a statement appropriate to the poet, to a particular love, to one mood, to one time, to one poem, but a quite general statement, so that wherever the speaker is in a position to make the statement "my love is" he must inevitably have in mind, as an already given fact, that she is "like a red, red rose".

But since poetry is not abstract, but a concrete non-symbolic language, we are entitled, in the next poem we write, to say

My love is a white, white rose,

or

If flowers be blossoms, my love is no rose.

But with an abstract non-symbolic language we would only be entitled to make this statement in a body of poetry other than the one in which we made the first, that is to say, in another language. A misunderstanding of this point makes Plato regard all poets as liars: and an understanding of it makes Sidney able to answer him by explaining that the poet "is no lyar, for he nothing affirms".

Thus this concrete character of poetry's subjective generalisation is just what makes it necessary to give poetry the half-assent of illusion—to accept its statements while we are in its phantastic world but not to demand that all the statements of all novels and poems should form one world in which the principles of exclusion and contradiction would apply, as they do in the real material world. This does not mean that no integration is necessary as between novels and poems. That integration is the very province of aesthetics. It is the essential task of aesthetics to rank Herrick below Milton, and Shakespeare above either, and explain in rich and complex detail why and how they differ. But such an act implies a standard, an integrated world view, which is not scientific—*i.e.* rational—but aesthetic. This is the logic of art.

This concretion and particularity applies also to the sphere of scientific argument, which, like poetry, is impure but is nearer the opposite pole. Everyone knows that biology, physics, sociology and psychology are spheres in each of which different laws apply, although there is a connecting principle which states that the law applicable to the more generalised sphere must not be contradicted in any less generalised sphere, *e.g.* the laws of sociology must not contradict those of physics. In the same way poetry must have this congruence, that its experiences always happen to the same "I", in whatever phantastic world, and novels must have this congruence, that they always have their scene laid in the same real world of human society whatever the "I" (character) may be; and the structure of this emotional "I" or real world determines the aesthetic judgment. This ego is in fact the "world-view" in which a logic of art is already given.

Does this "impurity" mean that neither science nor poetry are "really" true? On the contrary. *Because* truth can only apply to reality, to real concrete life, and because real concrete life is neither wholly subjective nor wholly objective but a dialectic active relation between the two (man's struggle with Nature), it is only these "impure" products of the struggle to which we can at all apply the criterion "true". Truth always has a social human reference—it means "true" in relation to man. Hence the criterion of mathematics, as Russell has pointed out, is never "truth", it is consistency. In the same way the criterion of music is "beauty". The fact that language in all its products contains a blend of both is because man in his real life is always actively striving to fulfil Keats' forecasts:

> Beauty is truth, truth beauty;

he is always struggling to make environment conform to instinct, consistency to beauty, and necessity to desire—in a word, to be free. Language is the product of that struggle because it is the struggle not of one man but of men in association and language is the instrument of associated struggle; hence language is stamped everywhere with humanity as well as with man's environment. Just as science is near the environmental pole, so poetry is near the instinctive. Consistency is the virtue of science, beauty of poetry—neither can ever become pure beauty or pure consistency, and yet it is their struggle to achieve this which drives on their development. Science yearns always towards mathematics, poetry towards music.

(g) *Poetry is characterised by condensed affects*

These affects are the affects proper to it, that is to say, *aesthetic* affects. A telegram, "Your wife died yesterday", may impart extraordinarily condensed affects to the reader of it, but these are not of course aesthetic affects. Here the language is used symbolically, and if the unhappy husband who received this telegram had previously known that his wife was in danger and (being of a parsimonious turn of mind) had arranged for the code word "Kippers" to be despatched to him as an indication of his wife's death, the affects accompanying the shorter message would be just as strong. This would be just as true even if the telegram were formally poetic. The scraps of doggerel in *The Times* obituary column have the formal characteristics of poetry and carry strong affects for those who insert them; but these affects are not aesthetic affects.

Now in both these cases another test could be applied. To other persons not bereaved, the words could not carry the same affects. The non-aesthetic affects are individual not collective, and depend on particular not social experiences. Therefore it is not enough that poetry should be charged with emotional significance if this emotion results from a particular personal experience unrealisable or unrealised in a social form. The emotion must be generated by the experience of associated men, and we now see of what the generality of the poetic "I" consists. It is not the "I" of one individual in civil society, any more than the infinity of mathematics is the infinity of one person's perceptual world. The infinity of mathematics is the infinity of the material world—of the world common to all men's perceptual worlds. And the "I" of poetry is the "I" common to all associated men's emotional worlds. How could bourgeois criticism, which never rises above the point of view of the "individual in civil society", solve the problem of what differentiates aesthetic objects and emotions from others? Aesthetic objects are aesthetic in so far as they arouse emotions peculiar not to individual man but to associated men. From this arises the disinterested, suspended and objective character of aesthetic emotion.

．　　．　　．　　．　　．　　．

To summarise: poetry is rhythmical, not translatable, irrational, non-symbolic, concrete, and characterised by condensed aesthetic affects.

These characteristics will suffice to detach the body of poetry from literature as a whole, and we can now proceed to a closer examination of its method, its technique, its function and its future.

VIII

THE WORLD AND THE "I"

THE characteristics of poetry flow necessarily from the nature of language and the active function of poetry in relation to society, man and reality.

When we speak of "man" we mean the genotype or individual, the instinctive man as he is born, who if "left to himself" might grow up into something like a dumb brute, but instead of this he grows up in a certain kind of society as a certain kind of man—Athenian, Aztec or Londoner. We must not think of the genotype as completely plastic and amorphous. It has certain definite instincts and potentialities which are the source of its energy and its restlessness. Nor are all genotypes alike. Men differ among themselves because of inborn characteristics. Society is not, however, opposed to this inborn individuality; on the contrary, the differentiation which comes with increase of civilisation is the means of realising men's particularities. Man cannot choose between being an artist or a scientist in a society which has neither art nor science; nor between biology and psychology where science is still no more than vague astrological superstition.

This genotype is never found "in the raw". Always it is found as a man of definite concrete civilisation with definite opinions, material surroundings, and education—a man with a consciousness conditioned by the relations he has entered into with other men and which he did not choose but was born into.

Men were originally drawn into these relations by their struggle with Nature or outer reality. There are certain laws of the individual—physiological and psychological. But in the extent to which man as one part of reality has separated himself from the other part (Nature) not in order to cut himself from it, but to struggle with it and thereby interpenetrate with it more closely in economic production—to that extent man has generated yet another field of laws, those of sociology. None of these sets of laws contradicts each other; they enrich each other.

But it is obvious that the field of sociology holds a special place because it is the field of the interpenetration of man and Nature, and the source of the generation ideologically of the other laws.

The struggle of man and Nature is a material movement which in the field of thought takes the form of the subject-object relation, the oldest problem of philosophy. It becomes an insoluble problem only because the division of society into classes, by separating the class which generates ideology from society's active struggle with Nature, reflects this cleavage into ideology as a separation of subject from object whereby they become mutually exclusive opposites.

In the field of thought as a whole this struggle of man and Nature in society is *reflected* as reality or "truth". This truth or reality is not something dropped down from on high, it is a living, growing, developing complex. Because it is truth about the Universe, it is a truth about matter. When we say the Universe is material we mean that all phenomena have under-ground connections, in the form of causes or determining relations, which have an ultimate homogeneity called "matter". This is the first assumption of science, because to include any-thing in the field of science is to assert it has connections of this kind. To deny such connectedness of any phenomena is to deny their knowability and therefore the possibility of their inclusion in the field of science. The history of science is the discovery of these connections, and their demonstration as objective. They cannot be discovered by contemplation alone, but at every stage experiment—the practical demonstration of connections—is necessary.

Thus truth is an organised product of man's struggle with Nature. As that struggle accumulates capital (technique and knowledge) and grows in complexity, so the truth which is the reflection of reality blossoms in man's head. Only a partial aspect of that truth, at any time, can be in any one man's head. Distorted, partial and limited, in one head, this perception of reality yet acquires the power of truth, of *science*, in the heads of all living men, because it is organised by the conditions of society which themselves spring from the necessities of economic production. Thus at any time truth is the special complex formed by the partial reflections of reality in all living men's heads—not as a mere lumping together, but as these views are organised in a given society, by its level of experimental technique, scientific literature, means of communication and discussion, and laboratory facilities.

In each man "truth" takes the form of *perception*—what he seizes of reality with his senses—and *memory*—what is active at any moment of former perception, affecting his present perception. Because these human consciousnesses acquire tremendous power when their contents emerge organised by association, and become truth, they reflect back again with increasing penetration on the individual, whose memory and perception thus become more and more modified by being in society. An individual's consciousness is, in this sense, a social product.

Truth is individual man's experience of the connections of phenomena, become organised by homologation with millions of other such experiences. It can be organised because these perceptual worlds are all phenomena exhibited by the one material universe of which all individuals are a part, and not phenomena of so many private subjective Universes. Without this common factor, there would be no congruence of private worlds and therefore no objective truth. Science, which is objective truth, therefore is concerned with demonstrating the material connections or "causality" of phenomena.

There is no absolute truth, but there is a limit to which the truth of society at any moment continually aims. This limit of absolute truth is the Universe itself. When man shall have completely interpenetrated with Nature . . . Yet even this theoretical limit supposes both a Universe that stands still and a truth which is outside the Universe. Truth, however, is a part of the Universe. Yet truth is generated by man's struggle with the rest of reality, and hence, with each stage of the struggle, new reality is generated and the world made more complex. As a result reality itself is enriched, and the goal-post of "absolute truth" removed a stage further by that very increase in the complexity of reality. Society can no more reach absolute truth than a man can be tall enough to look down on himself—yet just as man's height by continually increasing extends his range of view, so society's development endlessly extends its truth.

Language is the most flexible instrument man has evolved in his associated struggle with Nature. Alone, man cannot plough Nature deeply; hence alone he cannot know her deeply. But as associated man, master of economic production, he widens his active influence on her, and therefore enlarges the truth which is the product of that action. Language is the essential tool of human association. It is for this reason that one can hardly think of truth except as a statement in language, so much is truth the product of association.

How does truth emerge in language? The word is a gesture, a cry. Take, for example, a herd of beasts that give a certain cry in situations of danger. When one cries, the others, as a result of a current of primitive passive sympathy, are terrified too, and all flee together.

The cry therefore has a subjective side, a "feeling-tone", all *feel* terrified at the cry.

But the cry also indicates some *thing* terrifying, a foe or danger. The cry therefore has an objective side, a *reference* to something perceivable in reality.

Evidently for purely animal existence a few brief cries suffice. Some animals are dumb. But for the animal engaged in economic production in association—the animal called man—the cry becomes the *word*. Its "value" is now no longer instinctive—resulting from the relation of genotype to habitual environment—it becomes "arbitrary"—resulting from the relation of modified genotype to artificial environment in economic production. In becoming the word as a result of association for economic production, the cry still retains its two sides, its instinctive feeling-tone and its acquired perceptual value, but both are made more precise and complex.

The feelings of the herd have a general similarity, because of the similarity of their instinctive make-up. Their perceptions also have a similarity, because of the likeness in their way of living. These like feelings are not known to the individual animals as like, any more than each knows the other's perceptual worlds are like. The individual animal feels and sees *alone*. We, the onlookers, deduce the likeness in the emotional and perceptual worlds of the animals from the similarity of their behaviour; but the animals cannot be conscious in this way of a like world.

Man *knows* that there is a likeness in the worlds of men; this likeness is expressed for example in science, the world of perceptual reality. In the same way he knows there is a likeness in feelings. This likeness is expressed in art, the world of affective reality.

Man only came to know this likeness in his perceptual worlds when he entered into association with other men. Why did he so enter? In order to change his perceptual world. This contradiction is simply the basic contradiction of science —that man learns about reality in changing it. That is precisely what an experiment does; and the experiment is crucial for science. This characteristic contradiction reaches its final expression in Heisenberg's Principle of Indeterminacy, which declares that all knowledge of reality involves a change in reality. All laws of science are laws stating what actions produce what changes in reality. Science is the sum of the changes in perceptual worlds produced by men in their history, preserved, organised, made handy, compendious and penetrating.

In the same way, man learns of the likeness of the egos of other men by attempting to change them. This change is essential for living in association as men. Man's instinct is to do always such and such. Unless therefore these instincts can be modified to make him do something different, man will respond instinctively instead of in a conditioned way, and society will be impossible. Men live in a common feeling-world only in so far as they are able to produce changes in each other's feelings by action. This change in feeling is crucial for art. The sum of such changes, organised and made independent of men, is what art is, not in abstraction, but emerging in concrete living.

Both science and art exist nascently in the animal. The wooing of the female, the frightening of enemies, mean that the active animal must change feeling in the other. The courtship dance and the threatening preliminaries to a fight are art in embryo. But both are done instinctively. They lack freedom and are therefore unconscious. They do not belong to a socially conditioned world. Only those feelings which are changed by means not given explicitly in the nature of man or of the natural environment are the subject of art. In so far as art exposes the real necessity of the instincts by exposing all the various possible changes following from the various possible means of influencing them, art becomes conscious of the necessity of the world of feeling, and therefore free. Art is the expression of man's freedom in the world of feeling, just as science is the expression of man's freedom in the world of sensory perception, because both are conscious of the necessities of their worlds and can change them—art the world of feeling or inner reality, science the world of phenomena or outer reality.

The common flight of a herd from a terrifying object indicated by the cry of one, is science in embryo, but only becomes science when it is the consciousness of a change in the perceptual world produced, not by fleeing from danger instinctively, but by altering it economically—by, for example, making weapons or a snare and killing the dangerous animal, or retreating in an organised way, covering the rear.

Science and art, although expressions of the social commonness in perceptual and feeling worlds, do not reduce men to replicas of each other. On the contrary, because they deal with possible *changes*, and are expanded and enriched in proportion as new changes are discovered, they are the means whereby individual differences are realised. Differences which at the animal level reveal themselves as a hare-lip or an extra plumpness, now appear as subtle differences of emotional life or *Weltanschauung*, colouring and enriching the whole complex of reality. Language is the special medium whereby these changes are made social coin. Words are the money of the ideological market of mankind. Even as a few exchange transactions express all the bewildering complexity of modern social being, so a few sounds express all the rich universe of emotion and truth which is modern man's ideological world.

2

Let us study the Word. Just as that simple thing, a pound note, reveals a staggering intricacy when we pursue its reflection in the spheres of value and price, supply and demand, profit and cost, so the word is a microcosm of a whole universe of ideological elaboration.

The word has a subjective side (feeling) and an objective side (perception). But these do not exist in the word-as-itself, in contemplation, any more than a pound note exists in itself as paper and print. They exist only in the word as a dynamic social act, just as a pound note only exists in exchange.

The word is spoken and heard. Let us call the parties to this act speaker and hearer. The word indicates some portion of reality sensorily perceptible: this is its symbolic or referential context. The speaker wishes to change the hearer's perceptual world so as to include the thing the word symbolises. For example, he may say, "Look, a rose!" He wishes the hearer to see a rose, or be aware of the possibility of seeing one. Or he may say, "Some roses are blue"; in which case he wishes to modify the hearer's perceptual world to the extent of including blue roses. And so on up to the most elaborate and abstruse mathematical discourse.

But in order to do this, there must be a Common Perceptual World—common to both speaker and hearer—with Common Perceptual Symbols—symbols for indicating entities in that common world which are accepted as current by both speaker and hearer.

This Common Perceptual World is the world of reality or truth, and science is its most general expression. We have already seen how it was built up by men's experience of changing reality. It is sometimes described as the world of percepts or concepts (the distinction is artificial). Because "blue" and "rose" are common to this world, the speaker can change the hearer's perceptual world by the injection of a blue rose into it. Blue and rose are now combined and make a new entity—one which was not before in the Common Perceptual World, but now colour each other in a whole which is more than the sum of the parts.

What, then, has been the result of the transaction? A blue rose, which was in the *speaker's* perceptual world, but not in their *common* perceptual world or in the *hearer's* perceptual world, has been formed in the common perceptual world and introjected into the hearer's perceptual world. Hence both the hearer's perceptual world and the common perceptual world are changed. Thus, if now the speaker says, "A blue rose is scentless", the sentence will have a meaning it would not have had before, because blue roses now exist in the common perceptual world of speaker and hearer.

Notice that a new word is not essential to introduce a new entity to the common perceptual world, although it is some-times used. We might have said, "N is a blue rose", "N is scentless". Most new entites are introduced by recombination, expansion, condensation and displacement of existing symbols rather than by neologism.

But the transaction does not change only the hearer's per-ceptual world and the common perceptual world. For, in order to body forth his unique individual experience of a strange blossom to the hearer, the speaker had to transform it into current coin. From a unique blossom, unlike anything seen before or since, it had to become for him a blue rose—as a blossom, belonging to the order *rose*; as a visual rose, to the colour *blue*. Thus the act of communication changed his experience and as it were kept it on the social rails, just as it changed the common perceptual world and the perceptual world of his hearer.

But it would be inverting the process to suppose that the common world cheapens our impressions by making unique individual experiences conceptual and trite. We respond to experience with broad instinctive drives, which divide experience into "edible", "non-edible", "dangerous", "neutral", "light", "dark". The possession of the common world of experience enables us to discriminate flowers among the non-edible, roses among flowers, colours among lightness, blue among colours. Objective reality thus separates itself out by social means from a vague humming chaos on the threshold of consciousness. The more complex our social world, the more the individual phenomenon becomes an intersection of a number of concepts and therefore the more individual and unique it is. Once again we must repeat: society is the means of realising individuality and therefore the road of freedom. Keeping the perception on the social rails is merely keeping it conscious.

This change in the perceptual worlds of speaker and hearer and in the common perceptual world, is the essence of the Word. The lightest word produces such a change, however trifling. We measure the power of the word by the degree of the change.

The word is not fully realised except as a dynamic social act. We overlook this just as we overlook that a pound note only exists importantly as a social act, because the complexities produced by the division of labour delay the impact between producer and consumer by the interposition of a market. The pound note, like a word, is only the expression of a transfer between one man and another—of goods in one case, of ideas in another—but the conditions of commodity-production give them a mysterious existence in their own right as concepts— the concept of "value" in the one case, the concept of "meaning" in the other.

We must therefore picture men's heads as full of these private perceptual worlds and then certain percepts in common (or concepts) which form a common perceptual world, and therefore give them the means of modifying each other's private worlds. Truth is not just the lump-sum of all private worlds; it is the common world—the means whereby these private worlds modify each other. These private worlds have relations with each other just as do the men who bear them in their heads. This plexus of relations is Truth.

But neither truth nor perception exist as a self-contained superstructure. They only exist as reflections of *material* changes. The common perceptual world contains both truth and error. True or false means just this: "Living in the common perceptual world". Truth only separates out from falsehood by the active relation of the common perceptual world with material reality.

We saw that man's interaction with Nature was continuously enriched by economic production. Economic production requires association which in turn demands the word. For men to work together, that is, to operate together non-instinctively, they must have a common world of *changeable* perceptual reality, and by changeable I mean changeable by their actions; and by changeable by their actions I include predictable change, such as dawn and eclipse, and locatable change, such as "here" and "there", for man's control over himself makes it possible for him to be at such-and-such a place by night, for example, and so in effect change reality by his actions as a result of simple perceptual discrimination of sequence and location. Hence, by means of the word, men's association in economic production continually generates changes in their perceptual private worlds and the common world, enriching both. A vast moving superstructure rises above man's busy hands which is the reflection of all the change he has effected or discovered in ages of life. Presently this common world becomes as complex and remote from concrete social life as the market, of which its secret life and unknown creative forces are the counterpart.

This is the shadow world of thought, or ideology. It is the reflection in men's heads of the real world. It is always and necessarily only symbolical of the real world. It is always and necessarily a reflection which has an active and significant relation to the object, and it is this activity and significance, and not the projective qualities of the reflection, which guarantee its truth. Every part of the Universe projectively reflects the remainder; only man is conscious of his environment. The idea is not the thing: the reflection is not the object; but one expresses or reflects the other. The words are tied to percepts which are photographic memory-images of bits of reality. These percepts are fused into concepts, are organised and ordered in the broadest and most abstract way. Or, more accurately, out of the broad, humming chaos of "existence"—the simplest percept—other concepts and percepts arise by differentiation and integration. All this phantasmagoria is accepted by man as only symbolic, just as a remembered percept is accepted as symbolic. When man recalls a certain horse or dwells on the concept "horse", in neither case does he suppose a horse is actually in his head. Even when he dwells on the refined

K

concept "two" he still does not suppose all two things are in his head or that his head is double.

The word refers to this shadow world of thought, and conjures up portions of it in a man's head. The Common Perceptual World, with all the condensations, organisations and displacements it has undergone, refers to and symbolises outer reality. It is all the percepts of reality mobilised for action. It is a compendium of what happens to percepts when the underlying reality is affected. The word symbolises this shadow world which it has helped to create, and is therefore the symbol of a symbol.

This is the sphere of truth and error. The word expresses a social convergence of action. "X is here." This is true if a number of people arrive in practice "here" simultaneously. "S is blue" is true if there is a general similarity in society's reaction to S as a result of the message (for example, in comparing it with an already agreed colour on a chart). Of course we do not always refer to the concrete living of society—the Common Perceptual World is so organised as to make reference to it alone sufficient in most cases (logic, laws, records). But if there is any difference not solvable by recourse to this shadow world (contradiction between a hypothesis and experience) it can only be settled by a recourse to material reality (the crucial experiment) whereby the common perceptual world is changed (new hypothesis). In this way the shadow world is in organic connection with material reality and continually sucks life and growth from its contradiction. The contradiction between theory and practice is what urges on both. Only their organic unity enables them to contradict each other. *False* cannot contradict *hot* because they live in different spheres: they are not one. *False* is contradicted by *true, hot* by *cold*. Truth and error cannot rest within the framework of the shadow world; their resolution demands recourse to the real material world. Any dispute which remains within the confines of the shadow world is not a dispute about truth and error but about consistency. The whole use of this world is to be a correct and compendious reflection of material reality; not merely a still reflection but a dynamic one.

3

But now we must summon into being another world, also lying behind the word—the world of feeling—the ego. Just as the cry was connected not only with something outside and terrifying but also with some state inside, the being terrified, so all words, besides indicating some outer entity, include also an inner attitude towards that entity. *Brutes, animals, beasts, living organisms,* are words all indicating similar real entities, but each with a different group of feeling-tones.

It may be asked: Why not have a different word for the feeling-tone, another for the object, and so increase the plasticity of language and facilitate clarity? The answer is: it is not in the nature or possibility of experience; for the separation between feeling-tone and real object is an abstraction. In reality they are one—part of the one active subject-object relation. We may separate the conscious field into real (or objective) qualities and apparent (or subjective qualities), but the separation is artificial.

Mechanical materialism, for example, started from the position that only those qualities are real into which the observer does not enter. Thus, first the world was stripped of colour, feeling, scent and temperature, for these could easily be demonstrated to have a neural component. Einstein advanced this a stage further by demonstrating the dependence of size, weight, duration and motion on the observer—these too were therefore eliminated and only the tensor was left invariant; but the development of quantum mechanics impugned even this and nothing invariant was left but a probability "wave"—*i.e.* a mathematical function. Hence the search for complete objectivity only leaves us with a bunch of equations—that is, of thoughts. Mechanical materialism turns into its opposite—solipsism.

But the idealist's programme is just as disastrous. Starting from the opposite programme, "All is mind that has nothing material about it", he is driven to exclude everything but the absolute Idea or concept. But a concept is "something" in a human brain, and a human brain is matter. Thus the idealist is left with nothing but material human brains. Or if he denies that concepts are dependent on human brains, he is an absolute idealist, and his world is made up of real *things,* ideas existing objectively apart from men.

This dualistic see-saw is inevitable as long as the concrete genesis of experience is ignored—its active subject-object relation—man's struggle with Nature. For in every given experience there is a like and an unlike, *i.e.* something given in previous experience, and something not given. The something already encountered is the object, the something new is the having of the experience—that which makes us able to differentiate this object or this encounter with the object from others. For example, we may pass the same rose every day, but the "setting" of the day is different, and therefore our attitude to the rose. That newness or difference is, in that particular experience, our subjective attitude to the rose—the "feeling-tone" of that experience. Of course there is also something located "out there" which accounts for the feeling of newness. And there is in our experience, in the subjective side of it, also "recognition", recognition of the rose as a flower, as an object, as something real.

This "feeling-tone" inheres in all experience: there is the reality, the objective sector of the conscious field on the one hand, and on the other hand the subjective attitude towards it. One is the field of the "I", the other the field of the Universe. We may say that every real object has as a result of our experience subjective associations adhering to it, but of course these are not attached mechanically, but depend on the setting—internal and external. A rose in one setting has different associations from a rose in another.

This in its most general form is the law of the conditioned response, the law that fluid reality is classified by the instinctive responses, and that these classes elaborate, shift and change according to experience.

The simplest form of this instinctive classification of external reality is of course numerical—mathematics. The most elementary art of self-consciousness is that which separates the "I" from Nature, and this recognition of separation, of discontinuity, when sympathetically introjected into objects, makes possible the conception of numerous things. Thus mathematics

is that order of experience in which the subjective content is
almost nil, so primitive is it. It is not correct to speak of
mathematics as bare of quality, for already we have the difference between the qualities of the numbers, in itself a reflection
of the difference between "I" and other. But it is almost bare
of quality, and for that reason, as we have already noted, the
language of mathematics is most purely symbolic. But since it
is based on the most fundamental part of self-consciousness it
seems the least objective and most "ideal" of the sciences.

Since all other language, however rigidly objective and
symbolic, necessarily deals with categories of quality, since in
fact the sphere of any given science is defined by the particular
qualities with which it is concerned, all other language
necessarily contains varying amounts of feeling-tone—of that
subjective essence of experience which is part of "quality".

Quality can only be apprehended and distinguished subjectively. But directly it is no longer new and has become a social
fact, it can be established objectively and is drawn into the
sphere of quantity. Thus, once we have recognised socially the
colour blue, it can be associated with a certain wave-length,
and becomes an objective fact. It can then be considered
objectively. But from its first appearance as something strange
and unique to its last vanishing as a mere figure on a dial, it
retains some element of the subjective.

This shift of subjective experience into the more objective
sphere is important because it enables us to understand how
feeling-tone can never be completely separated from the object
in experience—and therefore in the word—and how we can yet
have words for feelings only—e.g. "afraid", "fear". But
"afraid" and "fear" indicate here *objective* realities. The mind
can introspect and then watch other people, so that its feelings,
projected into the social world, become objective, become
objects of contemplation for it. In the experience indicated by
"afraid", we have both the subjective state it objectively refers
to, and the subjective feeling-tone in thinking of people being
afraid.

Thus experience weaves back and forth on itself, always
modified by its settings, always generating fresh tones and
complexes and yet, in so far as it is activised by the Word,

always symbolic of external reality and internal feeling.

Just as the word refers to a portion of objective reality, *i.e.* is the stimulus for the idea of it, so it is the stimulus for a portion of feeling-tone.[1] Due to the limitations of vocabulary, any given word is in fact the potential stimulus for a whole series of possible classes, entities or movements in outer reality —for example, the word "sea". By combination grammatically with other words, however, only part of these meanings are released—it is seen to refer only to the sea, or to sea in certain conditions. The same selection applies to the possible feeling associations of a word, not all of which are generated at any time.

We saw that we were able to communicate part of our experience of outer reality to others because of the existence of a common perceptual world with agreed symbols. In the same way, we communicate our feelings to others because of a common feeling world with agreed symbols. This common perceptual world was nothing but the "real" world, or truth as reflected in the consciousness of society. What, then, is the common affective world? This common affective world is nothing but the "I" which men construct as a result of their social experience.

We know the dilemma of the critical idealist, who cannot know what matter is like in itself and so denies matter, and of his opposite the behaviourist, who cannot know how other men are for themselves and so denies consciousness. Now the idealist is refuted by practice, by showing that matter can be made to exhibit certain phenomena by certain operations, and when all these possibilities of change have been explored the thing-in-itself becomes a thing-for-us. In the same way, the behaviourist is refuted by practice, by our relations with our fellow men, in which we count on their having instinctual

---

[1] The distinction between the affective and rational significance of words is of course an old one. Hindoo philosophy recognised the "dhvana" or hidden meaning of words as characteristic of poetry. Dante distinguished between *signum rationale* and *signum sensuale*, which in turn was based on a division recognised by William of Occam. Milton's well-known definition of poetry as simple, *sensuous*, and passionate was no doubt influenced by this conception. Ogden's and Richards' analysis of meaning is based on a distinction between the symbolic and emotive meaning of words.

drives like ourselves, leading to like actions, and "feel ourselves" into them sympathetically, so that their consciousness-
of-themselves becomes behaviour-for-us.

The common lives of men in association—far more powerful
than the life experience of one individual—have summarised
symbolically a whole range of transactions with outer reality,
which are thus accessible to each and constitute the known
Universe. In the same way associated man has amassed a whole
world of affective experience which is thus easily accessible and
constitutes the common ego or Mind.[1] Now a civilised man's
view of outer reality is almost entirely built up of the common
perceptual world: he sees the sun as a fiery star, cows as
animals, iron as metal, and so on. The extraordinary power and
universality of language guarantees this. But it is just as true
that his whole emotional consciousness, his whole feeling-
attitude to the sun, iron, cows and so forth, is almost entirely
built up from the common ego which enables us to live in close
relation as men.

Once again we must emphasise that neither the common
perceptual world nor the common ego makes men think or feel
in a standardised way. On the contrary, they are the very means
whereby man realises his individual differences. To members
of an animal species, the world looks very much alike because
it is such a simple world: their lives cannot differ much within
a narrow range. To a human being born in a highly civilised
society, the world is so complex and elaborate that his life can
be unique—completely realisable of his genetic individuality.
In the same way, animals of one species must have a very
similar emotional life: their emotional world is so simple.
But the social ego has been so subtilised and refined by generations of art and experience, that an individual can realise

[1] One hesitates to use the word mind, which is so confusedly treated by
most philosophers and psychologists. Probably the most consistent use of the
word is that of gestalt psychology. Of any conscious field, mind consists of
those elements most closely adherent to the sensory or subjective pole. Idealist
philosophers use the word mind more loosely. All phenomena are counted as
mental because they form part of conscious fields, and since all objects are
only known as phenomena, all objects are counted as mental. Thus the
idealist reduces Reality to "Mind", and since he knows phenomena as part
of his conscious field, Reality is only "his mind".

his emotional peculiarities to the full within its frame.

A sunset is nothing to a beast; art makes it what it is to us. When words arouse a feeling-tone in us, we draw it from the social ego; otherwise how could a mere sound exactly arouse, like a note on a piano, a corresponding emotional reverberation selected from a socially recognised scale of values?

It is precisely because the complex social world and social ego offers such possibilities of realisation for the individuality, that we hear in modern civilisation so many complaints of the strangling of individuality by society. No such complaints are voiced in savage society, for the possibility of freedom does not yet exist. Man is too simple and cabined. When the development of the productive forces has been accomplished by a corresponding development in the social world and the social ego, giving man undreamed-of possibilities of self-realisation, and yet the *utilisation of these forces is manifestly held back by the productive relations,* then on all sides arise protests of "emotional starvation" and "crippling of personalities" in a world of rich consciousness, complaints which are the ideological counterpart of denunciations of malnutrition and unemployment in a world of plenty. They are part of the continually increasing volume of protest against modern society. They are the harbingers of revolution.

4

We saw that in experience neither object nor subject, matter nor mind, is ever completely "pure", and that this "impurity" is reflected in language. Therefore the common world and the common ego do not live apart, they interpenetrate. Always, given in the Word, is a certain subjective attitude towards a certain piece of reality. Science, concerned with objective reality, uses words as far as possible so as to eliminate or cancel out the subject: art to build it up.

All experience is organised, is *real*. There is not just a blur of phenomena, but things separate themselves out into a real spatial world. In the same way feelings are organised, they come to a point in the ego, they have stability and radiate out and have broad drives and homogeneities.

Words therefore cannot just be flung together in a hotch-potch. They must have organisation: express something real—a part of the universe, and a real attitude towards it—a part of the ego.

When we are making a scientific statement, we make it about observable things—observable operations of ordering, observable colours, actions and the like. We assume always there is "someone" doing this ordering and counting. The assumption is so implicit and naïve that scientists do not always realise that they are making this assumption and that they are referring everything to one observer. If queried, they will reply that this observer is any "right-thinking person" without explaining what right-thinking person could have so bewildering a range of experience, and maintain so neutral, so admirably judicial an attitude towards it. The scientist has tended to regard this understood observer as just a piece of scaffolding, and to assume that, if it were necessary, the scaffolding could easily be knocked away—it would make no difference to the building. But the latest developments of physics[1] have shown that if this scaffolding is knocked away—nothing is left. The building absolutely depends on the scaffolding for its support. This queer, universal "Mock Ego" of science is illusory and yet necessary: all the reality which science's language symbolises is attached to "him". Only mathematics seems to escape him, and then only because, as we have seen, it escapes from outer reality into the human brain and becomes a mere extension of the Mock Ego's personality. This Mock Ego is not of course taken seriously by scientists. He is appreciated as an *abstraction*. There is no interest in his home life or hobbies.

Now in precisely the same way when poetry—or literary art generally—wishes to "symbolise" the social ego, wishes to convey affective attitudes in an organised way, it is still compelled to make some statement about reality. The emotions are only found in real life adhering to bits of reality; therefore bits of reality—and moreover *organised* bits—must always be presented to achieve the emotional attitude. But the statement

[1] In particular, Heisenberg's Principle of Indeterminacy and the conflict of quantum physics with relativity physics.

about reality selected for the underlying emotional attitude is not supposed to be about *material* reality, any more than science's Mock Ego is supposed to be a real man. It is a mock world; it is an illusion, accepted as such. So, by a long road, we have arrived back at the illusion, the *mimesis*, which is the essence and puzzle and method of literary art.

This mock ego of science and this mock world of art are both necessary because object and subject are never parted in experience, but engage in the contradiction of an unceasing struggle. Science and art, separated out from mythology by an initial division of labour so that each can be better developed, keeps as a souvenir of separation a kind of scar or blind side like the Norwegian trolls which are hollow behind. This hollowness or blind side is the mock ego of science and the mock world of art. Science and art are like the two halves produced by cutting the original human hermaphrodite in half, according to the story of Aristophanes in Plato's *Symposium*, so that each half evermore seeks its counterpart. But science and art do not when fitted together make a complete concrete world: they make a complete hollow world—an abstract world only made solid and living by the inclusion of the concrete living of concrete men, from which they are generated.

What then is the *purpose*, the social function, of science and art? Why are reared upon this mock world and this mock man a frigid but true image of reality and a phantastic but warm reflection of man's own countenance?

Both are generated as part of the social process: they are social products, and the social product whether material or ideological can have only one goal, that of freedom. It is freedom that man seeks in his struggle with Nature. This freedom, precisely because it cannot be won except by action, is not a freedom of mere contemplation. To attain it a man does not merely relapse into himself—"let himself go". Just as the spontaneity of art is the result of laborious action, so freedom has as its price, not eternal vigilance but eternal labour. Science and art are guides to action.

(1) *Science* makes available for the individual a deeper, more complex insight into outer reality. It modifies the perceptual

content of his consciousness so that he can move about a world he more clearly and widely understands; and this penetration of reality extends beyond his dead environment to human beings considered objectively, that is, as objects of his *action*, as the anvil to his hammer. Because this enlarged and complex world is only opened up by men in association—being beyond the task of one man—it is a *social* reality, a world common to all men. Hence its enlargement permits the development of associated men to a higher plane at the same time as it extends the freedom of the individual. It is the consciousness of the necessity of outer reality.

(2) The other world of *art*, of organised emotion attached to experience, the world of the social ego that endures all and enjoys all and by its experience organises all, makes available for the individual a whole new universe of inner feeling and desire. It exposes the endless potentiality of the instincts and the "heart" by revealing the various ways in which they may adapt themselves to experiences. It plays on the inner world of emotion as on a stringed instrument. It changes the emotional content of his consciousness so that he can react more subtly and deeply to the world. This penetration of inner reality, because it is achieved by men in association and has a complexity beyond the task of one man to achieve, also exposes the hearts of his fellow men and raises the whole communal feeling of society to a new plane of complexity. It makes possible new levels of conscious sympathy, understanding and affection between men, matching the new levels of material organisation achieved by economic production. Just as in the rhythmic introversion of the tribal dance each performer retired into his heart, into the fountain of his instincts, to share in common with his fellows not a perceptual world but a world of instinct and blood-warm rhythm, so to-day the instinctive ego of art is the common man into which we retire to establish contact with our fellows. Art is the consciousness of the necessity of the instincts.

(3) It is important to understand that art is no more propaganda than science. That does not mean that neither has a social rôle to perform. On the contrary, their rôle is one which is as it were primary to and more fundamental than that of

propaganda: that of changing men's minds. They change men's minds in a special way. Take as an extreme case of science's way of changing man's view of outer reality, a mathematical demonstration. It cannot be said to persuade. A mathematical demonstration appears either true or false: if true, it simply injects itself into our minds as an additional piece of outer reality. If false, we reject it as mere word-spinning. But if we accept it, we are no more *persuaded* of its truth than we are persuaded of the "truth" of a house standing in front of us. We do not accept it: we *see* it.

In the same way, in art, we are not persuaded of the existence of Hamlet's confusion or Prufrock's seedy world-weariness, we are not persuaded of the existence of Elsinore or Proust's madeline cake. The whole feeling-complex of the poem or the play or the novel is injected into our subjective world. We *feel* so-and-so and such-and-such. We are no more persuaded of their truth than of the truth of a toothache: but the vividness or social universality of the emotional pattern is announced by the poignancy of the sensation we call Beauty. Music affords an even more striking example of this.

Thus neither Truth nor Beauty are persuasion, just because they are *guides* to action. Persuasion must be not a guide but a persuasion to action, a pressure to be or do differently. In fact science and art are opposite poles of language, and language has as its main function the rôle of *persuasion*. It has only evolved these poles as refinements, as tempered spearheads of the advance of life. Art and science are persuasion become so specialised as to cease to be persuasion, just as in the flower petals the leaves have become so specialised as to cease to fulfil the function of leaves.

Language sucks its life-blood from daily life, and in daily life all conversation which is not informative of outer reality regarded objectively (*e.g.* of events or the speaker's feelings treated objectively) or of inner reality (*e.g.* accent, angry or pleased "tones", facial expressions, circumlocutions, manner, polite, curt, surprising or warm phraseology), is *rhetorical* in the Aristotelian sense, that is, it is designed to persuade others to act in a certain way and feel in a certain way.

Now rhetoric stands in this relation to science and art, that

it is not a guide to action on outer reality or on the instincts
but is always mixed or counterpointed. Thus in so far as a
man already has an instinctive urge to do something in a certain
situation, then persuasion is directed to so explaining the nature
of outer reality that he will see the necessity of doing the
particular things to which we wish to persuade him. On the
other hand, if the situation plainly indicates action, our
persuasion is directed to arousing the emotional urge to fulfil
the action. Thus there is a kind of reversal of the use of words:
for emotional reasons objective statements are used, for
objective reasons emotional statements; but generally both
are mixed.

Rhetoric or persuasion is the universal mode of language
through which men freely guide and lead each other by appealing in day-to-day activity on the one hand to the necessities of
the task, and on the other hand to the demands of the instincts.
Rhetoric, too, is rooted in outer reality and the genotype, and
because it is more direct, urgent and prosaic it is more primitive
and everyday. It is the warp and woof of language as an instrument of association, from which science and art separate themselves as more specialised, more organised, more aloof, more
abstract and more *real and convincing in their special fields* precisely
because of their use of those unreal and illusory scaffoldings,
the mock ego and the mock world.

That persuasion can be used to mislead, that rhetoric can
be empty and hypocritical, is merely to repeat in another
form the well-known facts that truth and error both exist and
that man makes mistakes. It does not invalidate persuasion as
such. Science can be false, art trite, persuasion hypocritical or
misleading; as society develops historically, the false persuasion
emerges from the true.

.   .   .   .

We see, then, that language communicates not simply a
dead image of outer reality but also and simultaneously an
attitude towards it, and does so because all experience, all life,
all reality emerges consciously in the course of man's struggle
with Nature. This image of outer reality and this ego do not
confront each other stonily across a chasm; they emerge from

and return again into concrete living; they are the results of a dialectic development. Between them is the bridge of matter. Both are built on the soil which connects body and environment. The very nature of language is a proof of that interpenetration. Art and science therefore, through the means of social action, mediated by persuasion, continually play into each other's hands. Because man's life is educed from present reality by the contradiction between man and Nature, outer reality and inner feeling by this very contradiction mutually develop each other and themselves.

Poetry, like the human life of which it is an emanation, springs from the fruitful quarrel of mathematics and music.

THE PSYCHE AND PHANTASY

I

POETRY is written by a poet. The contradiction which generates it is a special case of the contradiction that drives on society and is fought out in the real life and real consciousness of men—the contradiction between man's desires and Nature's necessity. Poetry springs from the contradiction between the instincts and experience of the poet. This tension drives him to build the world of illusory phantasy which yet has a definite and functional relation to the real world of which it is the blossom.

The twentieth century has learned a good deal about the general nature of phantasy. Among its important discoveries are those of psycho-therapy, using the pioneer methods of Charcot, Janet, Morton Prince and, above all, Freud. Freud's disciples founded many rival schools, of which the best known are those of Jung (analytical psychology) and Adler (individual psychology).

Probably in no other field has the essential weakness of modern science been more clearly shown than in the subsequent development of the important data gained by Freud in his early researches. This weakness is the lack of any synthetic world-view in which to fit the empirical discoveries made. The researches of a brilliant investigator such as Freud increase instead of clarifying the hopeless confusion of modern ideology.

The scientist is left with two alternatives. On the one hand, he regards his discoveries as limited to his own particular sphere and adopts towards reality as a whole a complete eclecticism, which leads inevitably to a view of reality as essentially unknowable and to a conception of science as a mere collection of convenient summaries of empirical discoveries not necessarily capable of coherence or synthesis. Or, on the other hand, the scientist who has made some important discoveries may, in default of a world-view common to science as a whole, erect a complete ideology on the limited basis of the particular discoveries he has made. Naturally such an ideology will be a travesty of reality and will fail to account for most of the important features of reality and of the human mind. The things unaccounted for by its explanation are forcibly reduced to the level of the other few facts by the crude "nothing but" method.

If, however, this happens to be repugnant to the scientist, as will be the case if he is a scientist of some breadth of culture, then mystical explanations will be given for the other phenomena inexplicable by his limited world-view. A large portion of reality will be conveniently removed to the sphere of religion, as among the vitalists, holists, entelechists and spiritualists generally.

Freud is representative of empiricism with its reductive method, while Jung tends towards a more eclectic and mystical point of view.

Freud finds sexuality—using a somewhat broad definition of sexuality—present in all human ideology, but most clearly seen in the products of neurotic conflicts. This sublimated sexuality takes a number of forms: artistic, religious and philosophical. It is in fact the generating force of all human activity. "But then", the objector urges, "sexuality is something else besides sexuality, which by definition is a certain instinct directed to the accomplishment of the sexual act?" "No," Freud answers, "sexuality is unable to take this simple form, because it comes into conflict with the stern prohibitions of the super-ego and the ego in the psyche. The wealth of ideology is produced in its attempt to sublimate the conflict. This ideology includes religion, morals, art, philosophy, neuroses and dreams."

Freud takes the arbitrary, ego-instinct duel further by his concept of the Pleasure and Reality Principles. The pleasure principle represents the instinctive desires of the sexual part of the psyche. The ego is associated with the reality principle. Here we have nothing but a special version of the familiar biological opposition—the instinctive organism and its adaptation to the environment.

Freud's pleasure principle (which as he himself admits, must include hunger and other instincts beside the sexual) is the appetitive striving of life, and the reality principle is that conditioning or adaptation of its appetites produced by the environment. This adaptative instinct, seen in action, appears as the cat stalking the mouse, the otter fishing, the deer on watch and fleeing. But no hard-and-fast line can be drawn between the two. In seeking a mate, in seeking food or in evading danger, a pleasure principle is being followed, but the animal cannot ignore external reality; indeed it is only by the help of its adaptations to reality that it gratifies its appetitive instincts. Why then do the two not come into conflict in animals and so create a neurosis and an ideology? Why is the conscious ego in man associated with the reality principle and not with the more "egoistic" appetitive instincts of sex, hunger or self-preservation?

Freud is, in fact, only rediscovering in his new but *limited* sphere, categories as old as any known to human thought, and then applying them, with the nomenclature and special twist they receive in his domain, back to the whole sphere of human thought. It is the old contradiction between subject and object, between man and Nature, between instinct and environment, between free will and necessity, between life and matter, which appears in Freud's psychology in three different dresses: (*a*) as the pleasure principle and the reality principle, (*b*) as the life instinct and the death instinct, (*c*) as the ego (together with its emanations the id and the super-ego) and the libido.

Now we have already remarked about this subject-object dualism (which has been the constant ground of our study so far) that men have tended to separate them as mutually exclusive opposites and to give only one the status of reality. Thus all reality is reduced to those phenomena which do not contain any part of the other: since these two opposites are not exclusive but mutually interpenetrate, such a reduction eventually reduces the world to precisely nothing but a meaningless name.

Since he is a psychologist and not a philosopher, Freud does not treat of all reality but only of mentation, conscious and unconscious, considered objectively. Yet here, exactly as in the field of knowledge as a whole, the same interpenetration of environment and instinct takes place, and it is never possible

L

to separate any mentation as specifically instinctive and in no way conditioned by the environment. The attempt to do so, to discard as "additional" or "sublimated" all mentation which bears the stamp of the environment, involves excluding layer after layer of consciousness as secondary and unreal until one reaches as the only true psychic reality something vague and formless, a mere name—*libido*.

Yet this discovery was in fact given from the start in Freud's bourgeois approach to psychology. The bourgeois philosopher is unable to rise above the standpoint of the individual in civil society. All social activity is the product of the free will and dynamic urge of the individual as it emerges immediately in its own consciousness grappling direct with Nature. Since its instinctive centre is the source of its freedom, any restrictions placed on it by social relations cripple and distort its range of action.

This conception is, of course, appropriate to a class the conditions of whose existence are that he is free to produce exactly what seems best to him in view of the market, the market itself being but a kind of extension of Nature or the environment. To such a class, the initial condition of whose development was that it abolished all feudal relations, freedom necessarily seems to inhere in the individual by divine right, and freedom appears as the *ignorance* of the necessity of those social relations which influence the individual's desires.

Such a conception leads to a wholly false view of society and freedom, and in psychology, therefore, to a misinterpretation of the social contents of the psyche and of the way in which the instincts become free. It reflects the view of a class whose own developing freedom rests on its alienation from active struggle with the environment, and in whose ideology therefore there is already a cleavage between subject and object. Instead of seeing that subject and object are separated actively by their mutual struggle, such a view supposes that they are already separated contemplatively by their mutually exclusive nature. Such a misunderstanding can only lead to an interpretation of the world in terms of either subjectivism or mechanism, and Freud, although he regards himself as a materialist, *chooses the subject*. Libido, the source of free action,

creates the psychic environment which cripples it. Freud's
idealistic presumption is the simple presumption of Rousseau's
"natural man", who is born free and is everywhere in chains.

But we have already seen that the instincts, unadapted by
society, are blind and therefore unfree. The brute is not free;
the ant is the slave of its innate responses. Man's freedom is
obtained by association, which makes it possible for him to
acquire mastery over Nature through becoming actively conscious of its necessity and his own. This association of itself
necessarily imposes certain restrictions, conventions and obligations, such as those of good behaviour, language and mutual
aid. But all these things are not fetters on the free instincts
(*libido*); they are the instruments by which instinctive man
realises his freedom. The view of reality which is science, the
canons of feeling which are art and ethics, are imposed on the
instincts from without; none the less they are not fetters,
distortions, inhibitions or sublimations. They are the means by
which instinct realises its freedom because they give it understanding of Nature's necessity and its own and therefore are—
since Nature will not yield to a mere wish—the only means by
which the will can actively realise itself. And man's consciousness, with its ego, its sublimations, its distortions, and its
vivid rich complexity, is nothing but the adaptation produced
in man's psychic genotype by the conditions of working in
association with other men towards the realisation of freedom.
Consciousness, in the broadest sense (including therefore the
subconscious, which is also the product of modified instinct),
is a social product. It is not merely that consciousness has a
social component. The construction of consciousness is the
socialising of the psyche.

Of course individuals vary, and this individuality is reflected
in their consciousnesses, just as the difference in a man's
anatomy is reflected in his clothes. Yet clothes are clothes and
not flesh and blood, and these social adaptations of the human
psyche are the very means by which individual differences are
realised and accentuated. Also human experiences differ, and
since consciousnesses are determined by experience, individual
consciousnesses will differ, but this is only to say that society
itself by division of labour has so differentiated itself as to give

rise to the possibility of widely different individual adventures in the world of geography or of feeling; this difference contrasts with the simple sameness of lives among the members of a herd and once again shows that the development of society is the means by which differences are realised and personality attains its full worth.

Since consciousnesses are determined by the social complex made necessary by a given historical development of the productive forces, and it is not, as Freud assumes, that society is determined instantly by the make-up of the psyche, the historical production of ideology, phantasy, dream and the like must depend on an historical change in the structure of men's social complex. It must be plain that this is so, for if the innate qualities of the psyche determined the social complex and also the consciousness and ideological productions of its members, how could these vary so much from age to age and culture to culture, when man's genetic make-up barely varies at all in historical times?

It can be shown that the material productive forces of society, and the relations between men made necessary by these, vary and develop historically according to deterministic laws of a quality peculiar to the sphere of society, and since this development is fought out in the consciousnesses of the men who engage in these relations, it is possible to explain scientifically the ceaseless change of ideology and individual consciousness in spite of an invariant psychic genotype. To cut away all these material causes, as Freud does, is to cut away the only means of understanding scientifically the cause of historical changes in ideology.

It also robs his therapy of any but a local and particular value. Since the distortions and variations of consciousness, including all neurotic conflicts, are generated, not by material conditions of living but by the psyche torturing itself, by the ego separating itself and issuing stern demands to the libido, man can only be cured by becoming conscious of the cause of his conflict which, since it is all in the psyche, can by the same effort of will be removed. Hence Freud's therapeutic theory is solipsist and religious.

Empiricist as he is, he does not of course carry this out

consistently. He admits material causes for neurotic conflicts, such as family upbringing, psychic traumata derived from experience, unhappy surroundings and puritan education. But he does not fully see that if this kind of explanation is to be carried out in any scientific spirit of thorough-going determinism, it at once shifts the responsibility for the organisation of consciousness on to the material basis of society. He does not fully see that if the super-ego is a reflection of the parent, then —since the parent's behaviour to the child, and his status in regard to it, are reflections of the economic development of the era[1]—the formation of the super-ego, which is the key to most neurotic conflicts, is determined by sociological laws. To admit this fully would make psycho-therapy—once the connections between the psyche and the environment were understood— a matter of understanding how to modify the social environment itself. Of course with a rich neurotic the environment can be modified more easily, and since Freud's patients are mainly of this type, it suffices to state the problem of the environmental causation of neuroses in the partial vague way he does. But applied to society as a whole, any such therapy is—literally— revolutionary.

For although society is the instrument of man's freedom, it by no means follows that it is a perfect instrument. On the contrary its imperfections are what produce the constant development of society. The very nature of class society necessarily involves that the productive forces—on whose power men's freedom is based—tend in varying degrees to become stifled and crippled by the social relations which made possible their initial development. Class society itself is only a result of the division of labour which raised social productivity to new levels. At such periods it certainly seems as if man's social relations are crippling his possibilities of freedom. At such times he groans and travails and cries out because the forms and restraints—the morals, religions and all the conscious formulations of society—are crippling his "free" instincts. The very neuroses which Freud investigates, and which are so characteristically modern, are products of this travail—the labour pangs of a new society.

[1] See Engels' *Origin of the Family.*

Freud is always faced by the dilemma of deducing the changing phenomena of consciousness and mentation from unchanging instincts and an unchanging biological environment. This can only be done, as we have shown, by the introduction of a variable, the relations made necessary by economic production: but Freud ignores this. Hence he is driven to deduce historical change from the make-up of the individual psyche, and he therefore imagines to be a permanent part of the psyche what are merely reflections of a special social environment.

Jung is well aware of the contradictions in psychology. He regards them, however, as mechanical and mutually exclusive opposites—such opposites as "introversion" and "extraversion", or "energic quantitative finality" and "materialistic qualitative causality". He is never able to resolve the contradictions he raises, because he never passes from the contradictions of psychology to the sphere immediately beneath psychology, that of society itself. Instead he passes in the opposite direction, from psychology to the epistemology evolved by psyches, and gets lost in the old familiar metaphysical difficulties of subject and object. Thus by a more philosophical and less empirical path, Jung arrives at the same dilemma as Freud. Since the neurotic conflict is due to the conflict between life and reality, which religion in its various forms has been evolved to sublimate, how is the patient to be cured? Freud recommended telling the patient that the medicine was only water from the tap, in the belief that the shock would cure him. (Cure by abreaction.) Jung recommends that the patient should be allowed to believe in the water, should in fact be encouraged to spin his own fancies about it. (Cure by synthesis.) Jung justifies himself in this betrayal of science by the belief that back of all mythology are primeval structures inherent in the mind (the archetypes) which interact with the patient's ideology and so generate myths. These, although they are not truly true, are yet psychologically true. (Birth of the Hero.) Thus Jung also chooses the subject and a fundamentally idealistic approach. Their therapy is a therapy of will-power and mystic mind-control. In neither do the material, *i.e.* the *environmental* causes of mental disease figure candidly and openly, but only in the limited form of erotic transference to the analyst. The analyst tries to fill the rôle of society and necessarily fills it meanly and in a limited way. Neither see that the problem is of its nature one which cannot be solved only in the sphere of consciousness divorced from action.

Nor do Freud or Jung see that, in so far as religion is brought in by man to plaster up a decaying culture, man will have no difficulty in giving birth to new mythologies without the need of archetypes or the psycho-analyst's midwifery. Dying bourgeois culture has in fact evolved the vigorous religion of fascism, complete with mythology and choreagus, as seen in Germany and Italy. The neurotic conflict is a real thing and Jung and Freud are right when they see the germs of it in all civilised beings. But they are wrong in supposing it to be a pathological product of civilisation which would be removed if only we could do away with civilisation. The conflict between man's instincts and environmental reality is precisely what life is, and all the products of society—hats, art, science, houses, sport, ethics and political organisation— are adaptations evolved to moderate and cure that conflict. Since the successful issue of this conflict is freedom, it is nonsense to talk of these adaptations as crippling freedom *qua* adaptations. They only cripple freedom to the degree in which they grow obsolete and begin to stifle the developing freedom they have already generated. This crippling is not a sign that adaptations must be done away with but that fresh adaptations are needed. It is therefore pointless to ask oneself, as Freud does, whether civilisation is worth the price one pays for it in the frustration and crippling of the instincts, for it was precisely to moderate and lessen the frustration and crippling of the instincts by the *environment* that civilisation was evolved.

Hence psycho-analysts play a petty part during the breakdown of modern civilisation in war, unemployment, universal degradation, hatred and despair. Plainly there is a world-wide conflict between the instincts and the environment and all the tremendous and elaborate superstructure of society—religion, art, laws, science, states, patriotism, ethics, political aims and aspirations, liberty, comfort, peace, life itself—all these things tremble and collapse in ruins; yet it was just this splendid edifice that man constructed to *sublimate*, in Freudian nomenclature, to *resolve*, in ours, the contradiction between his environment and his instincts. This immense decaying superstructure fills with awe the mind even of the revolutionary who sees the cause of its collapse and the still more complex structure which will supersede it; but as a substitute for it the psycho-analysts solemnly offer the meagre constructs of Freudian philosophy or Jungian mythology, tattered scraps expected to heal the conflict which a whole Europe of human achievement cannot resolve.

On the surface Adler's approach seems more realistic. In his theory of the struggle for existence and the consequent development of an inferiority complex and a compensatory ability, he realised the way in which bourgeois competition strangles in its final stages all the best in man's individuality and ability. He recognised the environment.

Let us take a quotation from Adler:

In a civilisation where one man is the enemy of the other—for this is what our whole industrial system means—demoralisation is ineradicable, for demoralisation and crime are the by-products of the struggle for existence as known to our industrialised civilisation.

So far, so good. Here we have an analysis of the general effect of capitalism on the individual. What is his remedy?

To limit and do away with this demoralisation, a chair of curative pedagogy should be established. . . .

2

We see, then, that psycho-analysts are idealist in their approach to the practical problems of living, and in no way take up an attitude different from that of the great class-religions. For if man's subjective feelings of misery, unease and unhappiness, are not due to outer material causes but to Sin (as the religions put it) or Complexes (as the analyst puts it), then man's misery, unhappiness and unease can be cured by casting out sin, by self-control, by salvation, by abreaction

—whatever name one gives to a pure exercise of will un-accompanied by organised effective action. Indeed, many of the class-religions have gone further in that they have developed organisations for clearing up certain sectors of misery by material action—societies to care for the sick, for example.

If the root causes of broad areas of human misery are due to the surroundings in which the psyche develops, and the obstacles, possibilities, adaptations and attractions offered by the social relations of that environment, then they can only be eliminated by a material change, which will make possible a change of heart. This view is opposed both to that of religion and of psycho-analysis.

Aside altogether from the question of revolution, if the strife between man's instincts and environment can be cured by "education", by a mental self-change, why has man troubled to evolve factories, clothes, houses, cooking, language, art, religion, science and political organisations? These are all products of the struggle between the instincts and environment and are all unnecessary if Freud and the religious teachers are right, since man's conflict could be resolved merely by his becoming conscious of its causes.

Of course, faced with such an obvious instance as the hunger instinct, Freud could not maintain that its conflict with reality could be pacified by any means other than the material therapy of food. But the logical basis of his theory is certainly idealist or "yogi", and it is this which makes Freud-ians treat art, one of the instruments of men's freedom, as something childish and escapist in tendency. They do not see that the human conflict between man and Nature (of which the neurotic conflict is only a special form) drives men to free association, and that art is a necessity of this association, the means whereby it remains free, and because it is free reaches heights and depths inaccessible to a coerced association.

The whole of psycho-analytical writing flounders in the marsh of bourgeois epistemology, where subject and object appear as mutually exclusive opposites under a hundred will-o'-the-wisp disguises and where the problems of mind are insoluble precisely because in the society which generates this discussion "mind" has moved away from "matter"—subject and object have ceased to interpenetrate actively and so establish in practice their theoretical identity of opposites.

What is consciousness? Unconsciousness? Instinct? Reality? Mind? Illusion? Understanding of these concepts is evidently vital for a psychology—and it is not surprising that Freudism, with its naïve Rousseauistic idealism, cannot achieve a satisfactory psychology.

The individual is born with certain instincts, evidenced in action (response to stimulus) and changed in that action (conditioned response). That conditioning includes consciousness: memory, images, thoughts, percepts and recognitions are the conditioning of instincts.

But not all conditioning of instincts is consciousness. It is important to understand that there is nothing mysterious in unconscious mentation. The repetition which is subtly different, the circling rhythm which is a spiral, the reaction which is changed because of what has gone before, is not peculiar to mind or life, but is a general characteristic of the process of reality. The like, Space, is generated by the ingression of the unlike, Time. Only when this process evidences itself in the sphere of life do we call it psychic; but then we have no reason to call it conscious, any more than the purposeful activities of the autonomous nervous system are conscious. The thing to be explained and accounted for as an intruder is not unconsciousness but consciousness. Only our immediate experience of it can give us grounds for accepting it.

As soon as a mentation becomes conscious, it makes a qualitative leap and enters the sphere of free will. Conscious mentations are different in quality from unconscious precisely because they are conscious. Consciousness is a real material quality and not an epiphenomenon; it is the quality of freedom in mentation.

The behaviourists argue that we have no right to deduce consciousness in others, and that their actions can all be explained deterministically by the sufficient stimulus. Their argument as to the non-existence of mind is sound as long as it remains in the sphere of theory, just as is the subjective idealist's argument as to the non-existence of matter. It is disproved in practice. Aware ourselves of a qualitative difference in actions when they are associated with conscious thoughts, we find, in our active intercourse with others, that their actions show similar differences. In so far as we depend on their consciousness in our transactions with them, and these transactions are successful, we prove the reality of their consciousness.

This in itself gives us the clue to what consciousness is. Consciousness is the product of association: not of herd association which is mediated by instincts, but of association for economic production which is mediated precisely by consciousness—by specific adaptations of the psychic instincts. We can never prove consciousness in terms of the theory of the common perceptual world because it is entirely that world. In the same way we can never prove not-consciousness (matter) because it is entirely not that world.

Objects detach themselves as objects from the flux of perception in so far as they become objects for social men. The sun, a mere unrecognised source of phototropism for animals, becomes a socially recognised object for man, ripener of harvest, measure of the working day, clock and compass of the hunter. The field of perception is organised into figure and ground only in so far as figures have a significance for the conjoint action of men. Instinctual appetite is the basis of this organisation, but it is lifted to a higher plane, it becomes conscious, as soon as it is an organisation for society.

This is equally true of our affective world. This flowing penumbra of instinctive music only acquires a pattern, only becomes *conscious*, to the extent that social life itself organises feelings, sentiments, passions, enduring trends, aims and aspirations which draw their stability from the relations of associated men.

In the fashioning of consciousness the great instrument is language. It is language which makes us consciously see the sun, the stars, the rain and the sea—objects which merely elicit *responses* from animals. It is this which makes us capable of appreciating truth and beauty: for truth is a relation between a perception of reality and the common perceptual world, and beauty is a relation between a feeling-tone of reality and the common ego.

Thus we see that what makes the difference between the

unconscious brute that a man would be if reared like Mowgli by a wolfish foster-mother, and the conscious human he in fact becomes in society, is the active relation between his personal experience of reality and the common perceptual world and common affective ego. Science and art expand and develop this world and this ego. They are not contained in them; they are secreted in the whole complex of a working society. Science and art may for various reasons in some respect oppose or deny the perceptual reality and affective attitude given in concrete social experience. In such a case science or art seems to conflict with a man's consciousness.

The common world and the common ego are generated by the active struggle of associated men with Nature, as a living historical development; and the consciousness of an individual is formed in organic connection with this struggle. Once again we repeat that the common perceptual world and the common ego do not stamp a standardised pattern on the genotype: like the society of which they are products and reflections they are the means whereby the genotype realises its individual differences in the psychic sphere.

It is for this reason that consciousness and conscience have so close a connection: for the conscience—the imprinted summary of the ethical laws of society—is a special integration of the individual consciousness, just as truth, beauty and reality are other integrations, playing similar social rôles.

This is not to say that there cannot be a conflict of conscience, divided aims and the like. On the one hand man's struggle with Nature is never absolutely victorious, and just as "accidents", like an earthquake or an attack of malaria, may reveal the relativity of any victory, so in the psychological sphere madness, murder, neuroses or melancholy reveal that man's adaptations do not extend to the full conquest either of himself or Nature. Man is not yet completely free. The consciousness is not completely integrated—different layers may have different trends.

In addition man's struggle with Nature is complicated by contradictions generated in the very instrument of his freedom, society. This gives rise to local stresses and strains, giant upheavals, revolutions, or the ruin and decline of whole societies.

This is necessarily reflected in man's consciousness—moral problems; feelings of sin, worthlessness and despair; widespread death thoughts; vast spiritual needs; loss of faith—these emotional pangs are part of the travail of society.

In a primitive society where man is as yet undifferentiated, conscience and consciousness are similarly simple, direct and homogeneous, and for this very reason lacking in depth and vividness. Primitive communities seem to have "collective representations" and a *participation mystique*. When this consciousness is attacked, there is no complexity or balancing of forces to soften the blow; the collapse is complete. The primitive who is once convinced that he has sinned or is bewitched will promptly die—a fact well-attested by field anthropologists. The shallowness of his consciousness is revealed in the simplicity of his dissociation, the ease with which his psyche can be precipitated into hysteria, his high degree of suggestibility and the "all-or-none" nature of his emotional reactions—all symptoms pointing to a mentation more unconscious and instinctive than that of "civilised" differentiated man.

We are born not merely primitives but *brutes*. Our instincts are not adapted genetically but by the social environment. We have already pointed out that this is the whole meaning of consciousness. Because our instinctive adaptations are acquired, our mentation presents different levels of unconsciousness and is more or less instinctive. It has an outer layer of civilisation, below it a more primitive layer, and still lower a merely animal core. This has long been generally known; but it was the achievement of psycho-analysts, while in general misunderstanding the social basis of consciousness, to understand the importance of unconscious mentation and to devise a technique for probing it.

Because the interpenetration of subject and object is complete, because life and experience is always the struggle of the instincts with the environment, all mentation necessarily has in it a component of outer reality and an instinctual component. This is not peculiar to consciousness but is a feature of all living responses. The fact that even the autonomous nervous system responds to and may be conditioned by environmental influences reveals that it too has a "reality" component in its mentation. Hence the whole field of neural activity is interpenetrated both with environmental or acquired effects and innate or instinctive effects. Previous psychology was chiefly concerned with acquired effects—the "real things" in the conscious field: even the sentiments, feelings and instincts of earlier psychology were regarded objectively and figured as real things. Psycho-analysis therefore found a whole new field to conquer —the exploration of the instinctive or innate elements in mentation considered not objectively but in action, *i.e. in their own terms.* Unfortunately they went to the other extreme and rejected all the objective components, with the result that life reduced itself to a blind dynamic libido. This libido seemed something preformed which wandered into the world like a Christian soul incarnate, instead of arising from a process in reality itself.

When we divide man into instinct and environment, we must remember that man's instinct itself is the product of environmental adaptation (natural selection) but that this is inborn biological adaptation, whereas man's conscious adaptation is to the social environment and is therefore acquired cultural adaptation. Conflicts may arise between these two layers of adaptations—the biological or instinctive, the cultural or conscious. In normal life each has its own sphere. Purely biological adaptations attend to man's digestion, purely cultural adaptations to man's design of a house; but in so far as they overlap a mutual distortion may arise. Man's digestion may be upset by an ugly house; his design of a house may be done for money—*i.e.* to feed himself. Cooking becomes an art. Art a bread-and-butter activity. It is this distortion and over-lapping which psycho-analysis has studied. Since the biological instincts are closely connected with the generation of emotion and the feeling-tone in consciousness (the exact connection has not yet been satisfactorily established), the study by psycho-analysis of the distortion of the consciousness (including the volition) by the instincts has been largely a study of the influence of emotional associations and complexes on men's thoughts and actions. And since we have already discussed the organisa-tion of the affective elements of consciousness into a com-mon ego by art, it is plain that the discoveries of psycho-analysis must be an important aid in the understanding of art.

3

No satisfactory classification of mentation has yet been proposed. We are concerned with the flow of images (not necessarily visual) to which I give the name phantasy, to distinguish them from clear perception or memory. We will use the following classification of these: (*a*) Dream; (*b*) Day-Dream or Reverie; (*c*) Free Association; (*d*) Directed Thinking; (*e*) Directed Feeling.

Until the psycho-analysts, no psychologist seriously studied the dream. Thanks to Freud, we now see the absurdity of that omission. Because of its primitive character and strange features, the dream throws light on the nature of phantasy and the rôle of thought.

The dream has certain characteristics which distinguish it from other kinds of thought. By far the most important is the fact that in it thoughts—the memory-images of percepts condensed, displaced and modified—take the place of the real environment. This is the specific feature of dream. In all other forms of phantasy the thinker is still vaguely conscious of his environment and does not site himself in the products of his fancy; he does not give them the status of immediate surroundings. The dreamer does. Hence they acquire a vividness and rounded actuality such as always belongs to the immediate environment when it is the object of attention.

This "materialising" of thoughts is the result of introversion, of a withdrawing of sensory attention from the environment. This introversion is what constitutes sleep. Sufferers from anaesthesia of the skin have only to close their eyes—providing the room is quiet—to fall into slumber. All the aids to sleep—darkness, quiet, mental blankness—are devices for reducing external sensory stimuli.

The materiality and vividness of dream-thoughts are thus only *relative*. If one recalls dream faces, forms, words and scenes, they are all vague, blurred, colourless, full of holes, indefinite and incomplete. But because no external sensory reality existed to quarrel with them, they assumed the status and vividness of the environment. It is this concentration of attention which gives the dream material its reality and vividness and not its own internal coherence. On the contrary, the material of dream is confused and patchy.

Jung investigated ordinary "free association"—waking associations of one image to another formed by the mind freely, without conscious attention to reality. Dream is an elaborate form of continuous free association, in which the free flow of phantasy acquires the material reality of an environment. Freud laid bare the mechanism of this more elaborate free association of dream.

Surréalisme bases its technique on this free association. It hopes thus to realise a spontaneous artistic production. Here it only displays the classic bourgeois illusion that freedom is the ignorance of necessity. Freud's and Jung's experiments have clearly proved that so far from dream or free association really being free, they are subject to the iron determinism of unconscious necessity. Distortions of instinctive drives called complexes inexorably force phantasy to follow a mean and narrow groove.

MacCurdy's researches on the productions of maniacs revealed the same iron law hidden beneath apparent spontaneity. The seemingly effortless and bewilderingly profuse flow of manic raving proved, on the careful analysis of stenographic reports over a long period, to be in fact all determined by some wish of an infantile simplicity. Once the unconscious law was revealed, the raving was seen to be simply a few thoughts which oscillated within the bounds of the crudest symbols.

What is the function of dream? Freud and Rivers agree that it is physiologically "the guardian of sleep". Stimuli that might rouse the sleeper to action—that is, wake him—are switched into non-motor channels unless they become imperative. Such stimuli include not merely external stimuli, such as bells whose sound is woven into the dream, but also internal stimuli—pains, hunger, sexual wishes, all the nascent stirrings of instinctive desire which make even a dog execute running movements in his sleep.

Freud also saw that this explanation by no means ended the matter. Granted that dreams enable one to sleep on in spite

of disturbing stimuli, why do they take the particular form
they do? Freud showed that they must take the form of a
phantastic response to the external stimuli. It is a pity he gave
this general quality of dreams the particular description of
"*wish-fulfilment*", as it has misled his followers and has tended
to separate psycho-analysis from other fields of psychology, such
as behaviourism and gestalt psychology.

Suppose a sleeper has been called. The knock penetrates his
dream; the active response to this would normally take the form
of his getting up. His phantastic response therefore takes the
form of dreaming that he gets up—an experience most of us
have had. In the same way, if a sleeper is disturbed by hunger
pangs, his waking response would be to feed, and therefore
starving explorers dream perpetually of food.

Of course this is "wish-fulfilment", inasmuch as in phantasy one fulfils one's wish to get up or to feed. But wish-fulfilment is misleading as a general description, because "wish" is
a term usually used of a consciously formulated aim, and its
use here hides the close kinship of the phantastic response of
dream to the active response of waking life. All the countless
stimuli that move us in daily life to action—a command, an
incentive, something seen, curiosity, a memorandum, a letter,
a burning sexual desire—may be called wishes, since plainly we
would perform no action unless we had some instinctive
dynamism inside us to make us do so. But to use the term
"wish-fulfilment" of such actions, or of their phantastic equivalent in dream, gives them a queer and freakish appearance and
leads Freud into difficulties to explain "unpleasant" dreams
and "unsatisfying" dreams. It is a reflection of his idealist
subjective approach to the subject-object relations of concrete
life.

Dreams are conscious. Now we have already seen that the
data of consciousness are socially given, that man by language, education and social contacts finds his instinctive
responses conditioned by the common world and the common
ego and given the status of consciousness. Therefore society is
still with man in dream. Even in dream the social ego phantastically fulfils man's desires in the social world.

In the social world man may get up or eat in immediate

M

response to the appropriate stimuli. But the conditions of association demand that an instinctive desire to strike a certain man or kiss a certain woman be not gratified. In the social world therefore such illegal desire can meet with one of two alternative fates, to which Freud has given the names of "repression" and "sublimation".

If we "repress" the desire, we dismiss it from the conscious field by an effort of will. Now we already saw that consciousness corresponded to the "socialisation" or adaptation to civilisation of instinctive responses. Consequently a desire that has a conscious dress already has its barbaric nudity clothed; it is already half-civilised. If such a desire is so strong that it is not dismissed by other interests (*i.e.* other instinctive drives) but requires to be forcibly repressed into the unconscious by an act of will, then it is plain that this very repression strips the wish of its veneer of education and makes it barbaric and savage. Hence the evils of repression, which Freud's school has pointed out, are due to the very act which strips them of their social adaptation and makes them savage prisoners. From this barbarising of conscious wishes springs the terrible ferocity of the saint, the bitterness of the puritan and the unspeakable cruelties of a Holy Inquisition.

In sublimation the instincts are given a social adaptation which permits them to satisfy themselves in consciousness. To write a "strong" letter, to indulge in violent sport or economic competition, are ways in which society permits us to give our instinctive wish a conscious dress. To wrestle with nature, to give our hate a creative material outlet, are still higher forms of sublimation. To dance, to write love poetry, to pay the woman we love the compliments of service or speech are the ways in which we civilise our sex. Thus these instincts, whose blind strength might make us their blind slaves, acknowledge us as their masters and increase our spontaneity, because they are given a conscious and therefore social adaptation. Here too freedom is seen to be the consciousness of necessity.

But the range of possibility of sublimation, the width of consciousness and therefore of spontaneity, is not settled in the ideal world. It is part of the social product and like all the

freedom of society is generated by labour. In the past the
majority of consciousness and therefore the greatest range of
sublimation has gone to the class which has appropriated the
major share of the social product; and for the other class,
the sublimation of its socially-thwarted desires for leisure
and food have taken the crude form of religion and the phantastic structure of a dream paradise.

The "I" of dream is still the socialised "I", the instinctive,
unconscious, genotypical ego modified by contact with the
common ego. The world of dream is still the world of instinctive response to environment modified by the common
perceptual world. It is for this reason that as in real life so in
dream the hunger and getting-up urges are gratified by *direct*
phantasy—we dream of eating or dressing—whereas instincts to
kill or rape other human beings are sublimated or, as Freud
puts it, "distorted by the censor". Of course as instincts they
are neither to kill nor to rape—since killing and raping are
social conceptions, unknown to the unconscious instincts of
sex and self-preservation. However, these words must be used
in discussing the unconscious in the terms of the conscious.

The idea of a separate endo-psychic censor is obviously an
abstraction. In fact this censor and the distortion "he"
produces are not the work of a special department of the
psyche but are given in the nature of consciousness itself.
Any neural "engram" whose activity forms a part of a dream-
consciousness must necessarily respect certain social laws,
because that very consciousness is like a suit of clothes and
a shave—a sign that it has been civilised.

Why in that case do we in dream permit ourselves to do
things we should be ashamed to do in real life? Two factors
combine to produce this moral looseness of dream. It has
already been remarked that the genotype is born not merely
a savage but a brute, and hence the development or consciousness is a shaping of the outside, a carving of the intact trunk.
Consciousness begins as self-consciousness, as a detachment
of the self from the environment, but this alone does not
secure consciousness; it is in a sense opposed to it and merely
instinctive. It is only when self-consciousness returns on the
environment and by experience impresses the environment on

itself that it becomes conscious of reality, of "otherness". This is a social process. The baby grows conscious by becoming interested in its surroundings and learning about them by active experience. Because it does so by means of language and social activity, its experience of reality is an experience of the rich complex reality of the common perceptual world. In the introversion of sleep the environment sinks away and with it therefore vanishes much of the social world of reality. We tend to return to the introversion of childhood and the dawning self-consciousness of infancy, in which the "I" is everything and external reality as yet a vague chaos. This explains not merely the archaic and infantile character of dreams, but also the extent to which their analysis reveals the influence of infantile experience. When we sleep the face grows childish. For the same reason in dream the Mother, the return to the womb, incest, and all the other familiar infantile Freudian motives play an important part. The "I" of dream, though so important, is a petty ego, for social life is the means of its realisation. The "I" of dream is like the world of dream, only partly socialised. Thus dream is doubly detached from reality—external and internal. It is not completely severed on either side but it is loosened.

It would be wrong to deduce from dream to life without allowing for the difference. This difference is the more active rôle in life of the environment which in its consciously perceived form is a social construct. We are born a genotype—merely instinctive. We become self-conscious and, by interaction with the environment, receive an adaptation of the instincts which determines our infantile consciousness and our infantile hopes, aspirations and aims. Our growth to manhood is accompanied by an enrichment of consciousness—that is, by a still more far-reaching adaptation of our childish desires to the environment. Our adult consciousness is not determined by our infantile, any more than our infantile consciousness is determined by our instinctive genotype. There is a difference which consists in the difference in experience, and this experience rests on a deeper penetration of the environment as a result of living in society. We have lived and therefore are altered. Freudism, by taking the dream at its own valuation, constantly dismisses the adaptations of consciousness as fetters or inhibitions on the instincts, without seeing the vital fact that these adaptations are generated by the struggle of the instincts with the environment. Robbed of these adaptations the instincts would be so much the less free. To strip the tortoise or the crab of its shell would not free it but would expose it to the necessity of the environment. This does not of course exclude the possibility of these adaptations becoming *relatively* cramping—relative to the freedom of other adaptations already made possible by a change in the material conditions. For example, the horny integument of the cactus secures its free development in desert regions, but if it should grow moist, this integument would cramp its development and the skin would either be discarded or the cactus would be crowded out by more thin-fleshed plants. This applies still more powerfully to man whose social organisation secures a continuous and rapid change in his productive forces.

Thus the loose character of the dream is partly explained by its infantilism. Our social conditioning is closely associated with the environment, for reasons already explained. Any weakening in environmental strength tends to lessen our adaptation. We all know how we act differently away from the home circle, or with friends, or in a foreign country. We know that the instinctive outburst of rage or the non-social behaviour of drunkenness are accompanied by a weakening of the reality of the environment; "we forgot where we were". In sleep introversion robs the environment of absolute reality; hence a corresponding loosening of social coherence, which, however, cannot vanish as long as the dream remains conscious; yet conscious it must be to have value, for the instincts, owing to their long conditioning, cannot act except upon socially accepted reality, and all such reality is conscious.

Because of its archaic and instinctive nature, the reality which makes up the conscious material of dream is crude and limited as compared with the reality of waking consciousness. This applies not merely to the external reality which figures in a dream as "dream thoughts", but to internal reality, the "I" which experiences them. It is a mean, petty and selfish

"I". We are not conscious of any nobility or heroic quality in this "I"; on the contrary, it never does anything we can really be proud of. Even its achievements are gained too easily. After waking from dream we are only too glad we are not "really like that". And in fact we are not, for it is the process of association which makes men noble and heroic which gives their character more beauty and worth. Hence the "I" of dream, stripped of so much of its social adaptation, is stripped of its largeness and human value.

Yet we see phantasy even in the form of dream reaching out towards an ameliorative rôle. In dream the ego experiments in action upon reality, but it is now a plastic reality without the stiffness of material things. In the space of a night it is possible to combine and recombine, free from the immediate tension of a direct contact with reality[1] and the limitations of manipulating real stuff.

It is possible to experiment with new forms of reality more appropriate to our instincts and to experience in a provisional way what these forms would feel like and how our instincts would react to their achievement. Thus the illusion of dream has this biological value, that by experimenting ideally with possible realities and attitudes towards them it paves the way for such changes in reality. Dream prepares the way for action; man must first dream the possible before he can do it. It is true that the realisation of our dream is never the same as the dream; it looks different and it feels different. Yet it also has something in common with our desire, and its realisation was only possible because dream went before and lured us on, as the harvest festival made possible the harvest. Of course dream is too archaic and too phantastically isolated from social reality to be of much value in the concrete living of civilised man.

The "remedy" for the illusory character of dream is not to abolish dream but to so enlarge and extend it that it becomes increasingly close to the realisation it is made to anticipate;

[1] This plasticity and recombination of psychical elements possible in the introversion of sleep is perhaps a reflection of a similar physiological process in all the higher cells of the body and therefore the biological "reason" for sleep. In sleep the conditioning of the whole body may undergo a liquidation and digestion such as takes place with consciousness in dream.

to fill it more full of life and reality and vivid content. Once again freedom is extended by an extension of the consciousness of necessity. This programme calls for the socialisation of dream.

4

Imagine, therefore, the first sub-man leading his almost solitary life of the instincts in his nearly private world of reality, dreaming like the dog of the simplest actions that answer his desires, and faced by reality with the need for making that dream more real, more full of content, more useful.

His solution we have already recorded when we dealt with the birth of poetry. Man made a tremendous stride forward when he injected the dream into waking life, which forced it to answer the categories of waking reality.

But it was essential that he should do this without losing the very quality that made dream useful, its plasticity. Now if consciousness is faced with the demand of completely coinciding with external reality, it then becomes indistinguishable from perception—perception of things round-me-now, perception of feelings inside-me-now.

Hence the joints of this waking consciousness had to be somehow loosened. Imagine the "I" located at a point in the solid crystal of space-time. So far as the "I" is conscious of its relations with space-time, they are simply a perceptual glowing network running from the "I" out into infinity.

Two ways of "loosening" are possible:

(i) One involves a separation of the subject from the object. This in itself gives rise to the possibility of two further subdivisions—

(a) It is possible to concentrate on the reality of feeling-tone, and dissolve the crystal of external reality. This does not mean that external reality disappears; it means that external reality is manipulated not primarily according to its own laws but according to instinctive and subjective laws. Hence the plasticity of dream is retained, but the waking reality of subjective consciousness is injected into dream to enrich it.

This gives us the field of the illusory Mock World (but real common ego), the world of art.

(*b*) Or it is possible to concentrate on the reality of the object and dissolve the nucleus of internal reality. This does not mean that the "I", the observer, disappears; it means that the "I" is manipulated not according to its own desires but according to the necessity of external reality. Once again the plasticity of dream is retained, but the reality of the waking environment is brought into the world of dream to stiffen it. This gives us the real perceptual world of the impersonal, omnipresent, unemotional Mock Ego, the world of science.

(ii) It is possible, besides separating subject from object, to separate space from time, like from unlike, and quantity from quality. This does not mean that space or time disappears, but that one or the other is the manifold in which distortion takes place.

(*a*) Spatial organisation gives us the classificatory sciences and poetry.

(*b*) Temporal organisation gives us the evolutionary sciences and the story.

The classificatory sciences, of which mathematics is the queen and physics an important sphere, deal with space-like orderings which are independent of time. Time enters only as a homogeneous oscillation in which no new qualities emerge except that of entropy. This is the field of timeless order, of quality, of mechanical materialism.

The evolutionary sciences, which develop later, are historical in their approach. They deal with reality as a process, as the emergence of new qualities. Sociology, biology, geology, psychology, astronomy and physiology are all sciences which are interested in time, which roam about through time and therefore abstract by telescoping, condensing and generalising time, just as the classificatory sciences telescope, condense and generalise space. Obviously these fields penetrate. Only mathematics is purely classificatory and dialectics purely evolutionary. The rise of the evolutionary sciences from 1750 to 1850 was what altered the mechanical materialism of Condillac, d'Holbach and Diderot to the dialectical material-ism of Marx and Engels and made it capable of including all the active side of the subject-object relation developed by idealism.

The same division in the field of art gives rise to a similar distinction. In literary art the novel is evolutionary and the poem is classificatory. As this distinction is of fundamental importance, it must be considered in detail later.

Obviously the brute-man did not evolve these external-isations of dream, as we have done, by taking thought. They were generated by his struggle with Nature, by the need for association in that struggle, and by the development of vocal and visual symbols which that association made necessary. The real world discovered with the aid of the mock ego, and the real ego explored by means of the mock world are the conscious world and the conscious ego and, therefore, the social world and the social ego.

In the dance and the chant man retires into a half-sleep by dismissing the world of immediate reality. This enables him to play fast and loose with the world of external reality, to build and unbuild it. But not arbitrarily and lawlessly—there would be no point or object in such an occupation. He builds it according to the laws of the social ego, and he does this because in the dance and the chant, while withdrawing from the world of external reality, he maintains touch with the subjective world of his fellows by moving his body in rhythm, by repeating the same words in unison, by weaving between them an emotional network of common feelings evoked by socially common objects, such as notes of music, animals mimicked in the dance, words denoting socially recognised entities or experiences. Thus the items of the common perceptual world are selected, organised, blended and re-orientated round the social ego, the "god" of early Greek ritual who descended into his worshippers and who was nothing but the symbol of the heightened common ego formed by the dance.

Of course, as society develops, poetry detaches itself from the common festival. Civilised man more easily secures physiological introversion—the rhythm of poetry is sufficient to achieve it—and the collective subjective significance of words keeps him in touch with his fellows without the need for that collective festival which has been out-moded by the division of labour, a division reflected in the wider range and greater content of language itself.

Such art is timeless, for man himself is still timeless, still lives entirely in the Now from age to age, with only a fabulous past and future. This ideal timelessness reflects the fact that man's division of labour itself has not extended into time, that he lives from hand to mouth, that he does not, like modern man, inherit all the capital, the congealed labour, the technique and cultural achievements of changing generations of men. He has only the barest social relations with the dead and the unborn. A few tools, a limited technique and an unwritten language he has certainly, and this commonness with the past is reflected in a few time-myths—about heroes and a golden age and a Prometheus or Moses, bringers of knowledge to barbarous men. But, in general, the timelessness of poetry matches his own childish simplicity which thinks, like Traherne, that the wheat was golden and immortal, corn that had never been sown or reaped.

But as history develops, man's interplay with his changeful past is reflected in towns and temples and states and irrigation and finally in *stories*—in images of men's changing lives organised in time. So a new art emerges which reaches its height—the novel and film—exactly in that era from 1750 onwards when the evolutionary sciences rise to notice. All this new insight is in turn a product of the terrific historic changes in Nature made possible by industrialisation.

In the story, man is young and grows old, and we are interested in watching how in this process of maturing his external world and his own heart change. This distortion, organisation, condensation and selection of the subjective contents of the psyche and its real environment in relation to a temporal life-line distinguish the story from the poem.

This in turn reveals the greater sophistication of the novel. In the undifferentiated tribe it is easily and always possible for all men to be in one mind in one time in one place, and for a universal and timeless ego to emerge from this congress, speaking for all with one voice. But the more differentiated life of modern society is *contrapuntal*; men's lives blend and overlap and interweave in a complicated tapestry, and the moments rarely arrive when all their minds and emotions are gathered together in one public universal "I". Hence the hero of the novel is not like the "hero" of poetry, a universal common "I", but a real concrete individual.

How is the "collectiveness" of the novel assured? It inheres in the real environment that always figures in the novel—the realism of the actions, of the other characters, and the events considered as one social plexus. Thus external reality, dismissed by introversion from the immediate attention of the reader, returns in another guise—not as reality-now, not as the room in which "I" am sitting reading, but as the external reality which has been or may be; and this is only possible precisely because the novel is plastic in the time dimension. Hence the immediate reality of the reader is pushed out or blanked off by the verisimilitude of the mock world of the novel, which is therefore much more realistic and factual than the shimmering, dream-like mock world of poetry.

In this the novel resembles the day-dream. As compared with the ordinary dream the day-dream has more reality, it remains in the field of the possible, it does not contain the wild extravagances or abrupt transitions of the dream. It is more orderly and less primitive, and this is necessary because in the day-dream we are awake and therefore the phantasy has to have this material coherence, this stiffening of objects ranged in a real order so as to screen out the everyday environment and draw the mind to it. This quantity of "matter" in the day-dream and the novel makes necessary their temporal organisation, because without such an organisation the narrative would become overloaded and confused and would finally bulk out to coincide with the slow unwieldy movement of perceptual reality itself—at which point it would lose all value, or possibility of affective organisation. Dream by its sensory introversion, and poetry by its rhythm and concentration, escape the need for so great a stiffening of reality and so marked an "organisation" in time. Theirs is an organisation in space.

The day-dream is characteristically a more "civilised" form of phantasy. It is the expression of man as an individual plastic in reality, just as the dream is the expression of reality plastic in the man. One expresses man's power over Nature derived from altering himself: the other man's power over himself by altering Nature. In the day-dream, man experiments with adapting himself to reality; in the dream, with adapting reality to himself; both these characteristics are carried over into their respective arts.

Science in its dichotomy reveals the same parentage. In the classificatory sciences man does not introvert himself from present reality by interposing thoughts of another precedent or subsequent reality, but by spreading over present reality categories derived from himself. This is precisely what the field of order or quantity really is. Just as man derives from rhythm certain instinctive commonnesses, so he derives from perception certain perceptual commonnesses. Three cows, three sticks, three apples, when bare of subjective aspects (the cow appearing as one thing to one man, the apple as differently valued to another), yet have a perceptual commonness among men which is "threeness", number, quantity. All these qualityless categories of classification, by robbing the present of its peculiarities, enable man to "abstract", to blend, select and combine all reality in a timeless way. By purging from the common ego all those qualities which are peculiar to one man in one place, it becomes possible to give man a phantastic and flexible grasp of the whole field of reality. The process robs reality of the time in it—the emergence of new qualities.

It is for that reason that in man's daily life, counting, the herdsman's science (India), and geometry, the agriculturist's science (Egypt), emerge before the more qualitied historical sciences. In a more primitive community men have much the same experiences in common from day to day, and it is easy for them, meeting together in a group, to make of their experience a bundle of world-perspectives from one point of space-time, a bundle bare of quality, of feeling-tone—which is just what mathematics is. It is easy for them to "abstract" themselves from those surrounding by abstracting from the surroundings all feeling-tone and therefore all quality. Because they perform tasks in common it is easy for them to abstract the commonness in all tasks—the quantitive element in them, the number of cattle tended, of acres planted.

Thus dream becomes mathematics when, for the introversion of sleep shutting out all sensory stimuli from the environment, is substituted the introversion of mathematics, which shuts out all sensory qualities and so is able to extend its grasp beyond present reality to all reality. In sleep the rhythm of breathing and the flow of blood draw the perceptual world into the ego; in mathematics the rhythm of breathing and the flow of blood push the ego into the perceptual world.

It is only later, when civilisation becomes contrapuntal, and men's labours, aspirations and aims cross and interweave, that the evolutionary sciences arise. Here introversion from present reality is secured, not by abstracting all quality from consciousness but by substituting an ego whose appreciation of quality is limited, distorted and organised in time. This mock ego is not like that of mathematics, the ego gazing everywhere and nowhere seeing quality, but the ego gazing everywhere yet seeing only one particular type of quality, the qualities that demarcate the particular sphere of science in question. Hence, with the rise of the evolutionary sciences, science necessarily splits up into different spheres each with their own distinct qualities—the spheres of chemistry, biology, psychology, sociology, etc. These spheres do not contradict each other; they are selections from the one universal movement of qualities which is reality, but which without this division of labour would be beyond man's grasp.

The spheres are not arbitrarily selected, they are determined by the nature of reality and of man's active relation to it, and mark his successive concern with dead nature, with himself as body, with his own mind and with the society that is the matrix of their mutual relations. Because of the fullness of quality even in any one sphere, it is still necessary to organise and condense them in time, just as man organises in retrospect his own experience—by a condensation, blending and fusing of the qualities that emerge in this sphere in the process of reality.

Just as the hero of the novel is an individual surrounded by those very events and persons which will actively call forth the subjective reactions for which the novel is written, so the hero of an evolutionary science is a particular sphere of quality observed by just that mock ego or one-sensed man whose peculiarities of sight will call forth the relations which the science is evolved to organise and study.

5

This development of art and science is not the merely contemplative discovery of static realities, it is part of men's active relation with Nature. The phantasy of art, by the constant changes in organisation which it produces in man's ego, makes man conscious of the necessity of his instincts and therefore free. This is not an absolute freedom but relative to the means of change—the complex, rich, social ego against which man presses his own blind ego in the embrace of art. This social ego is in turn built up not of ideal stuff but of the real concrete emotions and aspirations that a man experiences from living in a real, concrete society.

This is revealed, for example, in the nature of the material of literary art—words; the very words that are tools to man in his associated operations, however ordinary; the language of court, camp and kitchen.

Science and art are the frontiers of phantasy. They embody the most abstract, the most general, the most essential laws of concrete feeling and perception. They are "pure" and for that reason they have separated out from each other. They are concerned with the new, with just those general items of social experience which negate the already existing common ego and common perceptual world, and therefore demand the extension of both ego and world (new art works, new hypotheses) to include them. This is the way practice unites with theory, because men's practical experience contradicts the already given consciousness of men and demands its modification. To those who think mechanically it seems as if science and art are not interpenetrated with living experience but are opposed to it, because they are the fruit of its contradiction.

Science and art are artificially separated from life when they are visualised as ideological spheres. As practice, as felt and known experience, they are at every step derived from the struggle of man with Nature.

The world of phantasy which arises as the "guardian" of slumber because in it man rests from the active struggle with Nature, and in accordance with his desires rearranges in his body the traces of his struggle, taking the symbol for the fact—this world, by being introjected into the social world of waking reality, is forced to split and on the one hand increasingly to reflect the necessity of external reality, on the other hand to take the imprints of men's hearts. Thus men are affected by each other's emotional experiences and experiences of reality. Men make each other what they are.

The artist and the scientist participate in that manufacture. They are men who acquire a special experience of life— affective with the artist, perceptual with the scientist—which negates the common ego or the common social world, and therefore requires a refashioning of these worlds to include the new experience. Just as the producer of material goods for society brings them to the common market, so the artist or the scientist brings his special experience to the ideological market in a fashioned form.

In order that products should have the stamp of social products, of *commodities*, they must have been endowed with a shape which gives them a social use-value. They must have been fashioned by labour to be denizens of the world of social utility. In the same way the artist or the scientist must give his experience a social significance; it must be included in the ideological world of society. It is precisely this fashioning which constitutes the *labour* of art or science, and which entitles the artist or the scientist to regard himself as a producer.

Jung contrasted phantasy, or free association, with "directed thinking"—thinking which is forced to follow a "rational" path, a path conforming with our conscious knowledge of reality. This conscious knowledge, as we have already seen, is derived from the common perceptual world. Hence directed thinking is scientific thinking; by directed thinking we fashion our experience of external reality into a social product.

To Jung's conception of directed thinking we wish to add that of "directed feeling". This is what we do whenever we direct our feelings along lines intended to conform with what we think right, with our "true" self, with the valid or the beautiful, with what we feel is the better part of us, with the ideal each has in his breast. Just as directed thinking is controlled by the reason and acknowledges the social criterion of truth, so directed feeling is controlled by the heart and acknowledges the social criterion of beauty or goodness.

It is the crime of class religion to have separated goodness from beauty and the conscience from the heart. Religion arises as mythology, as early poetry in which science and art are still mingled, for collective phantasy is still no more than collective dream. Man has not fully separated himself from the environment, is not yet conscious of the contradiction between the ego and the environment, and, because he is not conscious, is the slave of that contradiction, blindly tossed hither and thither by his feelings and events. But when science and art separate out, religion no longer plays a useful rôle. It attempts to combine both; therefore it distorts the truth of science and fetters the plasticity of art.

We saw that in the realm of science phantasy gained penetrative power, gained the ability to reflect more accurately the environment, because it replaced the real concrete ego with a mock ego or scaffolding whose flexibility enabled the mould of phantasy to adhere closely to the environment. But religion still mixes the subjective with the objective. It announces as truths what man hopes to be true. Its views of reality are distorted by man's affective drives. It takes poetic illusions, valued and considered true for their subjective content, and demands that men give them the status of statements symbolic of external reality. But since man's practical experience proves or disproves the truth of scientific hypotheses, religion can only protect its illusions from exposure by making them symbolical of another world than the material world—the kingdom of heaven, the "next world". Obviously this is a degeneration from primitive religion which stated its tenets scientifically, referring them to the visible material world, as in the performance of miracles, the moving of material mountains and so forth, and whose errors therefore, being accessible to practice, could by their self-exposure give rise to science.

But class religion, by carefully protecting its symbolical statements from material test, confines them to a kingdom of heaven which is either invisibly present behind the real world, or in more sophisticated forms is simply "in men's hearts", *i.e.* is after all subjective. In that case religion's truths are simply symbolical of feeling-tone, and religion thus reduces itself to art, with this difference, that the very method of its generation gives it a dogmatic and amateurish stiffness which is opposed to the flexibility and technical richness of conscious art—conscious of its rôle, of its materials, of its problems, of its technique and of its traditions.

Thus like all survivals which have had their functions taken over by other organs, modern religion exhibits the stigmata of degeneracy. And as we have previously shown, its whole ideological structure betrays the reasons that have kept it alive, the same reasons that have kept alive the monarchy, the aristocracy, feudal privilege and similar non-functional relics—the special conditions and ossifications of a class society protecting obsolete privileges.

The confusion of religion—a confusion between subject and object—reflects a society which has itself become confused by a divorce between the active relation of subject and object which alone procures the separation of each by a mutually reflexive movement. In a society where consciousness (the subject) has become separated from the environment (the object) because the thinking class has become separated from the working class, there is not possible that constant correction of men's ideological image of reality by practice which secures the health and movement of science. Science, which adheres closely to reality by active experiment in its particular spheres, cannot be integrated into the universal "philosophy" of a class, but decomposes into a chaos of highly specialised, mutually contradictory sciences whose separation impoverishes thought. Even a scientist has as a rule an unscientific world-view. It is therefore possible for a subjectively distorted picture of reality to arise and be, because of this cleavage, immune from correction by action. The slaves may know blindly they are not free and God is not good—but how are their masters to share *their* experiences? And in the same way the growth of another world, not this material world but painted in glowing affective colours, is generated by the misery of the material world endured by the suffering class, for which they are compensated by future delights. Hence arises the inverted world of religion, inverted because the world of society is inverted. These two factors combine to maintain religion at a time when the development of science and art have replaced it by keener tools—by the *conscious* illusion of art, by the *impersonal* truth of science, and the richer concrete living these two make possible.

Thus phantasy develops as the inseparable accompaniment of action, which creates it and which it in turn anticipates and calls into being in a richer form. And practice, enriched, corrects phantasy's anticipation and makes possible a new level of achievement. Thus phantasy adapts man in two ways— his instincts to the ego of society, and his perception to the perception of society. This adaptation ennobles and heightens and makes free the dumb brute of the genotype, because the ego of society and the perception of society is infinitely more penetrating and rich and complex than that of the unaided individual, just as man in association is more powerful against Nature than solitary man.

All thought, all feeling, reflects in some measure the categories of science or art. Science and art are generated in our daily existence. Scientific systems and art works are merely the highest forms of organisation, the essence of this daily concrete life.

Science and art become *practical*, they enter into concrete real life, directly we knock away the mock world from any artistic construction and substitute a real world, or knock away the mock impersonal ego from any scientific construction and substitute a real human being. In the first case we give an "unattached" human desire a real materialisation; in the second we give a part of reality the shape of an answer to human desire. Thus, in entering into real concrete life, artistic and scientific constructions become, as it were, blended or "impure", special instead of general, concrete instead of abstract, and the language we use to make this possible belongs to the realm of persuasion—the ordinary language of daily life, removed from the pure and "impractical" worlds of science and art. We must not regret this forced descent. Science and art were made for man, not man for science and art. But there is more to it than that. Science and art were made *from* man, not man from science and art. This issuing of science and art into real "impure" life-experience is what corrects, refines and develops them, so that they return to their heavens wiser, richer, still more abstract and pure as a result of their incarnation in life. And though so ethereal now, science and art in their infancy were as concrete as concrete living.

This phantasy, generated by association for economic production, is communicated by material symbols—gestures, sounds, drawings, touches. Because of the nature of man's senses, sound proved at first the favoured sense, leaving men's eyes free to con the external environment. The division of labour, which no longer made all men concerned at the same time with the environment, again restored advantages to sight and the sounds became visual symbols—writing. Language developed as the favoured tool for the communication of phantasy, superior to diagrams or "picture writing". Ignorance of this concrete function of language and concentration on its formal aspects make many philosophers approach language in a strangely patronising way.

They find it "imperfect", deviating from the ideal language, and illogical—rather as a biologist might study species and reproach them for their departure from some ideal animal. Such philosophers think consciousness is contemplation—a limpid image of reality. In the same way they think language exists to be a passive photograph of the universe. Wittgenstein's *Tractatus Logio-Philosophicus* is entirely based on this assumption. This is the error of philistines who imagine that a painting must be exactly like the scene it portrays. They do not see that it is a silly task to make an exact copy of something we already have, and that the relation of language and thought to reality is not a passive reflection but an active and tendencious reaction, and that it is this activity and tendenciousness which enables a mere reaction to become conscious and know. The mirror reflects accurately: it does not know. Each particle of the Universe reflects the rest of the Universe, but knowledge is only given to human beings as a result of an active and social

relation to the rest of reality. Knowledge is an economic
product.

Russell phrases the Wittgenstein conception thus: "The
essential business of a language is to assert or deny facts". But
this is not a business at all. Facts assert or deny themselves:
that is, they either exist or do not. A man sees them in external
reality or does not. He remains dumb. The business of language,
as an extension of life, is to decide what facts are worth asserting or denying: what facts exist for men and what do not. It
is the business of language to be the best possible tool for
siting facts in an ordered world-view, which can select or
condense or classify them hierarchically; and into such a world-
view the subject must enter. Society must appear twice, as ego
and world, and in both cases dragging its material history after
it. Russell's view of language is like that of the gushing lady
who said to Carlyle, "I accept the Universe". But man does
not accept the Universe, for the Universe does not accept him.
He must *change* it under penalty of extinction. And he can only
change it in association; therefore language reflects the relations
of men as feeling men and perceiving men in association for
economic production.

This historical function of language explains why existing
languages are so far from the "perfect" language postulated by
Wittgenstein. Such a perfect language would be perfectly useless. It would be a picture of the world, standing in the same
relation to external reality as a mirror-image to the thing
mirrored. But then it would be an inferior thing to the thing
imaged, and would be a useless construct. It would have no
hidden power over the world or the subject. It is precisely
because language expresses feeling, is a judging as well as a
picturing of parts of reality, that it is valuable. Language
expresses not merely what reality is (what reality is stares man
in the face) it expresses also what can be done with reality—its
inner hidden laws, and what man wants to do with it—his own
unconscious necessities. Language is a tool to express what
reality is in relation to man—not abstract man but concrete
human beings.

Is it not plain that the error of the philosophers regarding
language springs from the same source as religion—the

cleavage of the subject from the object in a class society? Then thought comes to seem merely contemplation and is cut off from the very activity which creates, develops and corrects it. Language, and the phantasy which has generated it, and the conscious psyche which is their offspring, and the man whose struggle with Nature in association has created all three, are bound together with a relation which Marx was the first to express in those hastily-scribbled eleven *Theses on Feuerbach* that marked the beginning of a new era in human thought: "The philosophers have only *interpreted* the world in various ways; the point, however, is to *change* it".

X

POETRY'S DREAM-WORK

I

In an earlier chapter we stated that modern poetry was composed of words, was non-symbolical, irrational, concrete, characterised by condensed affect, and rhythmical. Investigating dream we found that as compared with other forms of phantasy it also was non-symbolical, and irrational. Poetry is composed of words; dream is composed of memory-images. Dream-images do not follow rational laws drawn from external reality, but, as psycho-analysis shows, the flow of images is explained by affective laws.

Dream is neither directed thinking nor directed feeling, but free—that is non-social—association. Hence the associations of dream are personal and can only be understood by reference to the dreamer's personal life. The secret law of dream's structure is the "dream-work".

Poetic irrationality bears this resemblance to dream, that its flow of images is explained by affective laws; but it is not "free" association as in dream. Poetic feeling is directed feeling—feeling controlled by the social ego. Poetic associations are social.

As the dreamer lives entirely in the images of his dream, without reference to another reality, so the reader of poetry lives in the words of the poetry, without reference to the external world. The poet's world is *his* world. As he reads the poem he feels the emotions of the poet. Just as the pythoness or bacchante speaks for the god in the first person, so the reader under the influence of poetic illusion feels for the poet in the first person.

The images of dream, like the ideas of poetry, are concrete. In each dream, and in each poem, the memory-image and the word play a different part, and therefore have different meanings. Dreams and poems are inconsistent among themselves. Each dream and each poem is a world of its own.

Poetry is rhythmical. Rhythm secures the heightening of physiological consciousness so as to shut out sensory perception of the environment. In the rhythm of dance, music or song we become *self*-conscious instead of conscious. The rhythm of heart-beat and breathing and physiological periodicity negates the physical rhythm of the environment. In this sense sleep too is rhythmical. The dreamer retires into the citadel of the body and closes the doors.

Why is "physiological" introversion more necessary in poetry than in story, so that the poet accepts the difficulties of metre and rhyme? The answer is that introversion must be stronger in poetry. By introversion is not meant merely a turning-away from immediate environment—that could be secured by sitting in a quiet study, without disturbance. Such introversion is equally desirable for all kinds of thought, for scientific thinking and novel-reading as well as poetry, and it is not secured by the order of the words but by an effort of concentration. Some people can "concentrate" on a difficult scientific book or a book of poetry in conditions where others cannot. This kind of introversion does not therefore depend upon the order of the words. No one has suggested facilitating scientific writing by making it metrical.

But there is another aspect of introversion. In introversion for scientific phantasy it is true that we turn away from immediate environment, yet none the less we turn towards those parts of external reality of which the words are symbols. Ordinarily we see, hovering behind language, the world of external reality it describes. But in poetry the thoughts are to be directed on to the feeling-tone of the words themselves. Attention must sink below the pieces of external reality symbolised by the poetry, down into the emotional underworld adhering to those pieces. In poetry we must penetrate behind the dome of many-coloured glass into the white radiance of the self. Hence the need for a physiological introversion, which is a turning-away not from the immediate environment of the reader *but from the environment (or external reality) depicted in the poem*. Hence poetry in its use of language continually distorts and denies the structure of reality to exalt the structure of the self. By means of rhyme, assonance or alliteration it couples together words which have no rational connection, that is, no nexus through the world of external reality. It breaks the words up into lines of arbitrary length, cutting across their logical construction. It breaks down their associations, derived from the world of external reality, by means of inversion and every variety of artificial stressing and counterpoint.

Thus the world of external reality recedes, and the world of instinct, the affective emotional linkage behind the words, rises to the view and becomes the world of reality. The subject emerges from the object: the social ego from the social world. Wordsworth said correctly: "The tendency of metre is to divest language, in a certain degree, of its reality, and thus to throw a sort of half-consciousness of unsubstantial existence over the whole composition". In the same way Coleridge reached out after a like conception to ours: "Metre is simply a stimulant of attention"—not of any attention but a special kind of attention—attention to the affective associations of the words themselves.

We have here a distinction between poetry and the novel which it is vital to grasp. In the novel too the subjective elements are valued for themselves and rise to view, but in a different way. The novel blots out external reality by substituting a more or less consistent mock reality which has sufficient "stuff" to stand between reader and reality. This means that in the novel the emotional associations attach not to the words but to the moving current of mock reality symbolised by the words. That is why rhythm, "preciousness", and style are alien to the novel; why the novel translates so well; why novels are not composed of words. They are composed of scenes, actions, *stuff*, people, just as plays are. A "jewelled" style is a disadvantage to the novel because it distracts the eye from the things and people to the words—not as words, as black outlines, but as symbols to which a variety of feeling-tone is directly attached. For example when someone exclaims "Brute!" we do not think of animals and then of brutish qualities, but have a powerful subjective reaction suggesting cruelty and clumsiness. This is a poetic reaction to a word; the other is a story reaction.

Because words are few they are what Freud called

"over-determined". One word has many affective associations because it has many "meanings" (*e.g.* the word "brute" can mean a foolish person, a cruel person, the order of animals, etc.). In novel-writing the words are arranged so that all other pieces of reality are excluded except the piece required, and the emotional association is to the resulting structure. Poetic writing is concerned with making the emotional associations either exclude or reinforce each other, without a prior reference to a coherent piece of reality, *e.g.* in novel-writing, in the phrase "the Indian Ocean" the word "ocean" has been restricted to a specific geographical ocean, which *then* has emotional associations for the reader. In poetry "the Indian sea" has a different meaning, for the emotional associations are, not to a particular sea but to the word "Indian" and the word "sea", which affect each other and blend to produce a glowing cloudy "feeling" quite different from the novel-writer's phrase.

Of course there may be stretches of poetic writing in a novel (for example in Proust, Malraux, Lawrence and Melville) or of novel-writing in poetry (the purely explanatory patches in Shakespeare's plays), but this does not affect the general characteristics. The difference is so marked that it explains the strange insensitivity to poetry displayed by so many great novelists, and a similar fondness for bad novels on the part of so many great poets. This difference between the technique of poetry and the novel determines the difference between the spheres of the two arts.

2

What is the basis of literary art? What is the inner contradiction which produces its onward movement? Evidently it can only be a special form of the contradiction which produces the whole movement of society, the contradiction between the instincts and the environment, the endless struggle between man and Nature which is life.

I, the artist, have a certain consciousness, moulded by my social world. As artist I am concerned with my artistic consciousness, represented by the direct and indirect effect on me of all the art I have felt, and all the emotional organisation which has produced in me a conscious subject. This consciousness is contradicted by my experience—that is, I have a *new* personal experience, something not given in the social world of poetry. Therefore I desire what is called self-expression but is really self-socialisation, the casting of my private experience in such a form that it will be incorporated in the social world of art and appear as an art-work. The art-work represents the negation of the negation—the synthesis between the existing world of art (existing consciousness or theory) and my experience (life or practice).

Therefore at the finish the world of art will be changed by the incursion of my art-work. That is the revolutionary aspect of my rôle as artist. But also my consciousness will be changed because I have, through the medium of the art world, forced my life experience, new, dumb and unformulated, to become conscious, to enter my conscious sphere. That is the adaptative aspect of my rôle as artist. In the same way with the appreciator of art, his consciousness will be revolutionised by the incursion into it of a new art-work; but his appreciation of it will only be possible to the extent that he has had some similar experience in life. The former process will be revolutionary; the latter adaptative.

Rather than use the word revolutionary, however, it would be better to use the word evolutionary, restricting the other to cases where the new content of experience is so opposed to the existing consciousness that it requires a wholesale change, a complete revision of existing categories (conventions, traditions, artistic standards) for its inclusion, a revision which is only possible because concrete life itself has undergone a similar change in the period. The Elizabethan age was one of such periods. We are at the beginning of another such now.

It is plain that it is the emotional consciousness—that consciousness which springs directly from the instincts—with which the artist is concerned. Yet exactly the same relation holds between the scientist and his hypothesis (equivalent of the art-work) and the rational consciousness, that consciousness which springs directly from the perception.

Since the mediating factor in art processes is the social ego in its relation to the experience of individuals, it is plain that the integration performed by the art-work can only be achieved on condition that the item of private experience which is integrated (*a*) is *important*, concerned with deep emotional drives, with the unchanging instincts which, because they remain the same beneath the changing adaptations of culture, act as the skeleton, the main organising force in the social ego which ages of art have built up; (*b*) is *general*, is not a contradictory item of experience peculiar to the artist or one or two men, but is encountered in a dumb unconscious way in the experiences of most men—otherwise how could the art-work be meaningful to them, how could it integrate and give expression to their hitherto anarchic experience as it gave expression to the artist's?

Condition (*a*) secures that great art—art which performs a wide and deep feat of integration—has something universal, something timeless and enduring from age to age. This timelessness we now see to be the timelessness of the instincts, the unchanging secret face of the genotype which persists beneath all the rich superstructure of civilisation. Condition (*b*) explains why contemporary art has a special and striking meaning for us, why we find in even minor contemporary poets something vital and immediate not to be found in Homer, Dante or Shakespeare. They live in the same world and meet the same bodiless forces whose power they experience.

This also explains why it is correct to have a materialist approach to art, to look in the art-works of any age for a reflection of the social relations of that age. For the experience of men in general is determined in general by the social relations of that age, or to be more accurate, the social relations of that age are simply man's individual experiences averaged out, just as a species is a group of animals' physical peculiarities averaged out. Since art lives in the social world, and can only be of value in integrating experiences general to men, it is plain that the art of any age can only express the general experiences of men in that age. So far from the artist's being a lone wolf, he is the normal man of that age—in so far as he is an artist. Of course normality in consciousness is as rare as normality in vision, and, unlike the latter, it is not a fixed physical standard but one which varies from year to year.

Moreover his normality is, so to speak, the norm of abnormal experiences. It is the norm of the queerness and newness and accident in contemporary men's lives: all the incursions of the unexpected which shake their inherited consciousness. Hence the apparent abnormality of the artist.

This, finally, explains why in a class society art is class art. For a class, in the Marxian sense, is simply a group of men whose life-experiences are substantially similar, that is, with less internal differences on the average than they have external differences from the life-experiences of men in other classes. This difference of course has an economic basis, a material cause arising from the inevitable conditions of economic production. Therefore the artist will necessarily integrate the new experience and voice the consciousness of that group whose experience in general resembles his own—his own class. This will be the class which practises art—the class at whose pole gathers the freedom and consciousness of society, in all ages the ruling class.

This is the most general movement of literary art, reflecting the most general law of society. Because of the different techniques of poetry and the novel—already explained—this movement is expressed in different ways in poetry and in the novel.

Poetry concentrates on the immediate affective associations of the word, instead of going first to the object or entity symbolised by the word and then drawing the affective association from that. Since words are fewer than the objects they symbolise, the affects of poetry are correspondingly condensed, but poetry itself is correspondingly cloudy and ambiguous. This ambiguity, which Empson takes to be the essence of poetry, is in fact a by-product. Now this concentration upon the affective tones of words, instead of going first to the symbolised reality and then to the feeling-tone of that reality, is—because of the nature of language—a concentration on the more dumb and instinctive part of man's consciousness. It is an approach to the more instinctively common part of man's consciousness. It is an approach to the secret unchanging core of the genotype in adapted man. Hence the importance of physiological introversion in poetry.

This genotype is undifferentiated because it is relatively unchanging. Hence the timelessness of poetry as compared to the importance of time sequence in the novel. Poetry speaks timelessly for one common "I" round which all experience is orientated. In poetry all the emotional experiences of men are arranged round the instincts, round the "I". Poetry is a bundle of instinctive perspectives of reality taken from one spot. Precisely because it is cloudy and ambiguous, its view is far-reaching; its horizon seems to open and expand and stretch out to dim infinity. Because it is instinctive, it is enduring. In it the instincts give one loud cry, a cry which expresses what is common in the general relation of every man to contemporary life as a whole.

But the novel goes out first to reality to draw its subjective associations from it. Hence we do not seem to feel the novel "in us", we do not identify our feelings with the feeling-tones of the novel. We stand inside the mock world of the novel and survey it; at the most we identify ourselves with the hero and look round with him at the "otherness" of his environment. The novel does not express the general tension between the instincts and the surroundings, but the changes of tension which take place as a result of change in the surroundings (life-experience). This incursion of the time element (reality as a process) so necessary in a differentiated society where men's time-experiences differ markedly among themselves, means that the novel must particularise and have characters whose actions and feelings are surveyed from without. Poetry is internal—a bundle of "I" perspectives of the world taken from one point, the poet. The story is external—a bundle of perspectives of one "I" (the character) taken from different parts of the world.

Obviously the novel can only evolve in a society where men's experiences do differ so markedly among themselves as to make this objective approach necessary, and this difference of experience is itself the result of rapid change in society, of an increased differentiation of functions, of an increased realisation of life as process, as dialectic. Poetry is the product of a tribe, where life flows on without much change between youth and age; the novel belongs to a restless age where things are always happening to people and people therefore are always altering.

3

Yet all art is subjective. All art is emotional and therefore concerned with the instincts whose adaptation to social life produces emotional consciousness. Hence art cannot escape its close relation with the genotype whose secret desires link in one endless series all human culture. ·

Now this genotype can be considered from two aspects; the timeless and the timeful, the changeless and changeful, the general and the particular.

(*a*) Timeless, changeless, general in that on the whole the genotype is substantially constant in all societies and all men. There is a substratum of likeness. Man does not change from Athenian to Ancient Briton and then to Londoner by innate differences stamped in by natural selection, but by acquired changes derived from social evolution. Poetry expresses this constant instinctive factor.

(*b*) Yet beneath this likeness the genotypes, because they are bundles of genes, reveal individual differences. These genes are perpetually shuffled to reveal new personalities. Because men differ in this way among themselves they cannot be satisfied with the simple tribal life of collective civilisation. They demand "luxuries", freedom, special products which cannot be satisfied within the ambit of such a primitive economy. This leads to an economic differentiation of society which, as we have already explained, is not the means of suppressing individuality but of realising it. Hence these individual genetic differences produce change in time and also the realisation of *characters*, of man's deviation from the social "norm". Thus the very technique of the novel makes it interested in the way characters strive to realise in existing society their individual differences.

Poetry expresses the freedom which inheres in man's general timeless unity in society; it is interested in society as the sum and guardian of common instinctive tendencies; it speaks of death, love, hope, sorrow and despair as all men experience them. The novel is the expression of that freedom which men seek, not in their unity in society but in their differences, of their search for freedom in the pores of society, and therefore of their repulsions from, clashes with and concrete motions against *other* individuals different from themselves.

The novel was bound to develop therefore under capitalism, whose increase in the productive forces brought about by the division of labour not only vastly increased the differentiation of society but also, by continually revolutionising its own basis, produced an endless flux and change in life. Equally, as capitalism decayed, the novel was bound to voice the experience of men that economic differentiation had changed from a means of freedom to a rubber-stamp crushing individuality (the ossification of classes), and that the productive forces, by being held back from developing further, had choked the free movement of life (the general economic crisis). Necessarily therefore in such a period the decay of the novel occurs together with a general revolutionary turmoil.

Thus we see in the technical differences of poetry and the novel the difference between changelessness and change, space and time, and it is clear that these are not mutually exclusive opposites but are opposites which interpenetrate, and, as they fly apart, continually generate an enrichening reality.

This was the same kind of difference as that between the evolutionary and classificatory sciences. And just as the technique of poetry demands an immediate concentration on the word, so the classificatory sciences, such as geometry and mathematics, demand an immediate concentration on the symbol. The novel demands that we pass from the symbol to reality, and only then to the affective organisation; biology demands that we go first to the concrete objects, and only then to their rational organisation. Poetry passes straight from the word to the affective organisation, careless of the reality whose relation it accepts as already given in the word. Mathematics passes straight from the symbol to the perceptual organisation, careless of the concrete object, whose important qualities (to it) are already accepted as crystallised in the symbol. Hence the vital importance of precise speech—of the absolutely correct word or correct symbol—both to poet and mathematician, contrasted with the looser speech permitted to the biologist or novelist.

We have seen that music is an extreme kind of poetry, that just as mathematics escapes almost altogether from the subjective qualities of matter, so music (unlike poetry) escapes almost altogether from the objective references of sounds. Therefore the musician is even preciser in his language than the poet, and the affective laws of music's symbols are as careful and minute as are the perceptual laws of mathematical symbols.

We can now understand more clearly why poetry resembles dream in its technique. The characteristic of dreams is that the dreamer always plays the leading part in it. He is always present in it, sometimes (as analysis shows) in many disguises. The same egocentricity is characteristic of poetry. Quite naïvely the poet records directly all his impressions, experiences, thoughts, images. Hence the apparent egoism of poetry, for everything is seen and experienced directly. Poetry is a relationship of memory-images mediated by only two words—"I" and "like".

But this is not the egoism of dream; it is a social egoism. The particular emotional organisation of the poet is condensed into words, and the words are read, and the psyche of the reader experiences the same emotional reorganisation. The reader puts himself, for the duration of the poem, in the place of the poet, and sees with his eyes. He *is* the poet.

In a poem by Shelley, we are Shelley. As we read Shakespeare, we see with his profound shimmering vision. Hence the unexpected individuality of the poet. Though it is the common human creature, the genotype, and not the "character" who looks out in poetry on the common contemporary scene, he looks at it through the eyes of one man, through the windows of the poet's psyche.

How is this done? That is the peculiar secret of poetic technique. Just as poetry can be equated with dream, poetic technique is similar to dream technique. The nature of dream technique has been explored by analysts under the general name of "the dream-work".

A dream consists of two layers. Obvious is the *manifest* content. We are walking by the seaside, a ship comes alongside, we step on it, we land in France, certain adventures befall us, and so on. This is the manifest content of the dream as we tell it at breakfast next morning to our bored family, who cannot understand our interest in it. But our interest in it was due to the fact that the illusion was perfect. While they lasted, these things really seemed to be happening to us. And this vividness must spring from some affective cause. But we felt little real emotion in the dream, however surprising the adventures that befell us. If we felt emotion, it was out of all real proportion to our adventures. Surprising things happened and we were not surprised. Trifling things happened and we were appalled. The affects were displaced in relation to reality. If we are asked to give our associations to these various component images just as they spring to our mind, a whole undergrowth of displaced affective life is revealed. Each symbol is associated with memories in our life, not by association of ideas but by affective associations.

The characteristic of "dream-work" is that every dream-symbol is over-determined and has a multitude of different emotional significances. This we also saw was the characteristic of poetic words, and springs from the same cause, that dream-symbols are valued directly for their affective content and not as symbols of a consistent mock world in which we first orientate ourselves. Hence the inconsequence of dream matches the "illogical" rhythm and assonance of poetry.

The organisation of the psyche is such that in sleep all the conscious wishes, hopes, fears and loves of the instinctive are replaced by apparently arbitrary memory-images, but which really are associated by the affective ties of simple unconscious wishes. They are organised by the appetitive activity of the instinctive and therefore unsleeping part of the psyche which, because it is archaic phylogenetically, is unmodified and therefore anti-social, or rather non-social. This affective substratum does not normally appear in dream. It is "repressed". Only the arbitrary symbols, apparently unconnected, appear in the consciousness. But this affective basis is the "reasoning" of the

o

dream, and directs its course. It is the latent content. But the affects also have a "reason" for their relation to the memory-images of the dream. Thus there is a double distortion—a distortion of reality and of emotion—a double shift of subject and object.

Why cannot we achieve in sleep complete unconsciousness to any stimuli? For the simple reason that sleep is not death or complete unconsciousness but something in which part of our attention is still awake. In sleep attention, though turned from the outside world, is not completely asleep, otherwise external stimuli would never wake us at all. The attention of a sleeper can be attracted by a sufficiently loud noise. Obviously it is dangerous for animals to sleep too profoundly. All stimuli below the threshold, *e.g.* gentle outside noises, sunlight falling on the face, pressure on the limbs, internal digestive disturbances, are switched, not into their proper neurone paths, but into other paths dictated by the "sets" of the unconscious instincts.

The reality of an unconscious wish can be tested in practice. If a sleeper resolves before sleeping to hold a certain object in his hand, he will still be clutching it when he wakes, showing that throughout his sleep some unsleeping neurones continued to will unconsciously, and to send a continual stream of nervous impulses down the efferent nerves to the fingers to maintain a muscular tetany. If the affects were to be wakened by such stimuli, sleep would end. Therefore the associative paths from the instinctive unconscious neurones to the affective patterns are in some way side-tracked and the stimuli are switched instead into the patterns associated at one remove, *i.e.* the memory-images. These are connected with these side-tracked affective patterns by association, but are not themselves soaked with affects. These memory-images appear in the dream and thus give the flicker of attention something to focus on, which otherwise would be focused on the stimuli and so would wake the sleeper. It is no accident that sleep appears only in higher animals—those whose life is full of acquired adaptations which therefore require "working out" physiologically in sleep. Insects, with their elaborate innate adaptations, do not sleep. Or when they do "sleep", as in the chrysalis, it is a final and far more thoroughgoing adaptation, in which every cell in the body is re-orientated.

The emotional organisation of the memory-images—their latent content—is therefore given by the process of their generation. If a certain threshold value is exceeded by the stimuli, or anything goes wrong with the switching, too powerful affects are released; the sleeper, becoming more conscious, at once wakes. The lack of affective reality accounts for the ease with which dreams are forgotten, whereas nightmares, in which the sleeper wakes or almost wakes owing to the powerful affects, are generally clearly remembered. We wake because the affects were on the point of becoming realised and therefore of leading to action.

Dreams, then, contain a manifest and a latent content. The manifest content is imagic phantasy, the latent content is affective reality. Both have a double connection with a phantastic affectivity manifest in dream and an imagic reality connected with the latent content. Psycho-analysts have not made this distinction because the analysis of dreams is done verbally. They have not seen that in translating images and affects into language there is an epistemological leak. In language images and affects live simultaneously and cannot be separated: both are social and conscious. Ignoring this, the psycho-analyst meets a contradiction: in probing the latent content of dreams he can never be given by the dreamer a bundle of "unconscious" affects as associations, for the dreamer can only communicate by language, and in language affect is always attached to an image, to a symbol of external reality, and is itself a conscious feeling-tone. Therefore the analyst gets as the latent content of the dream-images—still more images with conscious affects attached. For this reason, not only does the psycho-analyst tend to equate unconscious affects with their social translations, but he overlooks the gap between dream, in which the affective organisation is unconscious and therefore *personal*, and art, in which the affective organisation is conscious and therefore *social*. It is the difference between free association and directed feeling.

4

This leads to *surréaliste* technique with its undirected feeling and personal affective organisation, where freedom, in true bourgeois style, is the unconsciousness of necessity, *i.e.* ignorance of the affective organisation which determines the flow of imagery and is conscious in good poetry. Hence the cerebral and visual character of *surréaliste* art. This bourgeois freedom was already contained in the philosophy of symbolism, from which *surréalisme* derives. Remy de Gourmont, the philosopher of symbolism, correctly said: "Above all it is a theory of liberty; it implies absolute freedom of thought and form: it is the free and individual development of the aesthetic personality". And Rimbaud, greatest of the symbolist poets, said: "I have come to hold sacred the disorder of my mind".

Poetry, like dream, contains *manifest* and *latent* contents. The manifest content can be roughly arrived at by paraphrasing the poem. It is the imagery or the "ideas". In a paraphrase the latent content, *i.e.* the emotional content, has almost entirely vanished. It was contained, then, not in the external reality symbolised by the words (for this has been preserved) but in the words themselves. The manifest content is the poetry interpreted "rationally". It is the external reality in the poem. It can be expressed in other ways and other languages. But the latent content of poetry is in that particular form of wording, and in no other.

How is the latent content contained in the original word and not contained in the *sense* of the words—*i.e.* in the portions of external reality which the words symbolise? The emotions are not associated affectively with the portion of external reality symbolised by the manifest content, for another language can be made to symbolise the same portion of external reality, and still it is not the poem. How then did the original words contain the emotional content "in themselves" and not in the things they symbolised? Dream analysis gives us the answer, by *affective* association of ideas. In any association of ideas two images are tied to each other by something different, like sticks by a cord. In poetry they are tied by affects.

If a word is abstracted from its surroundings and concentrated on in the same way as an analyst asked his patient to concentrate on any particular image of a dream, a number of associations will rise vaguely to the mind. In a simple word like "spring" there are hundreds of them; of greenness, of youth, of fountains, of jumping; every word drags behind it a vast bag and baggage of emotional associations, picked up in the thousands of different circumstances in which the word was used. It is these associations that provided the latent content of affect which is the poem. Not the ideas of "greenness", "youth", but the affective cord linking the ideas of "greenness" and "youth" to the word "spring", constitutes the raw material of poetry.

Of course the *thing* "spring" (the season) denoted by the word "spring" also has many affective associations. These are used by the novel. Poetry is concerned with the more general, subtle and instinctive affects which are immediately associated with the word "spring" and therefore include such almost punning associations as those connected with spring (a fountain) and spring (to jump). Hence the tendency of poetry to play with words, to pun openly or secretly, to delight in the texture of words. This is part of the technique of poetry which treats words anti-grammatically to realise their immediate and even contradictory affective tones. The novel uses words grammatically so as sharply to exclude all meanings and therefore all affective tones, except one clear piece of reality, and then derives the emotional content from this piece of reality and its active relation with the other pieces of reality in the story as part of a perceptual life-experience.

When we read a line of poetry these other ideas to which the affects are associated do not rise to the mind. We get the leaping and gushiness of "spring" in poetry's use of it as a word for the idea "season", but we do not get the fountain or the jump except in an open poetic pun. They remain unconscious. *Poetry is a kind of inverted dream.* Whereas in dream the real affects are partly suppressed and the blended images rise into the conscious, in poetry the associated images are partly suppressed and it is the blended affects that are present in the consciousness, in the form of affective organisation.

Why is there a manifest content at all? Why are not all images suppressed? Why is not great poetry like the poetry of the extreme symbolists, a mere collection of words, meaning nothing, but words themselves full of affective association? Why should poetry state, explain, narrate, obey grammar, have syntax, be capable of paraphrase, since if paraphrased it loses its affective value?

The answer is, because poetry is an adaptation to external reality. It is an emotional attitude towards the world. It is made of language and language was created to signify otherness, to indicate portions of objective reality shared socially. It lives in the same language as scientific thought. The manifest content represents a statement of external reality. The manifest content is symbolic of a certain *piece* of external reality—be it scene, problem, thought, event. And the emotional content is *attached* to this statement of reality, not in actual experience but in the poem. The emotional content sweats out of the piece of external reality. In life this piece of external reality is devoid of emotional tone, but described in those particular words, and no others, it suddenly and magically shimmers with affective colouring. That affective colouring represents an emotional organisation similar to that which the poet himself felt when faced (in phantasy or actuality) with that piece of external reality. When the poet says,

> Sleep, that knots up the ravelled sleave of care,

he is making a manifest statement. The paraphrase

> Slumber, that unties worry, which is like a piece of tangled knitting,

carries over most of the manifest content, but the affective tones which lurked in the associations of the words used have vanished. It is like a conjuring trick. The poet holds up a piece of the world and we see it glowing with a strange emotional fire. If we analyse it "rationally", we find no fire. Yet none the less, for ever afterwards, that piece of reality still keeps an afterglow about it, is still fragrant with emotional life. So poetry enriches external reality for us.

The affective associations used by poetry are of many forms.

Sometimes they are sound associations, and then we call the line "musical"—not that the language is specially harmonious; to a foreigner it would probably have no particular verbal melody:

> Thick as autumnal leaves that strow the books
> In Vallambrosa

is not musical to someone who knows no English. But to an English ear the emotive associations wakened are aroused through sound rather than sense linkages, and hence we call the line musical. So, too, with Verlaine's line, musical only to ears attuned to the emotive associations of French nasals:

> Et O—ces voix d'enfants chantant dans la coupole,

or the old fairy-tale title, "La Belle aux bois dormant".

It is impossible to have affects in poetry without their adherence to symbols of external reality, for poetry's affects (in so far as they are poetic) are social, and it is impossible for different subjects to be linked except by a common object (by "matter"). The logical conclusion of symbolism is not poetry but music. And here it may be objected—music consists of sounds which refer to no external reality and yet music is an art and has a social content. Exactly—because in music the symbols have ceased to "refer" to external reality and have become portions of external reality themselves and, in doing so, have necessarily generated a formal structure (the scale, "rules" of harmony, etc.) which gives them the rigidity and social status of external reality. The notes of music themselves are the manifest content of music, and they therefore obey not grammatical (subjective) but pseudo-mathematical (objective) laws: of course they are necessarily distorted or organised within the compass of those rules. In the same way architecture becomes external reality and is distorted or organised within the compass of the rules of use-function.

The technique of the poet consists in this, that not all the affects associated with any particular words rise up into the consciousness, but only those that are required. This is done by

the arrangement of the words in such a way that their clusters
of associations, impinging on each other heighten some affective associations and inhibit the others, and so form an
organised mass of emotion. The affective colouring of one
word takes reflected shadow and light from the colours of the
other words. It does this partly through their contiguity,
particularly in synthetic languages (Latin and Greek), and
partly through their grammatical connection, particularly in
analytic languages (English, Chinese); but chiefly through the
"meaning" as a whole. The manifest content, the literal
meaning, the paraphrasable sense, is a kind of bridge, or
electrical conductor, which puts all the affective currents of
each word into contact. It is like a switchboard; some of the
affective associations fade away directly they enter it, others
run down into other words and alter their colour; others blend
together and heighten a particular word. The whole forms the
specific fused glow which is that poem's affective organisation
or emotional attitude to its meaning. Hence the same word has
a different affective coloration in one poem from what it has in
another, and it is for this reason that a poem is concrete. It is
affectively concrete; each word has a special affective significance in that poem different from what it has in another. In
this way the emotional content does not float about fluidly in
the mind; it is firmly attached, by a hundred interweaving
strands, to the manifest content—a piece of external reality. A
poem's content is not just emotion, it is *organised* emotion, an
organised emotional attitude to a piece of external reality.
Hence its value—and difficulty—as compared with other
emotions, however strong, but unorganised—a sudden inexplicable fit of sorrow, a gust of blind rage, a blank despair.
Such emotions are unaesthetic because unorganised. They are
unorganised socially because they are not organised in relation
to a socially accepted external reality. They are unconscious of
outer necessity. The emotions of poetry are *part* of the manifest
content. They seem to be in the external reality as it appears
in the poem. We do not appear to take up an emotional
attitude to a piece of reality; it is there, given in the reality:
that is the way of emotional cognition. In poetic cognition,
objects are presented already stamped with feeling-judgments.

Hence the adaptive value of poetry. It is like a real emotional experience.

It is plain that poetry may be judged in different ways; either by the importance of the manifest content, or by the vividness of the affective colouring. To a poet who brings a new portion of external reality into the ambit of poetry, we feel more gratitude than to one who brings the old stale manifest contents. But the first poet may be poor in the affective colouring with which he soaks his piece of reality. It may be the old stale colouring, whereas our other poet, in spite of his conventional piece of reality, may achieve a new affective tone. Old poets we shall judge almost entirely by their affective tone; their manifest contents have long belonged to our world of thought. Hence the apparent triteness of old poetry which yet is a *great* triteness. From new poets we demand new manifest contents and new affective colouring, for it is their function to give us new emotional attitudes to a new social environment. A poet who provides both to a high degree will be a good poet. A poet who brings into his net a vast amount of new reality to which he attaches a wide-ranging affective colouring we shall call a *great* poet, giving Shakespeare as an instance. Hence great poems are always long poems, just because of the quantity of reality they must include as manifest content. But the manifest content, whatever it is, is not the *purpose* of the poem. The purpose is the specific emotional organisation directed towards the manifest content and provided by the released affects. The affects are not "latent", as in dream; it is the associated ideas which are suppressed to form the latent content. Just as the key to dream is a series of instinctive attitudes which provide the mechanism of dream-work, so the key to poetry is a cluster of suppressed pieces of external reality—a vague unconscious world of life-experience.

Poetry colours the world of reality with affective tones. These affective colours are not "pretty-pretty", for it is still the real world of necessity, and great poetry will not disguise the nakedness of outer necessity, only cause it to shine with the glow of interest. Poetry soaks external reality—nature and society—with emotional significance. This significance, because it gives the organism an appetitive interest in external reality, enables the organism to deal with it more resolutely, whether in the world of reality or of phantasy. The primitive who would lose interest in the exhausting labour necessary to plough an arid abstract collection of soil, will find heart when the earth is charged with the affective colouring of "Mother Nature", for now, by the magic of poetry, it glows with the appetitive tints of sexuality or filial love. These affective colours are not unreal because they are not scientific, for they are the colouring of the genotype's own instincts, and these instincts are as real as the earth is real. The significant expression projected by poetry on to the face of external reality is simply this, a prophecy of the endless attempt of the genotype to mould necessity to its own likeness, in which it obtains a continually increasing success. "Matter, surrounded by a sensuous poetic glamour, seems to attract man's whole entity by winning smiles." So said Marx and Engels of materialism before it became one-sided mechanical materialism, when it was still bathed in the artistic splendour of the Renaissance. That sensuous glamour is given by poetry; and materialism became one-sided when, afraid of feeling the self, it became aridly scientific, and matter vanishes in a logical but empty wave-system. Poetry restores life and value to matter, and puts back the genotype into the world from which it was banished.

5

Although we equated dream to poetry, we saw that there were essential differences. Poetry is creative; dream is not. Poetry is creative because it is *directed* feeling. In dream the associations are "free"—reality's images are manipulated according to the genotype's desires, just as iron filings over a magnet "freely" arrange themselves along the lines of force. In poetry, however, feeling is fashioned into a social form by being made to live in the common world of perceptual reality. Poetry externalises emotion. The self is *expressed*—forcibly squeezed out. Emotion is minted—made current coin. Feelings are given social value. Work is done. Dream-work is precisely *not* labour, poetic dreamwork is; because one produces social commodities, the other does not.

It is for this reason that poetry's technique differs from that of dream. Below the surface of the dream lie the unconscious instinctive wishes. Instinct is blind, it cannot alter itself as long as it is unconscious and incapable of self-conditioning, for it has no will but only automatic responses to stimuli. These instinctive wish-patterns dictate the dance of images in the brain, which are associated with the wish-patterns by indirect affective ties. But the ties themselves are suppressed in dream, for everything that wakes the affects to action must be avoided if the dreamer is to sleep on. The vast field of affect-laden images is "out of bounds". "Let sleeping affects lie" is the motto of dream-wishes. They are suppressed by being phantastically gratified as easily as one makes a thoughtless habitual movement.

In poetic illusion the process is inverted. Dreams ascend from the unconscious upwards and are therefore blind and un-creative. Poems descend from the consciousness downwards and are therefore aware and creative. Dream fearfully avoids the dynamic region of the emotions, so as not to wake the sleeper to action; poetry explores it courageously, so as to change the inner world.

The memory-images of dream blindly follow the wire-pulling of the instincts. But the words of poetry follow a pur-poseful path. Their mission is, first to stir up the affects and then to reorganise them. The only result of dream is a tem-porary and arbitrary pattern of images drawn from reality and rearranged at the behest of the instincts. "The world is not thus, but thus," say the instincts, and remould it in their dream, but sometimes the instincts are so modified that they quarrel with themselves, and the contradictions of the dream explode in affects that wake us.

Poetry, however, takes its words and arranges them in such a way that the affects are roused and forced to take up a new organisation towards reality, a new emotional attitude. Dream moulds reality to the instincts, and is therefore of little use except to guard the dreamer from external reality and so keep him sleeping. Poetry moulds the instincts to reality, and is therefore useful, for it does not protect the reader from reality but puts him in good heart to grapple with it. Poetry is inverted dream—inverted in direction, in aim, and therefore in technique. Poetry flows from reality down to the instincts, stopping only on the last outpost of perception where it encounters the instincts face to face. Dream flows from the instincts to the boundary of reality, at the limit of attention, and stops there, short of actual achievement, because it stops short of action.

We need not be surprised, therefore, that poetry is public and dream private, for consciousness is a social construction. The conscious psychic contents which the ego holds together are socially given contents. True, they cohere because the body which contains them is materially one object, but the materials that cohere—morals, knowledge, culture, aspirations, duties— are all socially given. Unsocial man is brute, unconscious, instinctive, and therefore without will. An instinctive uncon- scious organism has no will, but only an automatic reflex, responsive to internal or external stimuli. It has no freedom, for freedom requires a will. The essence of willing is that con- sciousness is aware of those reasons that make its choice inevitable, and it is just that inevitability which is will. The fulfilled will is the conscious dialectic of the psyche in which the strife between the instincts of the body and the necessity of outer nature is resolved by a conscious action which con- tains both feeling and perception. This conscious microcosm is creative because it can act voluntarily, for ultimately conscious action and creation are the same. Creation, as opposed to accidental appearance, is the will moulding instead of blind necessity evolving. Accident carves the rocks into strange un- premeditated shapes, but the will hews the stone into a desired sculpture. Both are aspects of necessity.

The poet, then, must be a man sensitive above all to the associations and affective tones of words—not the personal but the collective tones. How is he to differentiate between per- sonal and collective tones? He cannot consciously, and no poet can avoid the danger of writing verse which is meaningful to himself but meaningless to other people. All he can do is to live his affective life socially; to live with words. For indeed he can only live with words socially. He will meet them in books, in literature, in scientific papers, in journals, in speech, but always they will be met in public. Thus if he lives with words instead of memory-images, he will master the technique of poetry, for poetry is written with words.

The poet's mastery of word associations gives him his tools for his creative task. His task is this. An emotional reorganisation must be made public, must be expressed by words in a collectively accessible form. Let us give our phrase—emotional reorganisation—a more current psychological form. Psychotherapy has evolved the conception of the autonomous complex. A complex is a constellation of contents in the psyche which gather to themselves psychic energy. They become organised and full of dynamic power; they occupy a large part of the psyche. The psyche has many small complexes, but they only become complexes in the therapeutic sense when they are repelled by the chiefly conscious contents of the psyche (repression) and are unknown to the "ego", that is, to the consciously thinking and feeling portion of the psyche. They become dangerous when they develop a "will of their own", influence the actions of the psyche unknown to the consciousness, and give rise to neurotic conflicts, doubts and strange anxieties. The man seems torn in half. He has two motives and two wills. Similar symptoms are seen in Pavlov's dogs when they have been conditioned to make two different responses to, say, a square and a circle. If an object midway between these shapes is presented to them, they exhibit a canine caricature of the neurotic's hesitation. An emotional reorganisation is the resolution in some degree of an autonomous complex by making it socially conscious.

6

Psycho-therapy draws its conceptions from pathology. It is impossible fully to understand the relation of illusion to reality in man's mind and life without understanding the relation of insanity to the healthy functioning of thought.

In dream, as we already saw, the stimulus to action is phantastically gratified in a stream of affectively-toned images in which both affect and image are distorted in their relation to reality. This distortion is permissible precisely because the dream by definition cannot issue in action, since its purpose is to protect the living body from active relation with its environment.

Man makes a step forward when he injects the dream into waking life. But this very injection narrows the scope of the biologically permissible in phantasy. Because phantasy now issues in action it must be geared in some way to present reality, for present reality determines action.

But it cannot be geared to present reality on both sides, subjective and objective, for to do so simply equates phantasy with perception, with man's immediate vision of external reality and his attitude towards that reality.

It is therefore distorted in space to produce the mystic illusion, centring round the spell and the rite, which seems to drag all reality into the circle of the tribe by the power of magic and the word. It is distorted in time to produce the myth, or story. These two forms of phantasy, myth and magic, or theology and mysticism, correspond to the evolutionary and classificatory aspects of man's plastic relation to reality, but they are still impure—subjective is mixed with objective, science with art. They are still religion. To make the subjective more pure and internal, and the objective more precise and external, they must be separated out by the dissolution and manipulation of the "other" side.

Hence waking phantasy is distorted on one side. Art distorts phantasy on the side of external reality by the device of the mock world; science distorts it on the side of subjective reality by the device of the mock ego. Yet this distortion is not distortion for the sake of distortion on the distorted side; it is distortion for the sake of greater accuracy on the "other" side. Now that other side can only reach out to a greater precision beyond that of present reality by association with the consciousnesses of other men—by passing from the semi-consciousness of brute phantasy to the consciousness of a man.

Therefore the undistorted side of art—the subjective side—is developed by interaction with a social subjectiveness or social ego, and the undistorted side of science, the objective side, is developed by interaction with a social objectiveness or social world.

Science and art are merely abstract and generalised forms of the scientific and artistic elements in individual phantasies. Individual phantasies are, however, subject to disturbance. Men go insane. Study of these disturbances should throw light on the nature of phantasy.

Madmen are men whose theory has got out of gear with reality as evidenced by their practice—their action. This reality can only be a social reality because this is the only reality known to society. Madmen are men whose theory of reality differs markedly from that of society. They are socially maladapted. In them there is a conflict—a conflict between their social experience—their life in society—and their phantastic theory of life.

Psychiatry now tends to recognise two main divisions of insanity: (a) the manic-depressive or cyclothymic disturbances, and (b) the schizophrenic, catatonic or dementia praecox disturbances. The two groups are by Kretschmer closely associated with two types of body constitution, the pyknic (stout and fleshy) and the asthenic (thin and spare). Apart from insanity or the psychoses, there are disturbances of mental functioning —the psycho-neuroses. There is a general tendency to find a close association between hysteric neuroses and cyclothymic insanity, and between psychasthenic neuroses and schizophrenic insanity.

Jung's division of psychological types into extraverted and introverted is also based on the assumption that extraverted types, when mentally disturbed, tend to hysteric and manic-depressive states, while introverted types are more likely to suffer from the psychasthenic neuroses and schizophrenia. The former group is generally regarded as easier to cure than the latter.

Now we saw that dream is the vehicle of a tension which is resolved wholly in the phantastic plane by a double distortion of subject (affective tones) and object (memory images). Madmen solve their conflicts by detaching their theory from social reality and making it personal. They are awake and cannot solve their problems by this double dream-like shift. Their phantasy will be geared at one end to social reality.

It is our contention that the extraverted, cyclothymic

hysteric type is geared to reality externally. This is in fact clinically correct. Even the manic-depressive can "orient" himself correctly, find his way about, and generally notice what is going on.

MacCurdy points out that he reacts to real stimuli, but in an exaggerated way. For example, he hears whispering below and imagines it to be a conversation regarding his assassination. He then betrays all the fear appropriate to an attempt at assassination.

In adjusting himself to reality he has *desocialised his ego*. As a result it becomes unconscious and correspondingly violent and barbaric. It oscillates uncontrollably and explodes with the slightest provocation on the all-or-none basis. To observers, therefore, the manic-depressive seems a man of wild passions who has forgotten external reality. But to himself he does not seem like that, for his ego has become unconscious and primitive and has therefore retired from his conscious field. Of course this throws out of gear the external reality in his conscious field, so that it is always being distorted by unconscious forces. If he hears the word "lobster", he promptly assumes he is to be boiled alive. Because his ego has become unconscious and desocialised, he is its slave.

The schizophrenic, however, exhibits an emotional consistency and integration like the manic-depressive's orientation towards external reality. The classical clinical sign of schizophrenia, according to MacCurdy, is when the patient does not show an affective reaction proportioned to the stimulus. For example, he declares that he hears people whispering that they will assassinate him, but he shows no fear. Eventually he shows a complete lack of orientation, is unable even to feed himself, and finally passes into a private world of reality. As an introvert, attaching most value to the subject, he has resolved his conflict by desocialising external reality, so that he lives in a dream world—a personal world. This dream world reflects his conscious ego, which, however, because the dream world is an unchecked reflection of its movement, does not seem very evident to the observer. The observer, being a part of negated outer reality, is out of touch with the schizophrenic's ego. The schizophrenic's conscious ego is not roused to passion or emotion because the dream world does not annoy it but "conforms" to it. Hence the conscience and strong social content of the schizophrenic's mental world, which does not of course affect his conduct, for (as in paranoia) the outer world is always "in the wrong". It justifies his desires by altering itself to conform with them. This is why Freud calls the paranoiac narcissistic; and this explains his incurability and untouchability.

Now we regard the phantastic device of art as similar in its general mechanism to the introverted distortion of schizophrenia and psychasthenic neurosis, and the phantastic device of science as similar in its general mechanism to the extraverted distortion of cyclothymia and hysteria.

Does this mean that we regard science and art as in any sense pathological and illusory? No, for although there is a similar psychological mechanism at work, art is no more neurosis than thought is dream. And the difference consists precisely in this, that science and art have a social content. The reality around which the extraverted hysteric or cyclothymic distorts his theory is private reality, a reality that contradicts the whole of the social theory of reality in his consciousness. This contradiction, instead of leading (as in science) to a synthesis of his private experience with the social theory of reality (demanding a change of both), leads to conduct which denies the social theory of reality. The desocialisation of the cyclothymic's ego leads to an uprush of the instincts from the unconscious which distorts his relation to external reality and therefore his whole action. The desocialisation of the schizophrenic's conception of external reality leads to a slavery of perception to the ego which removes the "brake" from it so that its world becomes dream-like and unreal.

Thus the psychological mechanism of science, because its reality is public and true, produces in the sphere of theory an ego which is the very opposite of that of the cyclothymic extravert—an ego which is drained of affect and quality, which is neutral, passive and serenely conscious of necessity. Of course this very reality, because it is without the dynamism and appetite of the instincts, requires the emotional reality of art for its completion. It is true, therefore, that a world which

P

tried to live by science alone would deny its theory in practice and show the nervestorms of a cyclothymic, not because science is cyclothymic, but because it is only one part of concrete living.

The reality around which the psychasthenic neurotic or schizophrenic distorts the outside world is a private ego, his own private desires and appetites. Around this he "arranges" a whole mock world (the compulsive actions, obsessions or phobias of the neurotic, or the complete screen of fancy of the schizophrenic). But the psychological mechanism of art, because its ego is public and noble, produces in the sphere of theory a world which is beautiful and strong. This world, because it is drained of necessity, requires the mechanism of science for realisation. A world which lived by art alone would deny its theory in practice and live in a beautiful world of dream, while all its actions would produce only misery and ugliness.

7

Let us examine the difference between the two forms of extraverted mental disturbance. The hysteric does not deny the world of external reality (taking external in the sense of "external to the body"). He accepts this. The reality he distorts and desocialises is that of his body regarded subjectively. It is as if he does not dare to challenge social reality in that portion of it where society is most firmly entrenched, and he therefore selects his body as something in which he has a special proprietorial interest, and distorts that. Hence the famous hysteric-illnesses (hysteric dumbness, paralysis, blindness, hyper-aesthesia and anaesthesia) which are socially unreal in the sense that they are only functional and non-organic, and yet are real to the hysteric because he is, by definition, unconscious of their real cause.

Classic examples of the solution of a conflict between the instincts and the environment by hysteric means are the hysteric soldier, whose fear of death takes the form of an hysteric paralysis, and the hysteric woman, whose unsatisfied love or fear of domination takes the form of an hysteric illness. Hence the term "organ-language" for hysteric symptoms.

But if the conflict is unresolvable by this means, then the extravert's ego, forced into unconsciousness, challenges the whole domain of social reality, including that outside his body. He becomes mad in relation to his environment. Forces coming from he knows not where, irrupt into his environment and completely distort it. His ego, forced into the darkness of his soul, grimaces back at him from the environment, though he does not recognise it there.

The psychasthenic neurotic, however, is a man who challenges at first the social reality. Therefore, just as the conflict of the extravert is a conflict with an external reality (*i.e.* a perceived external reality) which is too hard for his unconscious ego, the conflict of the introvert is a conflict with a felt ego (conscious or morality) which is too hard for his unconscious environment. Hence the psychasthenic symptoms of lack of interest in external reality, in life—an inability to face up to its problems or to do anything about them. He invents such external realities as inimical men (paranoia) or objects (phobias) or processes (compulsions) in order to justify his desires. The psychasthenic neurotic does not deny the existence of the ego as a social individual, as an ego in touch with other egos, but claims to be excepted from the usual rules owing to its difficult environmental circumstances. Hence the endless martyrisation and introspection of the psychasthenic neurotic which makes such remunerative and almost incurable customers of the psycho-analyst. Because of his "special difficulties", this type of neurotic is always trying to create a specially "easy" world. He solves his conflict by "blaming" the emotion caused by it on to other details of environmental reality. The emotion generated by some sexual crisis, for example, is attached to some trifling object. The emotion generated by a soldier's being buried in a trench, or his fear of this, is in neurosis displaced to all dark objects or shut-in places.

Thus just as the hysteric does not deny external reality but adjusts it in the domain of his body considered as an object suffering from physical disease, so the psychasthenic neurotic does not deny his responsibilities as a social ego but adjusts them in his environment, which he distorts by elaborate rationalisations and inventions. The slightest detail is seized on and twisted. The hysteric speaks an organ-language; the neurotic a feeling-language. One asks society to believe nothing he does not see (and manufactures the proof); the other nothing he does not feel (and manufactures the cause). Thus just as the hysteric is unconscious of the real cause of his paralysis, the neurotic is unconscious of the cause of his "difficult" circumstances. He avoids fear by avoiding closed places; he does not realise that what he is really avoiding by his claustrophobia is going to the trenches.

But if the conflict is insoluble by this means then the neurotic denies social reality completely and becomes unconscious of his self. This is schizophrenia. He still remains conscious of external reality. An example is the Korsakoff syndrome. The patient knows everything external that happens to him, but does not know it is happening as to him. He lacks what Claparède called "moïeté". To take an example given by MacCurdy: a patient was pricked by her physician with a pin concealed in his hand. Next time he went to touch her she shrank away. Asked why, she replied hazily: "Hands sometimes have pins in them". She could not be persuaded that she, as an ego, had been pricked, but merely that a pricking had happened in her field of perceptual consciousness. When occupied with phantasy this type is simply a receptacle for phantastic panoramas, whereas the cyclothymic is a phantastic Napoleon, a hero, an enormous "I".

Now we have already compared the mechanism of extra-version with that of science. We will go further and compare the mechanism of hysteria with the classificatory sciences and of cyclothymia with the evolutionary sciences.

The hysteric distorts his body to provide a reality consonant with a wished reality. In the same way the mathematician "imagines" an ego ordering, classifying, *operating* everywhere in external reality. But precisely because with the mathematician this external reality is social, real and therefore conscious, the ego which thus operates is unconscious, abstract, drained of any distorting or qualifying subjectivity.

The cyclothymic loses grip even on his ego to achieve an

adjustment in accordance with his "difficulties". As a result his delusion looks out at him everywhere in his perceptual field. In the same way the biologist or sociologist imagines an ego passively observing, noting, feeling everywhere in the sphere of reality chosen. But because with the scientist this external reality is social, real and conscious, the ego which thus observes is bare of subjective or personal bias—is the all-observing neutral eye of concrete society which yet spreads the quality it is interested in everywhere.

In the same way, since we have compared the mechanism of introversion with that of art, we will go further, and compare that of psychasthenic neurosis with poetry and that of schizophrenia with the novel. The neurotic substitutes for the social environment a special personal environment which "accounts for" his subjective difficulties. He makes an unreal environment consistent with his desires. The poet, however, substitutes for the affects and "I" of his experience a still more real and social "I"; he forces his "I" completely to enter the social ego, and produces, but for the opposite reason, a mock "adjusted" external world. Hence all poetry, as we have seen, turns on the social "I".

The catatonic, however, does not even make his world a real world of exceptionally difficult circumstances. The real world vanishes from society altogether; and the catatonic's world becomes coincident with a world of "I-organised" environmental contents, an ego-created bundle of remembered percepts. The novelist, however, makes his "I" coincide not merely with a generalised human "I" (which is the way the poet lifts his "I" from an "I" in specially difficult circumstances to an "I" in all human circumstances) but with the concrete "I"'s developed by the individuation of society. Hence the novel is not seen with all its contents oriented round one "I", as in poetry, but it becomes an objective world, a world apparently like a selection of society surveyed from without, just as the catatonic's "I" is extended to become a world of apparently objective percepts.

Why is the hysteric and the cyclothymic (according to the experience of anthropologists) far more common in primitive societies? Because, in their primitive undifferentiated state, the environment or objective reality is far more likely to be the cause of acute mental tension and require the "healing" phantasy than is the ego or subjective reality. Primitives are held firmly to the demands of the simple social environment. Conscience is clear and imperative. The development of ideology, and the cleavage of conscience due to the rise of class antagonisms, produces the torn egos and suppressed selves of modern society. Psychasthenic neurosis is a characteristic bourgeois disease. In the war, hysteria was, according to Rivers, commonest in the ranks; psychasthenic neurosis more usual among the officers. It is the disease of a class thrown by the cleavage of society away from external reality on to the consciousness, just as hysteria is the disease of a class thrown away from consciousness on to external reality. It required the development of a class society to develop consciousness by its separation, but it requires the reappearance of a classless society to synthesise what has now grown pathologically far apart—thinking and being, theory and practice. Schizophrenia is the disease of philosophy and idealism.

Thus, although there is a correspondence between artistic and schizophrenic solutions, and between scientific and cyclothymic mechanisms, because there is a resolution of a social conflict by similar roads, the goal is in fact the opposite. As compared with existing normality, the mad road leads to greater illusion, unconsciousness and privacy, the scientific or artistic road to greater reality, consciousness and publicity. Hence in catatonia the affects are repressed and in art they are abundantly conscious; in cyclothymia the ego is "wild"; in science it is conscious of necessity.

For what it amounted to was this. Faced with a conflict in experience between social consciousness and real life experience, the mentally-deranged chose to solve it by eliminating what was conflicting in consciousness, by making consciousness less true and social, and more private and illusory; whereas the scientist or artist chose to solve it by the opposite route, by dragging the new in experience up into social consciousness, by making consciousness more true and social, less private and illusory. They meet a similar obstacle but go in opposite directions. Science and art are "divine madness" in this sense, that a contradiction in experience drives the madman to private error and drives scientist and artist to public truth. They are more sane than the "sane", who, because they experience no conflict or contradiction in their lives, are not faced with the possibility of resolving it creatively. The only difference between artist and scientist is that one is interested in the subjective and the other in the objective component of consciousness and life. The only difference between poet and mathematician on the one hand, and the novelist and evolutionary scientist on the other, is that one is interested in generalisation, in integration, in a human essence and an abstract reality, and the other in specialisation, in differentiation, in human individuality and a concrete reality.

Although the artist and the scientist in the problems they resolve go the opposite road to madness it does not follow that they are wholly sane. For they can only resolve those problems which are socially real problems and have a general meaning for society as a whole. The artist has subjective problems, the scientist objective problems, which are not susceptible of a social solution, just as with other men. And of course the artist faced with objective problems is like the scientist faced with subjective problems, both are at least as helpless as ordinary men. This is only to say that science and art, because they are social reality in abstraction, in the most generalised and essential form, cannot exactly coincide with concrete living which generates them, but can only continually enrich and develop it.

Psycho-analysis, and psychology generally, is unable to make any clear distinction between the psychology of pathology and genius, and between the process of mental creation and mental delusion, because it is unable to show any causal distinction between conscious and unconscious phantasy. The difference is a social difference, but psychology, being bourgeois psychology, cannot rise beyond the conception of an "individual in civil society"; it cannot separate and distinguish the biological environment from the social environment, and consciousness is a product of the social environment. We have already discussed the difficulties to which this gives rise in the Freudian philosophy.

The very cleavage of phantasy types is due to the fact that in dream, when the inactive body is released from concrete living, distortion from reality can take place on two planes—internal and external. This is not possible when dream is injected into waking life; hence the special types of madness.

At the same time, once madness has set in, the theoretical possibility arises of a return to sleep of a deeper character, in which adjustment takes place on a double plane once more, but in a more penetrating way. In fact MacCurdy and Hoch's work on benign stupors has revealed the clinical importance of a special, prolonged, deep form of sleep (stupor) as a prognosis of approaching cure in psychoses. Evidently, then, sleep and dream play an important part in the solution of private conflicts which arise during the day and are "solved" privately at night. Hence, too, no doubt the significance of the sleeplessness which is so well recognised as a symptom of approaching madness, and hence, too, the curative importance of bromides and sleep-inducing drugs.

8

Our demarcation of "psychological types" necessarily calls to mind Jung's classic work on the same subject. How far does our division correspond with his?

Jung's earliest division was into extraverted and introverted types. On the whole our division corresponds with his—extraversion involves valuation of externality, of perception, of the *object*, whether in action or consciousness; and introversion is valuation of internality, of feeling, of the *subject*, either in consciousness or action.

Of course this does not mean that the introvert is essentially sympathetic; on the contrary it is *his* feeling, not that of others, which he values. It is the extravert who is sympathetic, but with the weakness of a shallow feeling.

Jung found this vision insufficient, and therefore he distinguished four functions, irrespective of valuation of the object or the subject. Of these functions two are rational—feeling and thinking, and two are irrational—sensing and intuiting. A type has one main function and an auxiliary function which must be of a different character, *e.g.* a rational function can only be assisted by an irrational function, and *vice versa*. All four functions exist in all psyches, and therefore individuation —the development of one function at the expense of the other —means that the functions not used sink into the unconscious. Thus in a thinker feeling sinks into the unconscious and becomes correspondingly barbaric and crude. Here it exerts a compensatory influence, and may eventually gain in power until, at first sporadically and then completely, it becomes the main function, and there is an *enantiodromia*, a kind of conversion or complete reversal of personality, as when the cold, Christian-hating Saul becomes the ardent apostle Paul, or when the dry mathematical person becomes a raving maniac.

Now Jung's rich experience and subtle mind gives this classification great value and importance, It is confused, however, owing to Jung's epistemological confusion as to the meaning of consciousness. I regard Jung's cleavage between feeling and thinking as that between theory and practice. The thinking extravert is the theoretical extravert, the man of thought; the feeling extravert is the practical extravert, the man of action. The feeling introvert, however, is the theoretical introvert, and the thinking introvert is the practical introvert. Of course both the theory and practice of introvert and extravert is conditioned by their different valuations of object and subject—hence the apparent reversal of the functions in theory and practice; and hence Jung's initial mistake, afterwards corrected, in believing introversion and extraversion to be all-sufficient for the determination of psychological types. Our analysis of the two-sidedness of phantasy (which is matched by a similar two-sidedness of practice) explains how this reversal of functions occurs.

What are we to make of "sensing" and "intuiting"? According to Jung, "sensing" is appreciation of *external* phenomena by an act of unconscious apprehension, and "intuition" is appreciation of *internal* phenomena by an act of unconscious apprehension.

It seems to me that Jung has got himself into an epistemological confusion here. His types are real, but their mechanism is wrongly grasped. Sensing is not just irrational feeling, but the relation between them is the same as between poetry and the novel. Sensing is conscious but poetic, it is generalised feeling; this-sidedness reduced to the common instinctive ego. Feeling is conscious but concrete; it is individualised sensing, sensing given the status of particular differentiated egos. Sensing is thus more primitive than feeling. In the same way intuiting is not irrational thinking, but the relation between them is the same as between mathematics and biology. Intuiting is conscious but mathematical; it is generalised thinking, other-sidedness reduced to the abstract commonness of quantity. Thinking is conscious but concrete; it is particularised intuiting, intuiting given the content of spheres of quality. Intuiting is thus more primitive than feeling.

It has already been explained why poetry and mathematics emerged in the history of our race before the story and the evolutionary sciences. In the same way sensing and intuiting are the earliest forms of thought—the reasoning of the leaders, prophets, poets and lawgivers of primitive society.

Thus in general we agree with the importance of Jung's distinction between extraversion in which the object is valued, and introversion in which the subject is valued. We also agree with his warning that any one type may be introverted in relation to some spheres of activity and extraverted in relation to others, and that this may change in the course of his life. Hence a type has a fluidity and individuality even in his attitude to life. To take Spearman's conception of two factors in intelligence—g, a general fund applicable to all fields, and s, a special capacity, limited to one field—not only may g vary in its "attitude" as well as its quantity, but the various s-factors too may vary in attitude and quantity.

Our analysis differs from Jung in three respects:

(1) He does not allow for the difference between a theoretical and a practical approach to life, and the existence of some fields in which a man is theoretical, others in which he is practical, and others where he shows a balanced unity. The more a man is purely theoretical in some fields, the more he is likely to be purely practical in others, and because of their divorce, both theory and practice will show a special crude primitiveness which may make them seem of different quality from

what they are when they appear as an active whole. The thinking and intuiting extraverts and the feeling and sensing introverts are men predominantly theoretical precisely because their living behaviour exhibits a valuation of the object which is contrary to their phantastic valuation, and in the same way the feeling and sensing extraverts and the thinking and intuiting introverts have a predominantly practical approach to life.

(2) He regards sensing and intuiting as in some way unconscious forms of feeling and thinking, although he uses the word irrational. But the "intuition" on which mathematical reasoning is based cannot be regarded as irrational. Of course the word "intuition" begs the question, and it is not suggested that the view of mathematics represented by Poincaré's school was right and Peano and Russell's logistic theory wrong. Intuition is not used in a Platonic sense. It is simply applied to the abstract generalising approach characteristic of logic and a more primitive society, and so far from being irrational it is rational in that it leads (as in Platonism, scholasticism and Buddhist philosophy) to a glorification of the reason as against practice.

(3) Jung has no adequate definition of consciousness and unconsciousness except a reduction of "psychic energy" which makes the unconscious contents sink below the threshold. For this crude and unhelpful theory we have substituted the conception of the desocialisation of conscious contents, either ego-attached or environment-attached, due to the tension of concrete living, which causes them to become unconscious and correspondingly archaic and infantile.

If real external reality conflicts with my consciousness in life, I can actively and really change it. If I starve, I can get food; if I am too cold, I can put on clothes. Scientific phantasy is born from this kind of active change or practice, and though it is introversion, it is extraverted introversion—introversion with a view to changing outer reality. This change is its value, purpose and mode of generation. The experience in life which contradicts existing scientific consciousness and demands its change is always an experience in changing objective reality. Science develops as an abstract system of knowing Nature by its guidance of man's attempts to change Nature.

But if my social ego conflicts with my consciousness in life, I can actively and really change myself. I can want different things—satisfy my instincts in other ways open to me in existing life—by art-works for example. I then have an interest in objects which is introverted—it is extraversion with a view to changing my own ego. This change of the ego is the value, purpose and mode of generation of art-works. The experience in life which contradicts my existing ego and demands its change is always an experience encountered in satisfying my wants, that is, in changing myself. Art develops as a concrete group of objects, a mock world, whereby man changes himself and in doing so comes to know himself. The method of art is the method of science turned inside out. One knows to do; the other does to feel. One changes himself in order to change outer reality; the other changes outer reality in order to change himself. Both are necessary to each other, for the limits of outer and inner change are both set by necessity. Operating with existing consciousness, men change reality to new forms. Operating with existing forms, men change consciousness. The first is science in creative practice, the second art in creative practice. Reverse the rôles and we have science in creative theory, and art in creative theory.

Without this understanding of the relation of theory to practice, Jung moves without realising it from one definition of introversion to another.

Thinking and intuiting in introversion, *i.e.* in *theory*, are practical functions—functions orienting thought round the outer world. In practice, in extraversion, they are world-changing *actions*, actions changing perceptual reality. Feeling and sensing in introversion, in *theory*, are theoretical functions—functions orienting thought round the ego. In practice, in extraversion, they are self-changing, *i.e.* self-satisfying or self-expressing *actions*, actions satisfying the ego. This complex relation is precisely what makes the complexity of types, for no man lives in the same way, no one has precisely the same relation between phantasy and action. Hence Jung's thinking and intuiting extraverts are men of "theory", scientific men, just as his thinking and intuiting introverts are men of action, mysteriously practical men. His extraverted sensing and feeling

men are practical men, appetitive or sensual, and his feeling
and sensing introverts are theoretical men, mystics, prophets
or poets.

Jung's confusion regarding the "compensatory" rôle of the
unconscious springs from the same source. To say a function
becomes unconscious is to say that it becomes desocialised.
Jung's functions "sinking into the unconscious" through
repression or repulsion by the conscious contents are nothing
but man finding parts of the social ego or social reality in
himself at war with each other. His consciousness of himself
realised in his life experience conflicts with his consciousness
of the outer world. We have already seen that he can adjust
himself in phantasy in two ways—by orienting the consciousness of the outer world round his ego, or by orienting the ego
round the outer world.

If the outer world is major to him (the thinking intuiting
extravert) he will desocialise and adjust his ego round external
realities so that it becomes subjectively distorted; so that his
whole impression and valuation of it is false. In other words
the feeling side or the sensing side will become an unconscious
and archaic function; it will become desocialised and hence full
of instinct. As it emerges in objective action, the ego will *to us*
seem inflated and full of feeling. But precisely because it
emerges in action in this wild instinctive way, the subjective
content of the ego will be slight. The maniac does not feel
profoundly; but he acts like a man in an overpowering passion,
because he lacks that consciousness of self which moderates,
complicates and subtilises man's response to reality. He makes
an "all or nothing" response. Jung's compensatory unconscious
is really the extravert's adjustment of life to reality in phantasy
by a desocialisation of the ego and an unconsciousness of
subjective feeling, matched in action by a more passionate
behaviour, a *folie de grandeur* or wild inflation of the ego.

The correct response of this type is scientific—changing the
environment and injecting a greater measure of environmental
reality into consciousness as a result. The first route is the
route of *illusion*, of madness, of an unsocial and unconscious
ego leading to a false conscious perception of the environment
and therefore a destructive behaviour; the second is the route

of *science*, of *reality*, of a manipulation of the ego to produce a truer conscious perception of the environment and therefore a more useful behaviour. A movement of extraversion and introversion is involved in both cases.

But here the maxim "Physician, heal thyself" does not apply. The scientist's contribution to society as a result of his special tension is a deeper consciousness of environmental reality, and what he requires from it to heal his own one-sidedness is just what he cannot give but the artist can—subjective consciousness and inner reality.

In the same way with the feeling or sensing introvert, a conflict between consciousness and reality necessarily takes the form of a distortion of conscious perception owing to the over-valuing of the ego. This leads to the psychasthenic neurotic having a greater consciousness of emotion and a fictitious independence of his environment, which, because of the denial of the objective term, leads to a slavery to his environment in the form of "difficult circumstances". Nature, not his ego, becomes primitive and uncontrollable because it becomes unconscious.

This type of introvert is driven to artistic production—to change himself not by lowering his consciousness of outer reality but by injecting his ego's experience into the social consciousness. But this creative task in relation to society may lead to a one-sidedness of personality which can only be corrected by the healing consciousness of outer reality drawn from science.

The maladapted introvert attempts to free himself from his conflict with "nature" by cutting himself off from the object; but his unconsciousness of the object makes him its blind slave. The maladapted extrovert attempts to cut himself off from the subject; but his unconsciousness of himself makes him the blind slave of his own instincts. Thus they prove in their own persons that freedom is the consciousness of necessity. In theory they deny the ego or the world, only to prove it in a wild barbaric way in practice—and this cleavage in them between theory and practice is precisely wherein their madness consists. Thus art points the road to the hysteric's cure; science to the neurotic's. Science and art in relation to the consciousness are therapeutic—science for the introvert, art for the extravert. In relation to practical life they are reality-changing, science changing the world and art changing men.

Apart from these weaknesses, Jung's study is a profound encyclopedia of the human psyche as a part of reality, a study of how man realises or fails to realise his freedom in concrete living. It represents the deepest study of the psyche possible to a world-view which has not risen above the conception of an individual living in civil society.

Science and art are the most abstract and generalised forms of a way of phantastic adaptation *via* society which cannot be separated from the reality of action, both of which are generated in the act of changing nature and so oneself, that is, in the act of living. Science and art are nothing if they do not give to each of us an immediate guide to our personal lives in all their aspects—both a morality and an understanding, an impulsion and an instrument which is not merely general but guides each of us in every one of our concrete relations, which is a compass to every act whereby we change nature and ourselves. Our life is lived wrongly if this theory, which guides and impels our every act, does not suck from every act new theory and grow as a developing thing. Human activity is activity through objects. To separate science and art from "practical, critical-revolutionary activity" is to separate them from life. And this is what modern civilisation increasingly tends to do.

Modern culture has known well enough how to tear itself apart. It strove at first in its rise to cut itself off from the subject, to throw itself completely into the object. Hence the wild cyclothymic energy of the Elizabethan era of bourgeoisdom. Now it has passed to the other pole, from hysteria to psychasthenia, and, attempting to cut itself off from the object which it can no longer control, becomes the blind slave of necessity. This is the oscillation from mechanical material to idealism and thence to the helpless eclecticism of positivism, which, by attempting to cut itself off from both subject and object and so dominate them both, is the slave of both, a helpless victim of mere appearance.

Positivism leads to *surréalisme* in poetry. The dream-*work* of poetry is abandoned, and men float into air, cut loose both from subject and object—unconscious of both, and therefore the blind slave of both. "Free" association is compulsive dream. Poetry ceases to contain a dream-work; it becomes dream; the poet passes into a benign stupor. *Benign*, for Aragon has told us that the poet cannot rest on this position or return to an earlier one, but can only recover by winning into a world where subject and object again become social and therefore conscious, and the poet's relation to life again becomes free, revolutionary and laborious.

THE ORGANISATION OF THE ARTS

I

POETRY grasps a piece of external reality, colours it with affective tone, and makes it distil a new emotional attitude which is not permanent but ends when the poem is over. Poetry is in its essence a transitory and experimental illusion, yet its effects on the psyche are enduring. It is able to live in the same language with science—whose essence is the expression of objective reality—because in fact an image of external reality is the distributed middle of both propositions, the other term being *external reality* in the case of science, the *genotype* in the case of poetry. This is not peculiar to poetry; it is general to all the arts. What is peculiar to poetry is its technique, and the particular kind of emotional organisation which this technique secures. None the less, an analysis of poetry should also throw light on the technique of the other arts.

The other important artistic organisation effected by words is the story. How does the technique of poetry compare with that of the story?

In a poem the affects adhere directly to the associations of the words. The poet has to take care that the reader's mind does not go out behind the words into the external reality they describe before receiving the affects. It is quite otherwise with the story. The story makes the reader project himself into the world described; he sees the scene, meets the characters, and experiences their delays, mistakes and tragedies.

This technical difference accounts also for the more leisurely character of the story. The reader identifies himself with the poet; to both the words arise already soaked with affect, already containing a portion of external reality. But the novel arises as at first only an impersonal *description* of reality. Novelist and the reader stand outside it. They watch what happens. They become sympathetic towards characters. The

Q

characters move amid familiar scenes which arouse their emotions. It seems as if they walked into a world and used their own judgment, whereas the world presented by the poet is already soaked in affective colour. Novel-readers do not immediately identify themselves with the novelist, as a reader of poetry does with the poet. The reader of poetry seems to be saying what the poet says, feeling *his* emotions. But the reader of the story does not seem to be writing it; he seems to be living through it, in the midst of it. In the story, therefore, the affective tones cling to the associations of external reality. The poem and the story both use sounds which awake images of outer reality and affective reverberations; but in poetry the affective reverberations are organised by the structure of the language, while in the novel they are organised by the structure of the outer reality portrayed.

In music the sounds do not refer to objects. They themselves are the objects of sense. To them, therefore, the affective reverberations cling directly. Although the affective reverberations of poetry are organised by the structure of the language, this structure itself is dependent on the "meaning"—*i.e.* on the external reality referred to. But the structure of music is self-sufficient; it does not refer to outer reality in a logical way. Hence music's structure itself has a large formal and pseudo-mathematical component. Its pseudo-logical rigour of scale and chord replaces the logical rigour of external meaning. Thus in music, poetry and the novel the sound symbol has three different functions: in the novel it stands for an object in external reality; in poetry for a word-born mental complex of affective reverberation and memory-image; in music for part of a pseudo-external reality.

The social ego or subjective world is realised in artistic phantasy by the distortion of the external world. But for a world to be distorted into an affective organisation it must have a structure which is not affective (subjective) but logical (objective). Hence the socially recognised laws of music, which are pseudo-logical laws. They correspond to the laws of language, also socially recognised, which are pseudo-objective and are distorted by poetry, but not by the novel, which distorts the time and space of objective reality.

A logical external world can only exist in space and time. Hence the musical world exists in space and time. The space is the movement of the scale, so that a melody describes a curve in space as well as enduring in time. Although a melody extends in time, it is *organised* spatially. Just as a mathematical argument is static and quantitative, although it "follows on" in time, so a melody is timeless and universally valid. It is a generalisation, corresponding to the classificatory content of science. It is colourless and bare of quality in its essence. It draws from the ego a universal emotional attitude within the limits of its argument.

Harmony introduces into music a temporal element. Just as space can only be described in terms of time (a succession of steps), so time can only be described in terms of space (a space of time imagined as existing simultaneously, like a panorama). Time is the emergence of qualities. Hence two qualities sounding simultaneously describe time in terms of space. Just as the evolutionary sciences import from external reality a perspective of a whole field of qualities evolving (yet here visualised by an all-seeing eye as already fully developed), so harmony brings into music a whole rich field of temporal enrichment and complexity. It individualises music and continually creates new qualities. It was therefore no accident but a result of the way in which the bourgeoisie "continually revolutionises its own basis", that the richest development of harmony in music should have coincided with the Industrial Revolution, the rise of the evolutionary sciences and a dialectical view of life. There was a parallel temporal movement in story and symphony. It was equally no accident that this musical development should have coincided with a technical development which on the one hand facilitated the instrumental richness of bourgeois orchestras, and on the other hand by its increase of communications made men's lives and experiences interweave and counterpoint each other like a symphony.

In the world of melody undifferentiated man faces a universal nature or static society, precisely as in poetry. In the novel and the world of harmony a man contemplates the rich and complex movement of the passions of men in a changing and developing world.

Rhythm was prior to either melody or harmony if anthropological researches are any guide, and we assumed that a rhythmic dancing and shouting was the parent also of poetry. The external world of music exists, not to portray the world but to portray the genotype. The world has therefore to be dragged into the subject; the subject must not be squeezed out into the object. Rhythm, because it shouts aloud the dumb processes of the body's secret life and negates the indifferent goings-on of the external universe, makes the hearer sink deep down into himself in a physiological introversion. Hence the logical laws of music, in spite of their externality and materiality, must first of all pay homage to rhythm, must be distorted by rhythm, must be arranged round the breath and pulse-beats and dark vegetative life of the body. Rhythm makes the bare world of sound, in all its impersonality, a human and *fleshy* world. Melody and harmony impress on it a more differentiated and refined humanity, but a great conductor is known most surely by his time. The beating baton of the conductor says to the most elaborate orchestra: "All this complex and architectural tempest of sound occurs *inside* the human body". The conductor is the common ego visibly present in the orchestra.

When man invented rhythm, it was the expression of his dawning self-consciousness which had separated itself out from nature. Melody expressed this self as more than a body, as the self of a member of a collective tribe standing in opposition to the universal otherness of nature. Rhythm is the feeling of *a* man; melody the feeling of *Man*. Harmony is the feeling of *men*, of a man conscious of himself as an individual, living in a world where the interweaving lives of society reflect the orchestral pageant of growing and developing nature.

Just as the rhythm of music is physiological and distorts the object to its pattern so as to draw it into the body, so the periodicity and ordering which is the essence of mathematics is "natural" and logical, and squeezes the ego out of the body into the object, so that it follows the grain of external nature.

The collective members of the tribe do not conflict in their broad desires and do not require a mutual self-adjustment to secure freedom for each, because the possibility of large inequalities of freedom does not arise. There is no real surplus of freedom. The life of the primitive corresponds almost exactly to a blind necessity. So small is the margin that to rob him of much is to rob him of life itself. Therefore just because it is, in the sum, so scanty, it is shared equally by all, and Nature, not other men, is a man's chief antagonist. But the individuation produced by the division of labour and a corresponding increase in productivity, raises this mutual interplay of different characters in conflict to a vital problem. Appearing first with the static and logical simplicity of tragedy, it is in bourgeois civilisation developed as the novel with a more flexible and changing technique. The development of orchestration in music has a similar significance as a road to freedom.

The decay of art due to the decline of bourgeois economy is reflected in music. Just as the novel breeds a characteristic escape from proletarian misery—"escape" literature, the religion of capitalism—so music produces the affective massage of jazz, which gratifies the instincts without proposing or solving the tragic conflicts in which freedom is won. Both think to escape necessity by turning their backs on it and so create yet another version of the bourgeois revolt against a consciousness of social relations. In contrast to the escape from proletarian misery in bourgeois literature, there rises an expression of petty bourgeois misery. This characteristic expression is the anarchic bourgois revolt, the *surréalisme* that attempts to liberate itself by denying all convention, by freeing both the inner and outer worlds from social-commonness and so "releasing" art into the magical world of dream. In the same way, petty bourgeois music advances through atonality to an anarchic expression of the pangs of a dying class. The opium of the unawakened proletariat mixes with the phantastic aspirations of the fruitlessly rebellious lower stratum of the bourgeoisie.

Because the world of music with its logical structure is pseudo-external and drawn out of the genotype, like the logical content of mathematics, the "infant prodigy" is possible in both. The full development of the novel and the evolutionary sciences requires even in genius the maturity of concrete experience. Because the external reality of music is self-generated, it is as if music directly manipulated the emotions of men.

Language expresses both external reality and internal reality —facts and feelings. It does so by symbols, by "provoking" in the psyche a memory-image which is the psychic projection of a piece of external reality, and a feeling which is the psychic projection of an instinct. But language is not a haphazard group of symbols. It must be organised. This organisation is given in the arrangement of the symbols but cannot be itself symbolised by these symbols. Wittgenstein, to whom we owe this conception, saw it as a projective correspondence between the symbols and outer reality. But there is also a projectivity correspondence between the symbols and inner reality, and the final shape or pattern is the result of a tension or contradiction between the two organising forces. Both orderings are shared in common with the thing projected. If this is a part of external reality, we may say symbols and symbolised share the real world; if it is a projection of internal reality, they share the same affective manifold or social ego. Considered separately, these orderings are only abstractions. They cannot in concrete language be separated. In concrete language only their tense mutual relation is reflected, and this is the subject-object relation—man's active struggle with Nature.

In poetry the manifold distorted or organised by the affective forces of the common ego is the logical or grammatical manifold inhering in the arrangement and syntactical organisation of the words themselves. Of course this corresponds to a similar logical arrangement "out there" in the external reality symbolised. It corresponds, but it is not the same and therefore permits an affective organisation more direct, "languagy" and primitive than that of the novel, where the logical manifold organised by common ego is "out there" in the external reality symbolised. Hence poetry is more instinctive, barbaric and primitive than the novel. It belongs to the age when the Word is new and has a mystic world-creating power. It comes from a habit of mind which gives a magical quality to names, spells, formulae and lucky expressions. It belongs to the "taken for granted" knowledge in language which, when we discover it consciously—as in logic's laws—seems to us a new, unhuman and imperious reality. The poetic Word is the Logos, the word-made-flesh, the active will ideally ordering; whereas the novel's word is the symbol, the reference, the conversationally pointing gesture.

In music the logical manifold is the formal or structural element in music, corresponding to the grammatical or syntactical element in language. It comprises the stuff-ness, the conventions, laws, scales, permitted chords, and instrumental limitations of musical theory. It is the impersonal and external element in music. This is distorted affectively in time and space by rhythm, melody and harmony. *Wovon man nicht sprechen kann, darüber muss man schweigen,* ("whereof one cannot speak, thereof one must be silent"), ended Wittgenstein, asserting in a mystical form that since language corresponds to facts, it cannot speak of non-factual entities, but must fall back on mystical intuition. This is untrue. By arbitrarily limiting the function of language Wittgenstein excludes it from the provinces it has long occupied successfully. It is precisely art—music, poetry and the novel—which speaks in the affective manifold what *man nicht sprechen kann* in the logical manifold.

The even pulse of rhythmic time contrasts with the irregularity of time successions observed in the outside world. Man naturally seizes therefore on the few natural periodicities—day and night, months and years. Hence the conception of order and therefore number is given to us physiologically, and mathematical calculation consists in giving different names to different periodicity groups; at first digital symbols, later separate written characters. The ego is projected on to external reality to order it. Subjective affective periodicity is the parent of number, therefore in mathematics affective time must be distorted by orderings found in external reality. The outer manifold is the main organising force. In music external periodicity is affectively distorted to follow the instinctive ego. The affective manifold is here the organising force. The musician is an introverted mathematician. The "lightning calculator" is an extraverted conductor.

To summarise:

Mathematics uses spatial orderings of periodicities drawn from subjective sources, these periodicities being distorted to conform with external reality.

Music uses affective orderings of periodicities drawn from objective sources, these periodicities being distorted to conform with internal reality.

In poetry the affective rhythm is logico-spatial, not affective-temporal. Unlike the basic rhythm of mathematics, it is not distorted by cognitive material. It asserts the tempo of the body as against that of environment. Metre denies external time, the indifferent passing on of changing reality—by "marking time" and drawing in the object to it.

Music, language, mathematics, all mere sounds, can yet symbolise the whole Universe and express the active relation of internal to external reality. Why has sound, a simple physical wave system, become so apt a medium for the symbolisation of life in all its concreteness?

In the life of animals external reality has been explored by three distance receptors round which, as Sherrington has shown, the brain has evolved; these are physico-chemical smell, sound and sight. On the whole light-wave reception has proved its superiority for this purpose and sound therefore became specialised as a medium of inter-species communication. Among birds and tree-apes this would follow naturally from the engrossment of eye-sense by the demands of balance, aerial or arboreal. Long have cries—mere sounds—been the simple voice of the instincts among the warm-blooded animals from which we evolve. Long have our ears been tuned to respond with affective association to simple sounds. Birds, with their quick metabolism the most emotional of animals, express with sound the simple pattern of their instincts in an endlessly repeated melodic line. But man goes a step further, along the line indicated by the warning cry of birds. The demands of economic co-operation—perhaps for hunting— made essential the denomination of objects and processes in external reality not instinctively responded to. Perhaps gesture stepped in, and by a pictographic mimicking of a piece of external reality with lips and tongue, man modified an instinctive sound, a feeling-symbol, to serve also as the symbol of a piece of external reality. Language was born. Man's simple cries, born of feeling, of primitive sympathy, of gesture, of persuasion, became plastic; the same cry now stood for a constant piece of external reality, as also for a constant judgment of it. Something was born which was music, poetry, science and mathematics in one but would with time fly apart and generate all the dynamism of language and phantasy between the poles of music and mathematics, as the economical operation which was its basis also developed.

It is no mere arbitrary ordering of emotion which music performs. It expresses something that is inexpressible in a scientific language framed to follow the external manifold of reality. It projects the manifold of the genotype. It tells us something that we can know in no other way; it tells us about ourselves. The tremendous truths we feel hovering in its cloudy reticulations are not illusions; nor are they truths about external realities. They are truths about ourselves, not as we statically are, but as we are actively striving to become.

2

In addition to the sound-symbolical arts, there are the visual or plastic arts—painting, sculpture and architecture. It is easier to see how these fit into our analysis. The visual sense— in all animals, eked out by tactile corrections—has been that sense used most consistently to explore external reality, while the hearing sense has been used to explore that particular part of external reality which consists of other genotypes. Sound mediates between genotype and genotype—the animal hears the enemy or the mate. Light mediates also between genotype and non-genotypical portions of external reality.

As a result, when we make a visual symbol of external reality, such as a diagram or a drawing, it is naturally made projective of external reality and not merely symbolic. Except in onomatopoeia, words individually are not mechanically projective of things like a photograph, but are only symbolic and therefore "conventional". A drawing, however, is directly projective of reality without necessarily the mediation of pseudo-grammatical rules or conventions. This is shown by the resemblance between a drawing and a photograph.

In drawing and sculpture bits of external reality are projected into a mock world, as in a drawing of a flower or a sculpture of a horse. This picture must have in common with the external reality from which it is drawn something not describable in terms of itself—the real or logical manifold or, more simply, the "likeness".

But line and colour also have affective associations in their own right. These must be organised in an attitude towards the mock world, the "thing" projected. This must be an affective attitude, which is what the painting or sculpture has in common with the genotype, or affective manifold, and cannot be itself symbolised by a drawing, since it is inherent in the drawing. To the naïve observer this appears as a distortion in the drawing as a non-likeness to external reality. But of course it is really a likeness, a likeness to the affective world of the genotype.

For the purpose of this brief survey, the only distinction that need be made between painting and sculpture is that one is three-dimensional and the other two-dimensional. Thus painting selects two out of the three dimensions of external reality—or rather to be accurate, it selects two out of the four dimensions, for unlike music, poetry and the story, the plastic arts lack the fourth dimension, time. Pictures do not begin at one moment in time and end at another. They are static; they do not change. All arts must select from external reality in some way, otherwise they would not have any looseness at the joints to give play for ego-organisation. They must have one degree of freedom.

Line and colour, symbolising real objects, are organised by the ego-reality projected. The result is a new emotional attitude to a piece of reality. After viewing a Rembrandt or a Cézanne we *see* the exterior world differently. We still see the same external reality, but it is drenched with new affective tones and shines with a bright emotional colouring. It is a more "appetising" world, for it is the appetitive instincts which furnish the aesthetic affects.

Plainly the same criteria we have already established for

language hold good here. A Michael Angelo painting or a
Dutch portrait contains more of external reality than a Picasso,
just as a story contains more than a poem. But what is the
scope and degree of the emotional reorganisation in the visual
field that it effects? It is chiefly on this that the varying
estimates of greatness in painting are based. Just as in music
or poetry, so in painting, easy solutions or shallow grasps of
reality are poor art.

Painting resembles poetry in this much, that the affects do
not inhere in the associations of the things, but in the lines
and forms and colours that compose them. Certain scenes—for
example a funeral—have affective associations in themselves.
But the affective associations used by painting do not pertain
to the funeral as an event but to a brownish rectangle in a large
transparent box with circles at the end drawn by greyish horse-
shapes. The affective associations adhering to ideas of bereave-
ment could quite properly be used in a story, and the novelist
could legitimately bring in a funeral in order to utilise its
affective associations in his pattern. Again the mere *word*
"funeral" as a word has of course inherent affective associations
which can be used in poetry—the "funeral of my hopes"—
but only if it is thoroughly understood that the whole group
of such linguistic associations will be brought into the poem,
and must either be utilised or inhibited, *e.g.* suggestions of
darkness, of *purple*, of *stuffy respectability*, of a *procession*, or *pomp*
and *ceremony*, of *deep wells* (sound association with *funnel* plus
the *grave*). The affective associations used by painting are only
those of colour, line and combinations of colour and line, but
they are used to organise the meaning—the *real* object represented.

Hence the static plastic arts which are representational are
akin to poetry and mathematics—to the classificatory sciences
and the universal arts. Just as we slip at once into the "I" of
the poem, so we slip at once into the viewpoint of the painter.
We see the world both from where the poet and where the
painter stands.

We have already explained why this approach leads to a
"tribal" primitive attitude to living, why it tends to lead to
the realisation of a static universal human essence opposed to a

static nature, and is therefore the best medium for voicing universal cries of passion or insight. By a paradox which is not really a paradox, but is given in the nature of individuation, poetry and painting are also the best mediums for expressing individuality—the individuality however only of the poet. Painting, poetry and melody all have this in common—this timeless universal quality of the human *genus* rather than the interesting sub-complications of a group of human individuals. Hence too we find painting developed at an early stage in the history of civilisation—as early as Palaeolithic man.

In its first appearance painting is man's consciousness of affective quality in Nature, hence the "life-like" character of early Palaeolithic Art, when it deals with natural subjects. But with the development of man from a group of hunters and food-gatherers to a crop-raising and cattle-rearing tribe, man passes from a co-operating observation of Nature, seeking his own desires in it, to a co-operative power over Nature, by drawing it into the tribe and domesticating it. Hence he is now interested in the power of social forms over reality, which becomes "convention" in perceptual rendering. Therefore naturalistic Palaeolithic Art becomes in Neolithic days conventional, arbitrary and symbolic—*decorative.* Not only does this prepare the way for *writing,* but it also expresses a psychic change in culture similar to the passage from rhythm to poetry and to melody.

The passage from the gens or tribe to class society is marked by a further differentiation in pictorial art which takes the form of a return of "naturalism", but man now seeks in Nature, not the affective qualities of the solid tribe, but the heightened and specialised qualities of the ruling class. These are elaborated by the division of labour and the greater technical power and penetration of Nature this makes possible. This naturalism is always ready to fall back into "conventionality" when a class ceases to be vitally in touch with active reality and its former discoveries ossify into dry shells. Naturalism becomes academicism. The most naturalistic pictorial art is bourgois art, corresponding to its greater productivity and differentiation and more marked division of labour. Hence the rise of naturalism in bourgeois art, and its revolutionary self-movement, is connected with the rise of harmony in music and of the evolutionary sciences generally during the same period. Naturalism must not be confused with realism—for example the realism of bourgeois Flemish painting. This realism too may be conventional. Since painting is like poetry, and not the novel, the vital ego-organisation which is the basis of naturalism does not take place in the real world depicted, but flows from the complex of memory-images and affective reverberations awakened by the line or colour, and is organised by the "meaning", by the projective characteristics of the painting.

In later bourgeois culture economic differentiation becomes crippling and coercive instead of being the road to individuation of freedom. There is a reaction against content, which, as long as it remains within the bourgeois categories, appears as "commodity-fetishism". The social forms which make the content marketable and give it an exchange value are elevated as ends in themselves. Hence, cubism, futurism, and various forms of so-called "abstract" art.

Finding himself ultimately enslaved by the social form and therefore still "bound to the market", the bourgeois rebel attempts to shake himself free even from the social ego and so to escape into the world of dream where both ego and external world are personal and unconscious. This is *surréalisme*, with the apparent return of a realism which is however fictitious, because it is not the real, *i.e.* social external world which returns, but the unconscious personal world. We have already explained why *surréalisme* represents the final bourgeois position.

3

The plastic arts are static. A visual art moving in time is provided in the dance, the drama and (finally) the film. The dance is primitive story—quality separating itself from the womb of rhythm. In the dance, rhythm gradually ceases to be physiological and begins to unfold in time and share the qualitative movement of reality, in which things happen.

Painting shares with poetry the quality of having affects organised by the projective structure of the symbols. (A black oblong, *not* a coffin.) But directly the visual arts move in time this spatial or pseudo-grammatical organisation is no longer possible and therefore it must take place as in the story—the affective organisation is an organisation of the real object symbolised by the visual representation. (The *real* coffin.) The courtship of the dance, the murder on the stage, the riot on the films are the material which is affectively organised, and not the linked forms, prostrate figure, or scattered crowd, considered as a projective structure, as would be the case if they were frozen into a static tableau. This confusion between the projective organisation of the static arts and the real organisation of the temporal arts leads to all kinds of special expressionistic and scenic theories of drama—for example those of Edward Gordon Craig. The development of the ballet, the drama and the film is the equivalent of the development of harmony, of the counterpoint of individuals whose life-experiences criss-cross against a changing background of Nature because the division of labour has wrought a similar differentiation and individuation within the crystal of the collective tribe. Tragedy appears in the rapid evolution of Greek classes out of the Greek gens and blossoms again with the rise of bourgeois productivity in the drama of the Elizabethan stage. In both, *poetry* still soaks it because the drama is a transitional stage in class society. It is the product of a society passing from collectivity to individuality.

The dance, the drama and the film are mixed or counterpointed in their technique as compared to the affective organisations of language and music. Just as music's sounds are the objects of external reality and not symbols of such objects, so the dancing or acting human being or the scenery around him is the real object. Admittedly, the dancing or acting human being also refers to another object (the courting or dying human he mimics). But he is also an object of external reality in himself—a gracefully- or attractively-moving human being. Hence acting and dancing have a musical "non-symbolical component", but they also have the other component, the characteristic of referring to objects of external reality. There is a double organisation—the thing mimicked and the person mimicking. This double organisation has a

certain danger, and gives rise to a quarrel between actor and
author, cast and producer, which can to-day only be overcome
in the film, where the mechanical flexibility of the camera
makes the cast wax in a good producer's hands. However in an
era of bourgeois individualism this feature of the film cannot
be fully explored, and the film remains a "starring" vehicle,
except in Soviet Russia.

The dancer or actor as *himself*, as an object of contemplation,
is *static*, like the poetic word. The reality symbolised is like the
reality of story's objects—*in movement*. Hence there is a tension
in a play or film between the static close-up or actor's instant
and the moving action or author's organisation—this resembles
the tension in an epic between the poetic instant and the
narrative movement.

The individual passages in epic or play that we conceive of as
particularly poetic or histrionic—Homer's description of the
stars of heaven opening out, or the great moment of a Duse—
are almost like music: the affects are attached to the words or
actions and only released by the meaning, as if a dam had
burst. The play or epic halts. There is a poetic instant and as
time vanishes, space enters; the horizon expands and becomes
boundless. The art reveals itself as double. The things described
in turn have their own affects which are organised by the action
of the story or the play in time. It is this that makes us think
of the *Iliad* and the *Odyssey* as substantial and spacious worlds,
stretching back as far as the eye can reach. In the great Shakes-
pearean plays we feel this double organisation as a world of vast
cloudy significance, not only looming vaguely behind the
action but in the poetic passages actually casting lights on it
from underneath, so that the action itself is subtly modified
and glows with unexpected fluorescence. Hence the difficulty
of acting poetic plays. Act*ion* and poetry go together because
they live in different structures. But poetry and act*ing*—the
"I" of the poet and the "I" of the actor, are in the same
structure and blot each other out. Irving's "Hamlet", or
Shakespeare's—we have to choose. In a play which is read,
poetry can take the place of acting, hence the satisfaction from
reading Shakespeare's plays not to be paralleled by reading
Ibsen's. Of course in Shakespeare's time the actor was less

dominating, as is shown by the use of boys to take women's parts.

The same characteristic and good mixture of the real and symbolised objects which is to be found in dance and drama is to be distinguished from the same mixture occasionally found in music—the bastard kind of music in which nightingales sing, monastery bells toll, and locomotives whistle. These real objects, mimicked or symbolised by sound, disturb the logical self-consistent structure of music's world, and are therefore here impermissible.

In Palaeolithic Art the individual is only self-conscious and is still anchored in the perception of the object, giving rise to an atomic naturalism of exactly-portrayed, unorganised percept-things. So in the dance of hunting primitives, the natural object—the animal—is mimicked unaltered because it is only sought by man, not changed. The object draws the ego out of man in accurate perception. It is gained in co-operation and so becomes conscious, a fact which differentiates its qualities from those it possesses in brute perception, but it is sought, not created.

In Neolithic Art, when hunting or food-gathering man becomes a crop-raising or cattle-rearing tribe, the object is not merely sought by society but changed by it. The man realises himself in the percept as social man, as the tribe changing the object according to conventions and forms rooted in the means of communication. The dance becomes the formal hieratic movement of chorus and incipient tragedy. The hunting or food-gathering primitive's dance is violently naturalistic and mimicking; the food-raising or cattle-rearing dance has the formality of a religious rite and reveals the impress of the tribe's soul on Nature. It emphasises the magical and world-governing power of the gesture. The circling sun obeys the circling dancer; the crop lifts with the leaping of young men; life quickens with the dizzy motion. The tribe draws Nature into its bosom.

The elaboration of class-society causes the dance to develop into a story, into a *play*. The intricacies of the chorus loosen sufficiently to permit the emergence of *individual* players. Individuation, produced by the division of labour in a class society, is reflected in the tragedy. A god, a hero, a priest-king, people, great men, detach themselves from the chorus and appear on the stage, giving birth simultaneously to the static act*ing* and the moving act*ion* which were inseparably one in the danced chorus, just as were the static poem and the moving story one in the ritual chant, where the word is poetically world-creating and yet also relates a mythical story.

Of course the decay and rigidity of a class society is at any moment reflected in a stiffening and typification of the "characters". The individuation is not rooted in the class but in the division of labour. The class cleavage at first makes this division possible but at a certain moment denies its further development and becomes a brake, a source of academic ossification, a corset which society must break or be stifled.

We said that the cathedrals were bourgeois and not feudal, that they were already Protestant heresies in the heart of Catholicism, the bourgeois town developing in the feudal country. Hence the bourgeois play begins in the cathedrals as the mystery play frowned on by the Church authorities. When the monarchy allies itself with the bourgeois class, the mystery moves to court and becomes the Elizabethan tragedy. Here the individual is realised once again naturalistically as the prince, as the social will incarnate in the free desires of the hero.

Because of the special development of bourgeois individuality, after Shakespeare the mimed action falls a victim to the static actor. In Greek tragedy the actor is swaddled in the trappings of cothurni and mask; he is the pure vehicle of poetry and action. In the Elizabethan play the actor's personality is still stifled, and because the actor is subordinate to the mimed action the play is still poetic. In our day the actor's instant conflicts with the poet's; in Shakespeare's the boy-woman, muffled in the collective representations of the feudal court, was still a hollowness which gave room for the poetry of Cleopatra to come forward and expand. The incursion of woman on to the stage marks the rise of acting in the drama, and the death of narrative and poetry. The personal individual actor or actress becomes primary; his social relations with others or with the social ego—which constitute the story or poetry of the play—become secondary. The play, because of the collective

R

basis of its technique, is injured by the individualism of bourgeois culture.

The play, like painting, becomes increasingly realistic and then moves over to commodity-fetishism—the abstract structure of Expressionism in which the conventions or social forms are hypostatised, and the content or "story" is expelled, so that the play aspires towards the impossibility of becoming the pure social ego. And the play finally makes a bid to cut itself off both from social ego and external reality according to the mechanism of *surréaliste* dream-work.

This same basic movement is only what we have already analysed in poetry. For the cry, reproducing the authentic image (the bird call or animal cry) in the dance of the hunting primitive, becomes the elaborate chant or choral hymn, with strophe, antistrophe and epode, in the crop-raising or pastoral society which has sucked Nature into its undifferentiated bosom. The rise of class society and its individuation, based on division of labour, is reflected in the emergence of the bard, with his epic poetry, glorifying the deeds of heroes, stories in which he does not speak for himself but for a general class, and so his own personal instant does not conflict with a poetic instant which is only given in the acts of heroes. But the further individuation of society, due to still greater division of labour, gives rise to the *poet*, with his lyrical verse—amatory, epistolary and personal—in which the poetic instant coincides with the personal instant, in which the collective "I" (formerly general and heroic) has become personal and individual. With this goes a naturalism and "pathos" of the kind for which Euripides was reproached by his contemporaries and which seems to bourgeois culture so appealing and right.

The poet finds his full individuation in bourgeois poetry, where chanted lyrical poetry becomes written study poetry, and the social ego of poetry is identified with the free individual. Here too there is movement through naturalism to escape from the external world (symbolism) and escape also from the social ego (*surréalisme*).

4

Architecture and the "applied" arts (ceramics, weaving, design of clothes, furniture, machines, cars, printed characters and the like) play a rôle in the visual field similar to that of music in the aural field in that the "things" are parts of external reality and are "distorted" or organised directly by the affects. But architecture and the other arts are like *inverted* music. The "external" element is not a formal ideal "structure" as in music, with its pseudo-logical laws, but a human and social function. The external reality of a house or vase is its use—its coveringness or its capaciousness. This use-form is organised or distorted affectively either by the symbolisation of natural external reality (as when a carpet, vase or house is covered with sculpture or decoration) or when it is given shape, balance, harmony, curves and movement in space. This organisation is poetic; the "I" which organises the use-function is static and collective. Great architecture arises in the womb of a society where social "I" and individual "I" do not conflict but reinforce each other.

Hunting man expresses the use-value realistically. He finds in Nature the correspondence to his use. His house is a cave; his vase a gourd; his weapon a rough flint; his covering a skin. In this sense his applied art is as realistic as his drawings.

Crop-raising or pastoral man imposes on his materialised use-value a decoration which is conventional and distorting. He takes Nature into the bosom of the tribe, and moulds it plastically to his wish. The use-value is given a social form—it is minted. The stone implements are polished. Instead of seeking out a cave, he erects a rough hut in a convenient spot. He no longer clothes himself in skins; his covering is woven. Instead of gourds, he uses pottery, moulded to a shape and decorated.

The birth of a class society sees the birth of palaces and temples where "coveringness" is affectively organised to express the majesty and sacredness of a ruling class. This majesty and sacredness has accrued through the division of labour and the alienation of property whereby the increased social power seems to gather at the pole of the ruling class at the same time as the humility and abasement appears at the pole of the slave class. With the merchant class of Athens and Rome this reflects itself also in municipal buildings. In feudal society castles and basilicas express the affective organisation of social power. The cathedral and the *hôtel de ville* of medieval town life already reflect the growing power of the bourgeois class and are rebellious. The bourgeois class is still collective—it is gathered in self-governing and self-arming communes—tribal islands in the pores of feudalism. At first their social expansion appears in the palaces and cathedrals of princes, who wield for a time the power of the bourgeoisie against other feudal powers. Then it passes into aristocratic villas and State structures; finally, it appears in the form of gentlemen's residences. At first this is a naturalistic movement. Houses become less "formal" and more useful and domestic. This movement too passes into abstraction. Abstraction in painting is functionalism in architecture. Finally even the social ego is negated and architecture shows everywhere freakishness and personal whim, irrespective of the needs of function. The same movement of course takes place in ceramics, textiles and other applied arts. In general the products of a class society in this field show the same rich elaboration and aesthetic idealisation of the aims and aspirations of the ruling class as do the other forms of art.

5

The organisation of the arts can be shown schematically:

ART	EXTERNAL REALITY
I. SOUND:	
Music	Pseudo-Logical Laws of Musical Structure
Poetry	Syntactical and Grammatical Laws of Language
Story	Real External World described
II. VISUAL:	
Painting and Sculpture	Projective Laws of Structural Representation

Dance and the Play and Film	Real Action imitated by Real People
Architecture, Ceramics, Textiles, Furniture, etc.	Use-Function

Obviously the arts can also be arranged historically—beginning from their confused appearance in food-gathering- and hunting-man to their complex development in a class society where individuation is possible. We have already dealt with this movement in general. The three main periods are all sublated in modern art's methods of subjective organisation which therefore include the consciousness of man seeking himself in Nature, of man drawing Nature into the social but undifferentiated "I" of the tribe, and finally of man splitting the social "I" into living *individuals* and at the same time resolving Nature into a differentiated universe which *evolves*.

If we are asked the purpose of art, we can make an answer—the precise nature of it depending on what we mean by *purpose*. Art has "survived"; cultures containing art have outlived and replaced those that have not, because art adapts the psyche to the environment, and is therefore one of the conditions of the development of society. But we get another answer if we ask *how* art performs its task, for it does this by taking a piece of environment and distorting it, giving it a non-likeness to external reality which is also a likeness to the genotype. It remoulds external reality nearer to the likeness of the genotype's instincts, but since the instinctive genotype is nothing but an unconscious and dynamic desire it remoulds external reality nearer to the heart's desire. Art becomes more socially and biologically valuable and greater art the more that re-moulding is comprehensive and true to the nature of reality, using as its material the sadness, the catastrophes, the blind necessities, as well as the delights and pleasures of life. An organism which thinks life is all "for the best in the best possible of worlds" will have little survival value. Great art can thus be great tragedy, for here, reality at its bitterest—

death, despair, eternal failure—is yet given an organisation, a
shape, an affective arrangement which expresses a deeper and
more social view of fate. By giving external reality an affective
organisation drawn from its heart, the genotype makes all
reality, even death, more interesting because more true. The
world glows with interest; our hearts go out to it with appetite
to encounter it, to live in it, to get to grips with it. A great
novel is how we should like our own lives to be, not petty or
dull, but full of great issues, turning even death to a noble
sound:

> Notre vie est noble et tragique
> Comme le masque d'un tyran
> Nul drame hazardeux et magique
> Aucun détail indifférent
> Ne rend notre amour pathetique[1]

A great picture is how we should like the world to look to us—
brighter, full of affective colour. Great music is how we should
like our emotions to run on, full of strenuous purpose and
deep aims. And because, for a moment, we saw how it might
be, were given the remade object into our hands, for ever after
we tend to make our lives less petty, tend to look around us
with a more-seeing eye, tend to feel richly and strenuously.

If we ask why art, by making the environment wear the
expression of the genotype, comes to us with the nearness and
significance it does, we must say still more about art's essence.
In making external reality glow with our expression, art tells
us about ourselves. No man can look directly at himself, but
art makes of the Universe a mirror in which we catch glimpses
of ourselves, not as we are, but as we are in active potentiality
of becoming in relation to reality through society. The genotype
we see is the genotype stamped with all the possibilities and
grandeur of mankind—an elaboration which in its turn is
extracted by society from the rest of reality. Art gives us so
many glimpses of the inner heart of life; and that is its significance, different from and yet arising out of its purpose. It is
like a magic lantern which projects our real selves on the
Universe and promises us that we, as we desire, can alter the

---

[1] Apollinaire.

Universe, alter it to the measure of our needs. But to do so, we must know more deeply our real needs, must make ourselves yet more conscious of ourselves. The more we grip external reality, the more our art develops and grows increasingly subtle, the more the magic lantern show takes on new subtleties and fresh richnesses. Art tells us what science cannot tell us, and what religion only feigns to tell us—what we are and why we are, why we hope and suffer and love and die. It does not tell us this in the language of science, as theology and dogma attempt to do, but in the only language that can express these truths, the language of inner reality itself, the language of affect and emotion. And its message is generated by our attempt to realise its essence in an active struggle with Nature, the struggle called life.

All this is only the inverse picture of what science does. Science too has a survival value and a purpose, and it fulfils this by adapting external reality to the genotype just as art adapts the genotype to external reality. Just as art achieves its adaptative purpose by projecting the genotype's inner desires on to external reality, so science achieves its end by receiving the orderings of external reality into the mind, in the phantastic mirror-world of scientific ideology. Necessity, projected into the psyche, becomes conscious and man can mould external reality to his will. Just as art, by adapting the genotype and projecting its features into external reality, tells us what the genotype is, so science, by receiving the reflection of external reality into the psyche, tells us what external reality is. As art tells us the significance and meaning of all we are in the language of feeling, so science tells us the significance of all we see in the language of cognition. One is temporal, full of change; the other spatial and seemingly static. One alone could not generate a phantastic projection of the whole Universe, but together, being contradictory, they are dialectic, and call into being the spatio-temporal, historic Universe; not by themselves but by the practice, the concrete living, from which they emerge. The Universe that emerges is explosive, contradictory, dynamically moving apart, because those are the characteristics of the movement of reality which produced it, the movement of human life.

Art and science play contradictory and yet intermingled rôles in the sphere of theory. Science in cognition gives art a projected selection from external reality which art organises and makes affectively appealing, so that the energy of the genotype is directed towards imposing its desires on that external reality. Thus, attention, moving inwards from action, through art moves outwards again to action. Attention to change of externals causes the inward movement of cognition; attention to change of internals the outward movement of action. For the outward-moving energy to effect its aim, science is again needed, and the original memory-images, now modified affectively, must be rescanned to grasp their inner relationships so that the desires of the genotype can be effected. Science in cognition now becomes science in action. In effecting those desires with the aid of existing memory-images, more knowledge is gained of the real orderings of external reality. Its object achieved, attention returns with fresh empirical experience to add to its treasure. This richer content is again organised affectively by the genotype, and again flows outwards as energy directed to an end. Energy is always flowing out to the environment of society, and new perception always flowing in from it; as we change ourselves, we change the world; as we change the world we learn more about it; as we learn more about it, we change ourselves; as we change ourselves, we learn more about ourselves; as we learn more about that we are, we know more clearly what we want. This is the dialectic of concrete life in which associated men struggle with Nature. The genotype and the external reality exist separately in theory, but it is an abstract separation. The greater the separation, the greater the unconsciousness of each. The complete separation gives us on the one hand the material body of a man, and on the other hand the unknown environment. Spreading from the point of interaction, the psyche, two vast spheres of light grow outwards simultaneously; knowledge of external reality, science; knowledge of ourselves, art. As these spheres expand, they change the material they dominate by interaction with each other. The conscious sphere of the genotype takes colour from the known sphere of external reality and *vice versa*. This change —change in heart, change in the face of the earth—is not just a consequence of the expansion of the two circles, it *is* the two expansions, just as the flash of light is the electromagnetic wave group. As man becomes increasingly free and therefore increasingly himself by growing increasingly conscious of Necessity, so Necessity becomes increasingly orderly and "law-abiding", increasingly itself, as it falls increasingly within the conscious grasp of the genotype.

Art therefore is all active cognition, and science is all cognitive action. Art in contemplation is all active organisation of the subject of cognition, and in action all active organisation of the object of cognition. Science in contemplation is all cognitive organisation of the subject of action, and in action all cognitive organisation of the object of action. The link between science and art, the reason they can live in the same language, is this: the subject of action is the same as the subject of cognition—the genotype. The object of action is the same as the object of cognition—external reality. Since the genotype is a part of reality, although it finds itself set up against another part of it, the two interact; there is development; man's thought and man's society have a history.

Art is the science of feeling, science the art of knowing. We must know to be able to do, but we must feel to know what to do.

Art is born in struggle, because there is in society a conflict between phantasy and reality. It is not a neurotic conflict because it is a social problem and is solved by the artist for society. Psycho-analysts do not see the poet playing a social function, but regard him as a neurotic working off his complexes at the expense of the public. Therefore in analysing a work of art, psycho-analysts seek just those symbols that are peculiarly private, *i.e.* neurotic, and hence psycho-analytical criticism of art finds its examples and material always either in third-rate artistic work or in accidental features of good work. In *Hamlet* they see an Oedipus-complex; but they do not see that this does not explain the universal power of the great speeches, or the equal greatness of *Antony and Cleopatra*, which cannot be analysed into an Oedipus complex.

The psycho-analyst can sometimes cure the neurotic who cannot cure himself unaided, because he provides a force or point of leverage outside the psyche of the neurotic. He is a member of society, and can therefore work from the outside inwards, into the socially created conscious psyche, the neurotic's "better self", and so attack the unconscious, his "worse self". The better self, the conscious psyche, the *conscience*, is society's creation, while the "worse self" is genotypical, the animal in us.

The psycho-analyst is only one man, and is also the possessor of a worse self which may get between himself and his patient. He is a luxury who can be afforded only by the well-to-do. In art, all society, the sum of all conscious psyches engaged in social creation, speaks to a man's "better self". All the better part of humanity, endlessly attacking and solving life's problems, stands ranged behind the artistic culture of a nation. They are men not gods; like him they suffered and fought, but when they died they left behind the enduring essence of their transitory lives. Hence the consoling, healing and invigorating power of art.

The emotional attitude of the neurotic or the psychotic towards reality is permanent. That of the poet in creation, or the reader in experiencing, is temporary. The essence of genuine illusion is that it is non-symbolic and plastic. The neurotic is deluded because the complex is in his unconscious; he is un-free. The artist is only illuded because the complex is in his conscious; he is free. We take up the attitude when reading a poem, and experience the emotions, and then when the poem has been experienced the attitude is thrown away. The attitude was released by the conscious emotions; as the neurotic attitude may be unfrozen if he becomes conscious of the complex; as the sleeper wakes if the stimulus demands willed-action. The artist releases the autonomous complex in a work of art and "forgets" it, goes on to create anew, to experiment again with the eternal adaptation of the genotype to its eternally changing environ-ment. If poetry becomes religion, if the non-symbolic is taken to be symbolic, the emotional attitude becomes frozen like the neurotic attitude. Thus the value of poetry's illusions in securing catharsis, as compared to religion's, is that they are known for illusion, and as compared to dream, that they are social.

If poetry's emotional attitudes pass, what is their value? It is this; experience leaves behind it a trace in memory. It is stored by the organism and modifies its action. The Universe to-day is not what it was a million years ago, because it is that much more full of experience, and that much more *historic*. Society is not what it was two thousand years ago, because its culture has lived through much and experienced much. So too a wise man, in the course of his life, has endured and experienced. He has not acquired knowledge of external reality only, for such a man we call merely "learned", and think of his learning as something arid, devoid of richness. The wise man has also learned about *himself*. He has had emotional experience. It is because of this double experience that we call him wise, with a ripeness, a poise, a sagacity given to him by all his history. Of course neither science nor art are substitutes for concrete living: they are guide-books to it.

The wisdom of a culture, our social heritage, inheres both in its science and its art. Either alone is one-sided wisdom, but both together give ripe sagacity, the vigour and serenity of an organism sure of itself in the face of external reality.

What, then, is the illusion of art? In what does it consist? Not in the affective element, for artistic emotion is consciously experienced, and is therefore real and true. Real and true as applied to emotion mean, simply: Has it existed in reality?— Has it been present in a psyche? The emotion of poetry is certainly real in this sense. The illusion of poetry must therefore inhere in the piece of external reality to which the emotion is attached—in poetry to the meaning, in novel to the story. The purpose of this piece of external reality was to provide a subject for the affect, because an affect is a conscious judgment, and must therefore be a judgment of *something*. Art is therefore affective experimenting with selected pieces of external reality. The situation corresponds to a scientific experiment. In this a selected piece of external reality is set up in the laboratory. It is a mock world, an imitation of that part of external reality in which the experimenter is interested. It may be an animal's heart in a physiological salt solution, a shower of electrified droplets between two plates, or an aerofoil in a wind tunnel. In each case there is a "fake" piece of the world, detached so as to be handled conveniently, and illusory in this much, that it is not actually what we meet in real life, but a selection from external reality arranged for our own purposes. It is an "as if". In the same way the external reality symbolised in scientific reasoning is never *all* external reality, or a simple chunk of it, but a selection from it. The difference between art's piece of reality and science's is that science is only interested in the relation of that selected piece to the world from which it is drawn, whereas art is interested in the relation between the genotype and the selected piece of reality, and therefore ignores the whole world standing behind the part. If by the words "mock world", we denote the illusory piece of external reality, the symbolical part alike of poetry and science, we get this relation:

External Reality	Mock World	Social Ego
Science		Art

Hence it is just "illusion" that art and science *have in common*. The *distinctive* concern of science is the world of external reality; art is occupied with the world of internal reality. The ordering or logical manifold characteristic of scientific language is that internal structure in its mock world projected from the relationships of external reality. The ordering or affective manifold characteristic of artistic language is that internal structure in its mock world projected from the relationships of internal reality. Hence another schematic representation:

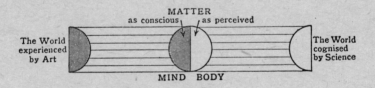

But since the genotype is itself a part of external reality, we can also represent it thus:

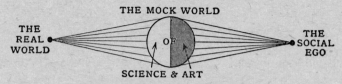

Hence science and art together are able to symbolise a complete universe which includes the genotype itself. Each alone is partial, but the two halves together make a whole, not as fitted together, but as they interpenetrate man's struggle with Nature in the process of concrete living.

XII

THE FUTURE OF POETRY

I

THE future was once a place to which one relegated one's hopes and aspirations: a place where one took revenge for the world's unkindness by holding its future richness to the narrow categories of the present.

Of the future one can only dream—with greater or less success. Yet to dream is not to associate "freely" but to have certain phantasies, a certain reshuffling of memory-images of past reality blended and reorganised in a new way, because of certain real causes in present reality. Even dream is *determined*, and a movement in dream reflects perhaps a real movement into daylight of material phenomena at present unrecognised. That is why it is possible to dream with accuracy of the future—in other words, to predict scientifically. This is the prophetic and world-creating power of dream. It derives its world-creating power, not by virtue of being dream—this is denied by the phantasies of madmen—but because it reflects in the sphere of thought a movement which, with the help of dream, can be fully realised in practice. It draws its creative power, like the poetry of the harvest festival, from its value as a guide and spur to action. It is dream already passed out of the sphere of dream into that of social revolution. It is the dream, not of an individual, but of a man reflecting in his individual consciousness the creative rôle of a whole class, whose movement is given in the material conditions of society.

Again and again we have emphasised the importance of studying poetry as an organic part of society, historically—that is, in movement. But movement for its complete specification requires that we state not only *from* where but *to* where. In our survey of its past we were already standing in its future—our present—but now, to understand its present, we must think ourselves into the future. We can only do this broadly; we can only predict a quantitative movement produced by the most fundamental and elementary forces. Sociology as a real science is still only in its infancy because science is not mere contemplation; it arises from an active struggle with reality, whose successive changes are generalised in a scientific law. The science of sociology is therefore a product of revolutionary activity, for this is the activity which changes social reality. Man has not yet learned fully to control himself.

This movement will be fought out in our own consciousnesses and will be the very force enlarging and transforming them. Thus a whole new world of values will be born, which we can no more describe in terms of quality than a man can look down on himself.

The first limitation must make us careful of any predictions too exact and detailed—a small alteration can often make a quality transform itself into its opposite. The other limitation should set us on our guard against reducing the novelty of the future to the stale terms of the present.

The productive forces released by capitalism have developed to a stage where they are no longer compatible with the limitations which engendered them. These limitations are now being shattered and more or less rapidly transformed. These changes do not happen "automatically", for history is made by men's actions, although their actions by no means always have the effect they are intended to have. The results of history are the net product of actions willed by men, but the results of history are by no means willed by any men.

To-day all bourgeois culture struggles in the throes of its final crisis. The contradictions whose tension first drove on the development of society's productive forces are now wrecking them and a new system of social relations is already emerging from the womb of the old—that of communism. Communism is not an ideal, it is the inevitable solution of the ripening contradictions in capitalism. On the one hand the increase of organisation in the factories; on the other hand the increase of competition for private profit between the factories. On the one hand an unparalleled development of productive forces; on the other hand a system of economy continually generating crises which result in a restriction of production. On the one hand an increase in international communication, unity of consciousness and interweaving of production; on the other hand an increasing nationalism and enmity. On the one hand a growing desire for peace; on the other hand an increasing preparation for war. Abroad idle capital wildly searching for profit; at home idle hands vainly searching for work. At one end of society the creation of a diminishing number of plutocrats with an income, power and purchasing capacity increasing beyond the dreams of earlier society; at the other end the growth of an army without possessions, without work, without hope to a degree unknown to any previous civilisation. On the one hand an efflorescence of the sciences and the arts in a new universe of technique; on the other hand their separation into spheres whose disintegration and contradiction reduces knowledge to chaos and men to spiritual despair.

These contradictions could be multiplied indefinitely, because they represent at various levels of social organisation the working-out of the basic bourgeois contradiction—freedom as the anarchic ignorance of social relations. This ignorance can only mean freedom to one class, the class whose existence depends on its continually revolutionising its own basis and therefore on its continually preparing the conditions for its own destruction. The "free" market—the blind lawlessness by means of which the laws of anarchy brutally assert themselves —has governed the bourgeois mind for four centuries. For four centuries it has idealised this one freedom, freedom from all social restrictions except that by which the bourgeois class lives —restriction of the means of production to itself. This formula means that freedom must increasingly be elevated to a vague ideal plane, for to interpret bourgeois freedom materially is to announce openly the claim of one class to monopolise the means of freedom. The social product is the condition of freedom, and to monopolise it means monopolising such freedom as society has produced. Stripped to its naked essence the bourgeois formula of freedom is all too true—*for the bourgeois class*. So stripped, it exposes its true significance. It shows that all the bourgeois demands for the equality of human souls, for the freedom of the individual, for the realisation of personal worth, stop short of the one issue which could make these demands real for the exploited majority. They stop short of attacking the private property of the few which is the condition for the annihilation of property for the many. They stop short of attacking the monopolisation of the surplus social product by the few which is the condition of the slavery of the many to necessity. This does not, however, shame the bourgeois into withdrawing his claims and ceasing altogether to talk about freedom and personal worth. On the contrary, this understanding by the unfree of the essence of his formula forces him to detach it still further from material reality and lift it completely into an ideal realm where it blossoms and spreads without restraint, forming an inverted world of ideal freedom which is at once a protest against real misery and an expression of real misery—a wholly bourgeois phantasy, the religion of *humanism*. It is precisely as the sum of human freedom diminishes in society that this phantastic ideal world of liberty and personal worth reaches its most characteristic development.

A class exists whose unfreedom is dependent on bourgeois private property. Its road to freedom is the destruction of the bourgeois right and therefore the destruction of the class whose continued existence depends on that right. This unfree class has long been famous as the proletariat. It is not merely the most suffering class of modern society. This typically bourgeois conception of it overlooks its most important rôle. History has always known a most-suffering class since classes existed. Slaves in ancient society, serfs and peasants in medieval society, wage-slaves in modern society, their miseries have been apparently ineradicable from the conscience of society since the day when economic production reached a level where a man could produce more than his means of subsistence and it became profitable to exploit other men. "The poor ye have always with you." Buddha, Christ and Luther accepted the sufferings of the major part of humanity as part of the necessary lot of life on this world, and called into being a whole phantastic other world to redress the balance, to soothe the suffering and therefore the revolt of tortured men.[1]

[1] In so far as Christ preached a Kingdom of Heaven realisable for the poor in this world, and not in Nirvana or the next world, his teaching had a revolutionary content. This is fairly evident from the persecution of the early

S

But the movement of capitalist economy lays the foundations of its destruction by the way in which it creates its most suffering class. Its organisation of the proletariat into huge factories creates the conditions for a shadow, workers' state behind the bourgeois state; the use of the exploited by the bourgeoisie in their early struggles for power educates the proletariat politically; the need of the proletariat to form its own organisations to protect itself in its struggle for part of the surplus value of its labour raises its political education to a higher plane; the improved communication and universal education necessary for capitalist economy welds it into a compact mass; the bourgeoisie proves its final incompetence to rule by the onset of *permanent* crisis in which it is unable to secure its slaves in the conditions of their slavery, and instead of being fed by them is forced to feed them, to hurl them into the concentration camp or the fighting line. The rise of permanent unemployment is the doom of an epoch; it foreshadows the end of the prehistoric or class era of society, when men's actions made history, but a history quite other than what they meant to make.

The relentless law of capitalist competition, with its tendency to a falling rate of interest only offset by actions which hasten its own fall, accelerates the rise of monopolies which compete still more bitterly among themselves, until the contradiction between social organisation in the factory and individual ownership of the factories reaches its height.

The vast majority of the people see themselves faced by a few who have increasingly monopolised the means of production. This concentration, so far from easing the passage to socialism, makes it more painful and disturbed, because the increasing irrationality of the privilege on which all capitalist economy turns forces the bourgeoisie to employ increasingly brutal, conspiratorial and autocratic methods for its maintenance.

Christians by physical torture and "atrocity" slanders. However, since this Kingdom of Heaven was to be achieved by non-resistance, by heavenly forces and a general change of heart, it was bound to become mere reformism and end as a machine for tying the oppressed of the Empire to the throne of Constantine. If primitive Christianity is primitive Communism, Roman Imperial Christianity is Social Democracy.

It costs the keenest of human pangs to produce a man; and events in Russia, Germany and Spain have only proved the correctness of the communist warning that a new society would be born only in suffering, torn by the violence of those who will do anything to arrest the birth of a world in which the freedom of the majority is based on their unfreedom.

This rebellion of the suffering people, which has already taken place in Russia, is for the majority no clear-headed passage to a common goal. All classes injured by the final explosion of capitalism—workers, peasants, small farmers, shopkeepers, artisans, technicians, artists, specialists—compose that rebellious mass: all are agreed as to the intolerableness of the situation; but only one class is organised by its conditions of life to overthrow the old system and build a new. The other classes are organised only as part of the system—the capitalist State—and to overthrow it is to dissolve their only means of organisation. Only the industrial workers, *via* their trades unions, co-operatives and political parties, are organised *against* that system, and can therefore provide a structure able literally to overturn society and bring the bottom to the top.

This special feature of the industrial working class gives it the leadership in the struggle. All odds but its numbers and its organisation are against it. The bourgeoisie rule the old system and everywhere monopolise the key points of judiciary, police, army, civil service, finance and business. All men's minds are distorted by bourgeois presuppositions through living in a bourgeois economy. But the pressure of material conditions not only drives on the proletariat to revolt as did slaves and peasants before it, but unlike them puts the means of success in its hands—its own organisation and the concentration of capitalism. The organisation of the proletariat, which gives it the *de facto* leadership of revolt in this first period, is expressed after the success of this period in the dictatorship of the proletariat—the most abused and least understood of categories in the Marxian analysis because it expresses the creative rôle of a class which the bourgeois can sometime regard as "most suffering", but never as "most advanced".

The suffering majority are demanding the overthrow of the old, they do not all see that this means the construction of a new. Always it seems to the petty bourgeoisie that one may roll history backwards and return to an age when private property was not the means of exploitation, for tools were undeveloped enough and scattered enough to be owned by the man who worked them. Owner and producer were one. The proletariat knows that the factories cannot be owned individually like tools. The proletariat does not regret this, but understands that the whole development of capitalist economy, in so far as it has led to organisation in factories and the socialisation of labour, has raised the productive forces of society to a level where the freedom of a few no longer depends on the unfreedom of the many.

The social product can suffice to provide the freedom of all. The raising of the level of social productivity which follows on a proletarian revolution is the special task of the dictatorship of the proletariat. In it the other classes learn by practice that history cannot be turned back; that it is a question of storming new heights. And, when they understand that, the people as a whole becomes socialist, and the dictatorship of the proletariat begins to decay. This is already forecast by the birth of the new Soviet Constitution, which gives equal rights to all, not as the climax of communism but as the beginning of a new advance towards communism. Only when communism comes into being will the conception of equal "rights" pass from the fabric of the State, and the State, too, wither away. The very "right" of man to realise his freedom by association with others negates the bourgeois conception of equal right, which was the highest ethic to which bourgeois culture could aspire. Its average man was a reflection of the equalisation of labour power in the market. "From each, according to his powers; to each, according to his needs." When men's innate ability and desires vary, how could such a creed—that of communism—be compatible with equal *rights*? A right implies something exercised against another, and communism is a state of society in which material conditions no longer force man to be the enemy of man.

The State came into being to prevent a strife between the haves and the have-nots, a strife which would have paralysed society. The cessation of open strife does not remedy the inequality, for this inequality is the condition at this time for labour reaching a level of increased productivity. The division between haves and have-nots is produced by the division of labour. The State makes possible the continued existence of this inequality, without the shipwreck of society. Since the interests of haves and have-nots are opposed, it can only maintain this continued existence of inequality by coercion. The State is the coercive organ whereby the conditions for exploitation by the ruling class are forcibly maintained. As long as men are sundered by a property right and by the material conditions of society into classes of opposed interests at secret war, a truce can only be maintained by the emergence of a coercive power apparently above both classes. This power is the State.

The property of the bourgeois class which secured its freedom is the condition of unfreedom for the majority. When this majority in turn secures its freedom by expropriating the bourgeoisie, the condition of its freedom is the unfreedom of the bourgeoisie; but whereas the bourgeoisie, like all other ruling classes, requires an exploited unfree class for its existence, the proletariat does not require to maintain the bourgeoisie in order to maintain its own freedom. Thus the conditions are prepared for the ending of class-society.

As long as the bourgeoisie and its camp followers exist either inside a nation or outside it, so long must the proletarian State exist as a coercive organ to maintain the conditions of freedom for the proletariat. The remnants of bourgeois education and the unique experience given them by their privileged life make the expropriated bourgeoisie dangerous enemies, ready at any time to assert the material basis of their ideal of freedom by plunging society into violence to regain it. But the conditions of their existence are not rooted in economy—the means of exploitation have been done away with. State by State the bourgeoisie withers away, and as it withers the State too withers, for the State is the expression of a class division in society, rooted in the material conditions of economy and affecting the consciousness of men. When all human consciousness is the consciousness of men who have never known bourgeois conditions of production, then the State no longer needs to exist as something separate and towering over society. The seemingly endless war, now secret, now open, but always tragic and brutal, can cease, for at last the misery of a suffering class has not been diverted against God or the Devil or the Jews or other members of their own class in other countries or any other fancied sources of evil, but against the material conditions which produced their suffering as a class. Once rightly directed against its source, this hate and misery ends. It does not end peacefully, for the majority find themselves opposed by the class whose happiness is rooted in just those conditions the majority wish to end, and who are therefore prepared to defend those conditions with violence.

But it is the last fight. The rôle of the proletarian party in this tremendous revolution is to be the vanguard of the class whose objective conditions make it the leader of the whole transition. To be the vanguard is to lead, not to be swept along; it is also to remain in touch with the class of which it is the organised front, to be the active expression of that class's guiding theory and shaping will.

How then could the party fulfil this rôle and not be what it is in Russia to-day?—in relation to the expropriated class to express the dictatorship of the proletariat, the final use of coercion which will make coercion no longer possible; in relation to the liberated majority to be the leader, not by any coercive right but because it expresses most clearly and completely the aims and aspirations of the led. Hence the unique spectacle of a party which is a minority in the State, and has no rights or powers as a party, and yet which—by the tutelage its members exert in all the organs of contemporary soviet society—guides everywhere the activities of the class whose experience it never ceases to epitomise and express. But the organisation of the leading members of society as a separate organisation, however uncoerced, indicates a residue of unfreedom in society due to the still imperfect level of social production. Only when it is raised to a plane where all members of society are able fully to realise their physical and mental individuality can the era of socialism end and that of communism begin. Then the party too will have withered away, for it will have expanded to a stage where it includes all, and therefore will no longer be a party. Only then will men pass completely from the realm of necessity to that of freedom, not by ignoring necessity but by becoming through action completely conscious of necessity. In the past man had attained consciousness of the necessity of the physical environment, but not of society itself, and so he was enslaved to the forms of society—the machine, the harvest and the relations they generated. How could he become fully conscious of the necessity of society except in the same way as he became conscious of the necessity of the environment—by experience in changing it? How could political science be anything else but the science of revolution? Thus man realises in particulars and concretely the general and abstract formula of freedom which is expressed as follows:

Men, in their struggle with Nature (*i.e.* in their struggle for freedom) enter into certain relations with each other to win that freedom, which consists of the social product resulting from the change of Nature by men in association for economic production. But men cannot change Nature without changing themselves. The full understanding of this mutual interpenetration or reflexive movement of men and Nature, mediated by the necessary and developing relations known as society, is the *recognition* of necessity, not only in Nature but in ourselves and therefore also in society. Viewed objectively this active subject-object relation is science, viewed subjectively it is art; but as consciousness emerging in active union with practice it is simply concrete living—the whole process of working, feeling, thinking and behaving like a human individual in one world of individuals and Nature.

An analysis of the kind we have just completed, an economic and political analysis of the movement of society to-day, would be ordinarily regarded as foreign to a study of poetry. But no one who has patiently followed the argument thus far can fail to see its relevance to contemporary art, and the importance of understanding the revolutionary transformation of the basis of society which is everywhere affecting art and the artist.

2

This tremendous revolutionary transition, in which the whole superstructure is "more or less rapidly transformed", is not accomplished in the realm of ideology by a simple instantaneous movement. The transition is a material one, a change of a whole system of productive forces and social relations, and these material movements are reflected in men's consciousnesses where all struggles are fought out to an issue. This transition has only begun, but already its effects are felt throughout the sphere of art, in all the variety and rich development of the struggle. It is impossible to understand modern art without some understanding, not only of the nature of the revolution, but also of future society, the pressure towards which is expressed in the trajectory of every flying fragment from the explosion taking place below the level of consciousness.

We speak of proletarian art; it is an art which expresses the movement of the proletarian class itself, and this movement is to annihilate its existence as a class by becoming coincident with society as a whole. It was the rôle of class society to gather at one pole all consciousness and so enrich the development of science and art. How then could proletarian art exist, as a higher form than bourgeois art, before proletarian society had developed its own distinctive consciousness? And this could only happen in any full measure when proletarian freedom had exceeded bourgeois freedom—for consciousness is the reflection in ideology of the social product which secures its existence. Art also is a productive problem.

Proletarian consciousness, when it has even equalled bourgeois consciousness, will be of a higher quality, for the reason that bourgeois freedom and consciousness was the monopoly of one class in society and expressed only the aspirations and aims of that class. Bourgeois art, because of this, is the art of a man, half of whose organism has been cut away. The bourgeois class is not a class or a minority in the sense that it is a group of men more or less taken at random: such men may excellently express in any sphere a complete and rounded consciousness of reality—artists or scientists in any society will be such a minority. But the bourgeois class is an *economic* class—a class defined by a difference in its whole material surroundings and mode of life; it is a class, not a self-sufficient society. It therefore handles only part of the concrete living of society. The rest of life's movement goes out into the eternal night of the other class and returns from it into the day of consciousness, transformed—no bourgeois knows how. To know how would be to cease to be a bourgeois. Hence the final incompleteness of the bourgeois vision, and as the material contradiction which is the cause of the separation of classes increases, so the gap between thinking and acting widens. Social consciousness is torn from social action like flesh from bone. The ravages apparent in modern consciousness show that man can hardly endure the pangs of this dismemberment.

The consciousness which remains adhering to the pole of the ruling class contracts and stiffens because it is separated from its organic nexus. It becomes academic, reactionary and fascist and petrifies in a living death. The bulk of artistic consciousness cannot survive this fission. A part is attracted—by all the blindness and instinct in it—to the pole of the exploited class, but the effect of this is to explode the whole field of consciousness into fragments. This unendurable tension is shown in the chaotic and intoxicated confusion of all *sincere* modern bourgeois art, decomposing and whirling about in a flux of perplexed agony. It is expressed by the cries of the Lawrences and their followers, demanding a release from the torments of modern intellectual consciousness; and the schizophrenic vision of Joyce, condemning the whole Witches' Sabbath of bourgeois experience.

Pulled to the opposite pole by instinct and dumb experience, retained there and clarified by the *organising* force of the proletariat's life, part of the bourgeois artistic consciousness separates out, adhering to the pole of the exploited and revolutionary class. It fuses there with such consciousness as has already formed during the developing process of their separation: this already formed consciousness is scientific rather than artistic; intellectual and active rather than emotional and expressive.

This new consciousness gradually attracts all the dispersed elements of the old. The pattern of the old consciousness almost vanishes. Organised along the "lines of force" of the bourgeois categories, it was necessary that it be wholly broken up before the old elements could enter into a richer pattern, a pattern that now becomes the creation, not of a limited part of society but of a class which has expanded to include the whole of concrete living. This expansion will be evidenced in the fuller content of the new consciousness, which will now be fed by the whole process of human reality and can therefore blossom as organically as a flower, just as it did in tribal society, but with all the technical elaboration evolved since then. *Proletarian* art in realising itself will become *communist* art.

This process is simply a parallel in the sphere of ideology to what will take place in the sphere of material economy. Here the elements of bourgeois production, the productive forces, are bursting into anarchy as a result of the repulsive movement between the poles of the classes, generated by the development of the categories of bourgeois economy. Only when these are dissolved can the elements be arranged in the more fruitful organisation of socialism, but meanwhile the first clarifying outline of the forms of socialist economy has already appeared as an organising power at the proletarian pole, developing from trade unions to soviets of workers' powers.

All this is fought out in the consciousnesses of men. In the sphere of art this appears as the fugitive or confused alliances of bourgeois artists with the proletariat, and the emergence (at first within the limits of bourgeois technique) of proletarian artists.

The bourgeois artist has three possible rôles in relation to the proletariat—opposition, alliance or assimilation. Opposition means a return to discarded categories: it is no longer possible to return to the discarded forms of yesterday; they have annihilated themselves. It is necessary to "regress" and return to almost mythological themes, to interpret the world in terms of the blood and the unconsciousness. It is necessary to barbarise both the ego and the external world in order to find a sanction for an opposition which can only be an alliance with the privileged forces of reaction. This attempt to roll history back gives us Spenglerian, "Aryan" and Fascist art.

Most bourgeois artists are at present treading the road of

alliance—Gide in France; Day Lewis, Auden and Spender in this country—and many of the *surréalistes* have signed the same treaty. Such an alliance can only be an "anarchist" alliance. The bourgeois class cannot generate any higher organisation than that which it has generated—the organisation of the nationalist State, which reaches its extremest form in the Fascist State. If, therefore, any artists reject this organisation and become revolutionary, they can only be organised in the higher forms created by the proletariat. But this is the road of assimilation, and we are discussing now bourgeois artists who enter into an alliance, which means they do not enter the proletarian organisation but remain outside the ranks as "fellow travellers". Their attitude to existing society therefore can only be destructive—it is anarchist, nihilist and *surréaliste*. They often glorify the revolution as a kind of giant explosion which will blow up everything they feel to be hampering them. But they have no constructive theory—I mean as artists: they may as economists accept the economic categories of socialism, but as artists they cannot see the new forms and contents of an art which will replace bourgeois art.

They know "something is to come" after this giant firework display of the Revolution, but they do not feel with the clarity of an artist the specific beauty of this new concrete living, for they are by definition cut off from the organisation which is to realise it, and which therefore alone holds in its bosom the nascent outlines of the future. They must put "something" there in the future, and they tend to put their own vague aspirations for bourgeois freedom and bourgeois equality. They attempt to visualise the brave new world in terms of their desires: this is in appearance not so different from the Fascist haters of communism, who attempt to hold back the new world to the measure of *their* desires. In both cases a sketch of the future is produced which is curiously pathological and spiritually hysterical; but in the one case it is evolving backwards, in the other case it is full of forward movement and blind presage.

Of course this anarchic position of the contemporary bourgeois artist is only a variant of the old tragedy of bourgeois revolt. At each stage the bourgeois revolts against the system by the assertion of contradictory categories which only hasten on the advance of the things he hates. But it is a *new* variant of the tragedy. Actively to help on the development of bourgeois economy at this final stage is to help on its destruction; hence these allies of the proletariat are genuine revolutionaries and the destructive element in their activity is not fake, it is real and complete. Their cleavage arises from the impossibility of a constructive approach to the Revolution.

This Trotsky-like element in their orientation expresses itself in many ways. The younger are Romantic Revolutionaries: it is the wild and destructive part of revolution that seems to them most picturesque: and in many cases it is evident that a revolution without violence would be disappointing. Baudelaire expressed this revolutionary spirit which is anarchic in an extreme form when he said, referring to his fighting at the barricades in 1848: "Moi, quand je consens à être républicain, je fais le mal le sachant . . . je dis: Vive la Révolution! comme je dirais: Vive la Destruction! Vive la Mort!"

It gives even the revolutionary element in their art a Fascist tinge, because they draw their hate at the same source, petty bourgeois suffering from bourgeois development. However, with them this hate is directed against its true source, capitalism, whereas with Fascists it is directed against mythical sources—Marxists, Jews, and other nations. (The destructive element in genuinely proletarian art arises from proletarian suffering, which is a different kind of misery.)

On the constructive side the affective context of their work is often vague, disorientated and confused: it always conceals in some form or other a demand for "freedom for me" or "freedom from social restraints". There is a slightly *anxious* preoccupation with personal liberties and a scurrying hither and thither for reassurances or corrections in the proletarian revolutionary theory because of its suspicious deviations from petty bourgeois limitations and ideals.

This is a source of confusion in their art, which too often reduces it to chaos, or may even silence them. It must be understood that this "refusal" to be assimilated in the proletarian organisation does not *necessarily* mean that they stand completely outside the proletarian revolutionary ranks. The proletarian revolution takes place under the hegemony of the proletariat; and this means that these artists must accept to some degree the marching orders of the proletarian general staff unless they are to condemn themselves to complete nullity in action, which few of them now do. They must work with the proletariat somehow, and this necessarily involves their accepting the obligations of united action. This is educative and has had, for example, a considerable effect on Spender and Day Lewis. In some cases it may even extend to their joining the party of the proletariat—the Communist Party—but the extreme reluctance of most of these artists to take this step is symptomatic. None the less, even if they join the party, this anarchist quality in their alliance takes a characteristic form. They announce themselves as prepared to merge with the proletariat, to accept its theory and its organisation, in every field of concrete living except that of art. Now this reservation —unimportant to an ordinary man—is absolutely disastrous for an artist, precisely because his most important function is to be an artist. It leads to a gradual separation between his living and his art—his living as a proletarian diverging increasingly from his art as a bourgeois. All his proletarian aspirations gather at one pole, all his bourgeois art at the other. Of course this separation cannot take place without a mutual distortion. His proletarian living bursts into his art in the form of crude and grotesque scraps of Marxist phraseology and the mechanical application of the living proletarian theory—this is very clearly seen in the three English poets most closely associated with the revolutionary movement. His bourgeois art bursts into his proletarian living in the form of extraordinary and quite un-necessary outbursts of bourgeois "independence" and indis-cipline or quite apparent bourgeois distortions of the party's revolutionary theory. It leads to an unconscious dishonesty in his art—as of a man exploiting the revolution for his own ends. This is due to the fact that he sees the revolution as a path to a bourgeois heaven and is aware that his fellow revolutionaries have different ideas. However, he is prepared to co-operate for the sake of overthrowing the present system. This is only dis-honest because it is unconscious—if open, it would be a fair working alliance, an acknowledged treaty like that which politically unites the different parties of the People's Front.

Since the reservation extends chiefly to the field of art, this artist's main preoccupation with the revolution is to secure guarantees of his freedom in the field of art after the revolution. He is not at all concerned about what would to most people seem more important—his freedom in concrete living. He understands that his other activities will be freer then, because in these other matters he already has a proletarian point of view. He is concerned as to whether art will be free, whether there will be a "censorship" on art. All his conceptions of freedom are in fact summed up in one word—"censorship". He goes to Russia not so much to see if the people are free, but if the artists are "interfered with" by the authorities. And this leads him to a typically bourgeois conception of the artist as a man whose rôle is to be a lone wolf, a man who realises beauty for society only because he is exempt from contemporary social restraints; and he attempts to patchwork this conception into proletarian theory.

Of course this is not peculiar to the artist. Scientists, for example, will make an alliance with the proletariat in the same way; *they* make reservations only in the field of science. They go to Russia prepared to "sacrifice" everything, provided scientific theory is not interfered with. They develop a typically bourgeois conception of the scientist as a "lone wolf". And this extends to everyone—teachers, peasants, administrators, historians, actors, economists, soldiers and factory managers who see the necessity of an alliance with the proletariat, freely and consciously choose it, and are prepared to accept proletarian leadership in every field except the one which is valuable to them, and where they demand the retention of bourgeois categories. The fact that if *all* these different petty bourgeois claims were granted they would, when lumped together, negate any proletarian society at all, and simply equal the retention of the present system against which they revolt, does not of course affect the individuals who make the demand, for they have carefully segregated their particular fields of interest from the field of life as a whole, and the artist is, for example, quite content to see the scientist proletarianised. It is for this very reason that the more the petty bourgeois becomes revolutionary, the less he can operate in his own organisations with other bourgeois revolutionaries, and the more he becomes an individual under the hegemony of the proletariat.

This dichotomy between life and the most valued function is only possible because the development of bourgeois culture has produced a flying apart of all ideology into separate spheres of art, philosophy, physics, psychology, history, biology, economics, music, anthropology and the like which, as they increase their internal organisation and achievement, mutually repel each other and increase the general confusion. This is merely an equivalent in the field of thought of the way in which organisation within the factory has increased disorganisation between the factory; it is the struggle of productive forces with productive relations; it is the quarrel of real elements with bourgeois categories; it is part of the basic contradiction of capitalism. The task of the proletariat is just as much to integrate this ideological confusion and raise it to a new level of consciousness, as it is to integrate the economic confusion and raise it to a new level of production. One task is the counterpart of the other, and both have a common aim—to win more freedom for humanity.

To all these bourgeois revolutionaries the conscious proletariat therefore addresses the same kind of words:

"Your conception of freedom, because it is rooted in a part of society, is also partial. All consciousness is determined by the society which produces it, but because you are ignorant of this mode of determination, you imagine your consciousness to be free and not determined by your experience and history. This illusion you exhibit so proudly is the badge of your slavery to yesterday, for if you could see those causes which determine your thought, you would be like us, on the road to freedom. The recognition of necessity in society is the only passage to social freedom.

"But when we say that consciousness is determined by the society which produces it, we say that thought is ultimately inseparable from concrete living, from *practice*. Each secures and develops the freedom of the other. You think that by separating theory from practice—and from the social obligations and forms that go with practice—you are making thought free from 'censorship'. You hope to segregate thought from life, and so, by surrendering everything but this, in some way preserve a part of man's freedom, like the man who wrapped his talent in a napkin rather than adventure it in the market. However, freedom is not a substance to be preserved and isolated but a force generated in an active struggle with the concrete problems of living. You would deliver thought to the bondage of unconscious bourgeois categories; you would rob practice of its soul.

"There is no neutral world of art, free from categories or determining causes. Art is a social activity. Yours is the fallacious freedom of dream, which imagines itself spontaneous when it is rigidly determined by forces outside consciousness. You must choose between class art which is unconscious of its causality and is therefore to that extent false and unfree, and proletarian art which is becoming conscious of its causality and will therefore emerge as the truly free art of communism. There is no classless art except communist art, and that is not yet born; and class art to-day, unless it is proletarian, can only be the art of a dying class.

"We shall not cease to criticise the bourgeois content of your art. You indignantly reject these 'economic' categories, not because they are incorrect but because they are economic. But what are correct economic categories except categories drawn from concrete living? Ours is simply a demand that you should square life with art and art with life, that you should make art living. Cannot you see that their separation is precisely what is evil and bourgeois? Cannot you see that in this one matter you line up with our enemies—you, our ally—which is why on this point we fight your theory so bitterly?

"Our demand—that your art should be proletarian—is *not* a demand that you apply dogmatic categories and Marxist phrases to art. To do so would be bourgeois. We ask that you should *really* live in the new world and not leave your soul behind in the past. It is your artist's soul for which we value you; and how can your soul be in the new world if your art is bourgeois? We shall know that this transition has taken place when your art has become *living*; then it will be proletarian. Then we shall cease to criticise it for its deadness.

"Ours is not a demand that you should accept in the realm of art what you call proletarian dictatorship. On the contrary, we shall say you are still bourgeois as long as you impose a proletarian dictatorship on yourself and import formulations from other fields of proletarian ideology to apply them mechanically to art. It is a demand that you, an artist, become a proletarian *leader* in the field of art; that you do not take either of these easy roads which are in essence the same—mechanically shuffling the outworn categories of bourgeois art or mechanically importing the categories of other proletarian spheres. You must take the difficult creative road—that of refashioning the categories and technique of art so that it expresses the new world coming into being and is part of its realisation. Then we shall say your art is proletarian and living; then we shall say, your soul has left the past—it has dragged the past into the present and forced the realisation of the future. You are not now 'just an artist' (which means in fact a bourgeois artist); you have become a proletarian artist."

The proletariat addresses what is in substance the same message to the scientist, the engineer, the factory manager, the historian and the economist. But in each case the message is not understood; it is regarded as formal or even insincere. The debate cannot be solved in theory, for the essence of this dispute is that the antagonists live in two worlds—one of bourgeois categories and the other of proletarian. It can, however, be solved in the world of practice, for both are living in the same real world. Hence the progress of the socialist revolution hastens the assimilation of its bourgeois allies. Still, the bourgeois consciousness drags at the bourgeois revolutionary and produces in certain characters a hopeless cleavage, which makes the degeneration of some of its leaders a law of revolution. The record of Trotsky, Zinoviev and Kamenev are examples of how this may lead to complete treachery. On the other hand it may act as a "drag" to hold back the artist from full ripening. The lives and work of Yessenin, Mayakovsky, Pilnyak and Yury Olesha are examples of the conflict involved in this inability to recast creatively the categories of bourgeois

T

art after the Revolution. Meanwhile, at the proletarian pole, the whole process of assimilation is hastened by the development of the socialist revolution.

On the one hand men with proletarian lives attempt to interpret these in terms of existing bourgeois categories, that is, they use the already existing bourgeois artistic technique. Necessarily marked at first by an uncertainty, a poverty in handling alien categories, this attempt gives rise to what is sometimes regarded as being essentially proletarian art, although it is really an art in transition. This art has a simplicity and openness of theme which goes with a certain crudity and clumsiness in handling the technique; rather like a proletarian occupying for the first time a rôle in administration which hitherto had been peculiarly the prerogative of the bourgeois. Yet it is by this means that bourgeois technique and bourgeois administration will be lifted to a new level by a laborious refashioning, in which at first every mistake is made except the fatal bourgeois mistakes.

On the other hand artists with bourgeois consciousnesses attempt to refashion these in order to express proletarian life. These meet the others, as it were, tunnelling from the opposite side. One group attempts to push proletarian living (practice) into bourgeois consciousness (theory); the other to push bourgeois consciousness into proletarian living. Both tasks demand a complete refashioning of consciousness and neither can be successful alone. The bourgeois attempt produces a characteristic art which is also sometimes regarded as really proletarian art instead of being bourgeois art in transition, an art in which the rich but vague, fumbling and disorganised elements in bourgeois art are imperfectly transformed into large, concrete, proletarian realities.

Great *proletarian* art can only arise from a synthesis of the two, from the complete assimilation after breakdown of the old consciousness by the proletariat, which assimilation raises that consciousness to a new level, the level of communist consciousness.

Because then the proletariat has become coincident with the whole of society, this consciousness is no longer partial and torn apart from life, like flesh from bone. Society and its reflection in man is no longer rent and wounded. Art returns to life, and becomes a reality to all men.

3

Poetry expresses in a generalised and abstract way the dynamic relation of the ego to the elements of outer reality symbolised by words. This very generalisation is the source of its ability to voice with unique power the instinctive emotional element in man—the physiological component of the social ego.

Poetry begins, we recall, as the cries of primitive hunters and food-gatherers in which man attempts to master Nature by changing himself—by throwing himself into Nature so that his way of associated life conforms with the desired objects, just as his social perception expressed in art strives to conform with the track of the beasts, its special outline, its specific ferocity and vulnerability. This introjection of the self into Nature is conscious because it is social; man could only hunt and gather food successfully in co-operation even at this early stage. This is the poetry which summons from the breast of man a mimicry of Nature that is not a mere reflection, but a Nature as man desires her woven from the strands of Nature as men share her in common effort. There is a tense bareness about the art of this stage.

This passes into the poem as myth and ritual, as *chorus* or chant, where Nature in the shape of herds and crops is taken into the heart of society. Men, instead of changing their associated perception and action to conform with the outline of Nature, change Nature's outline to conform with their own. The world process is extravagantly distorted to suit man's whim. Yet the society into which Nature has been dragged is still undifferentiated and collective. Society is passive yet creative, like a pregnant woman. It has a certain closed complacency. Life is now in it—not outside.

In the next stage the introjection of Nature into society has led to society itself splitting into antagonistic parts or classes. Division of labour is reflected in a division of society. The development of agricultural and pastoral civilisation leads to the creation of a ruling class which becomes ossified and has as its counterpart a class of serfs and slaves. The struggle with Nature is transformed into men's struggle with each other. The first emergence of the ruling class is seen as the transformation of mythology into the epic, and into story, and in the evolution of ritual into play. The conflict of society is reflected in a poetry sombre and clouded with moral issues—questions of right and wrong—balanced by a poetry concerned with delight—with love and joy. Doubt, pathos, nobility, serenity, fear and a conscious beauty all enter the field of poetry. And the development of classes, by rendering possible the differentiation of function, gives more freedom to individuality. For the first time men speak personally in poetry. The lyric is born.

The bourgeois class comes to rule—a class the conditions of whose existence is the continual revolution of its basis. Poetry becomes dizzy, tragic, full of contradictions. Its technique undergoes the most rapid transformations. Its law of formation decrees that each step it takes in revolt against the conditions of its existence only urge on the ripening of those conditions and its own fall. The continual revolt of poets against the negation of poetry and individual freedom by concrete bourgeois existence only calls into being a whole world of poetry precisely fulfilling the conditions of concrete bourgeois existence. It flies away from life into a heaven of pure art, whose assertion of personal worth and open denial of concrete living increase in proportion to the rate at which concrete living strangles the realisation of personal worth. This withdrawal in itself reflects the movement of the bourgeois class from reality, the development of the contradiction between bourgeois consciousness and proletarian reality, between the productive forces of society and the social conditions of existence of the capitalist class.

Poetry reaches technically an unprecedented competence; it draws more and more apart from the world of reality; it asserts with increasing success the personal perception of life and the personal feeling until it becomes so desocialised that at first perception and then feeling cease to exist at all. The great mass of men no longer read poetry, no longer feel the need for it, no longer understand it, because poetry has moved away from concrete living by the development of its technique, and this movement was itself only the counterpart of a similar movement in the whole of society.

Thus the poet was forced by life—*i.e.* by his experience—to concentrate on just those words and organising values which were becoming steadily less meaningful to men as a whole, until poetry, from a necessary function of all society (as in a primitive tribe), becomes the luxury of a few chosen spirits.

The movement forward from bourgeois culture to communism is also a movement back to the social solidarity of primitive communism, but one which includes and gathers up all the development of the interim, all the division of labour which has made possible an increase in freedom, individuation and consciousness. It is a movement back to the collectivism and integrity of a society without coercion, where consciousness and freedom are equally shared by all.

Such a society primitively was a society which, because of its low productivity, had an integrity that was crude and bare, and a sum of consciousness and freedom so scanty that although shared by all each share was small. It was necessary for freedom and consciousness to be monopolised, to gather for a time at the pole of a ruling class, for man to develop all the productive powers that slumbered in the lap of social labour. And when this gives rise to a contradiction which can only be solved by communism, the productive powers based on division and organisation of labour have developed to a stage where individual differentiation can take place freely within the integrity of one society, where freedom and consciousness are sufficient for all to share and yet be rich in liberty; a society where freedom and consciousness, because it is general, is higher than in a class society, where it is perpetually maimed and torn. Individuality reaches a new and higher realisation.

This means a great expansion in the poet's public. As freedom and consciousness become the right of all and not the prerogative of a class, the poet's public must become gradually coincident with society, and poetry once more fulfil a function similar to that of poetry in the primitive tribe, but with this difference—that the tremendous growth of the productive

forces has differentiated poetry from the other arts, the arts
from the sciences, and changed poetry itself from the poetry
of a tribe to the poetry of individual men. By becoming collective, therefore, poetry in the era of communism will not become
less individual but more so. This individuation will be artistic
—carried out by the change of the social ego, not personal and
dream-like—carried out by the reduction of the social ego to
unconsciousness.

The increase of the poet's public can already be seen in the
Soviet Union where poets have publics of two or three million,
books of poetry have sales of a size unknown previously in the
history of the world.

The same change is reflected in the poet's vocabulary.
The vocabulary of the bourgeois poet became esoteric and
limited. It was not limited in the sense of limitation of
number of words but limitation of useable public values of
words. In fact the number and type of words useable by the
bourgeois poet increased, paralleling the continual revolution
in technique which, because it is the condition of capitalist
existence, continues right down to the end of capitalism. But
this increase and enrichment in technique is paralleled by a
decrease and impoverishment of the social associations in
words which can be used by the poet.

One after another these associations became vulgar, common,
conventional, insincere, trite, jaded or commercialised because
the life from which they sucked their souls was becoming these
things. Hence modern poetry grows barer and barer of life, of
real social content, and the only word-values useable by poetry
become increasingly personal until poetry is altogether esoteric
and private. It was for this reason that poetry became no longer
acceptable to most people, submerged in the conditions of
bourgeois civilisation. It was too rebellious, too openly critical
of concrete living. It was rebellious, not revolutionary, but
neither was it opiate. It did not take their vulgarised values
and outraged instincts and soothe both in an ideal wish-fulfilment world like that of religion, jazz or the detective novel.
It quietly excluded all those vulgarised values, but in doing so,
it step by step excluded more and more of concrete living, and
it was this process that called into being the world of art for

art's sake, of otherness and illusion, the towering heaven of dream which ultimately became completely private and turned into an abyss of nightmare and submarine twilight.

Thus poetry lost that simplicity of outline, that grandeur and searching nobility which comes to it from being sited in the heart of concrete living and able to voice the most general and important experiences in the most universally meaningful way.

Though rebellious, poetry was not revolutionary, for revolution remains within the sphere of material reality and operates with the common values and outraged instincts of men. It does not organise them to soothe them in a phantastic heaven, but bends their hate and aspirations, however limited, to the task of wiping out the real cause of their misery here in the world of concrete life. The poet cannot be the leader of revolution (although at a certain stage he can be its singer and inspirer), because his world has become by the pressure of alien values too small a part of the real world and it is part of the task of the revolution to widen it.

The change of values, the de-vulgarisation of life, the growth of collective freedom and the release of individual consciousness which takes place in communism, means the return of these social values, regenerated and ennobled, to the palette of the artist. His vocabulary may at first be even simplified as to number of words, precisely because the world of reality released by those words for poetry is complicated and enriched. Now he can speak in the old noble way. The world of values behind language will expand for poetry in the same way as it did during the Elizabethan era—then by the revelation of a whole world of values, before personal to the poet but for the first time made social; now by the injection into poetry of a whole world of purified social values for the first time made personal to the poet. This change in the technique of poetry is a reflection of the way art returns into the life from which it has flown away, bringing back with it all the development produced by the cleavage.

The individuality developed by bourgeois economy, which became anarchic and stifled itself, is still further elaborated by the categories of communism, and at the same time integrated, given a collective wholeness and sanity. This is likely to be expressed in two ways. On the one hand the development of broadcasting will give to poetry a new collective appearance, on the other hand the individuality of the actor will no longer conflict with the poetic instant, and poetry can return to drama making it once more collective and real. It seems also (though this is bare conjecture) that the film, because it realises the highest possibilities of the bourgeois stage in a more collective, more richly powerful and more flexible form, will only come into its own in communism.

As conductor is to orchestra, so producer is to film, the incarnation of the ego in which the story takes place, but his power is far greater than that of the conductor. It must not be supposed that communism involves the stifling of actor, "star" or author. On the contrary, it is just then that their individuality will be given a more elaborate and deeper meaning because it will be a collective meaning. It is no accident that the final period of bourgeois culture, which raised individuality to its height, produced no "heroes", no great authors, artists, actors or poets. The great man is not just an individuality but an individuality given a collective embodiment and significance. The shadow is so enormous because it is cast over the whole of society. Bourgeois culture mocked the proletariat because it had in its first struggles produced Marx, Lenin and Stalin, while according to bourgeois culture communism "does not believe in great men" or "in the individual" and so had here contradicted its own teaching. In this mockery bourgeois culture only exposes the fallacies in its own conception of the relation of the individual to society.

It will be seen that the final movement of society has this parallel to primitive communism, that once again man turns outward from the ego to reality, and looks the world steadily in the face. But now the world is not the world of a few beasts and crops and a wandering sun, but a world enriched by the taking in of Nature into society during the period of class formation. It is a reality elaborated by centuries of interpenetration of Nature and man, evident in the division of labour in society, and due to the attempts of man to change Nature, at first solely by drawing her into himself without regard to the whole world of social relations this movement necessarily produces.

When this period is ended men can look steadily at this whole world of social relations with all its richness and complex values. Before it was only known to them by distortions in their cognised world, as secret presences or forces or gods, as a mere abstraction—man, the "human essence", civil society. This concrete world of life which gathers up within itself as a rounded, developing whole the divorced and simpler abstract worlds of man and Nature, is the peculiar concern of the communist poet. He is interested in his own individuality, not in and for itself—a conception which conceals the contradiction that wrecked bourgeois society—but in its developing relation with other individualities in a communicating world that is not just a fluid amorphous sea, but has its own rigidity and reality. The communist poet is concerned to a degree never known before with the realisation of all the values contained in the relations of human beings in real life.

Every phase of art, every stage of culture, has its moving principle which is the source of its tragedy, its beauty, its satisfaction and its creative power. To primitive culture, the tragedy of the strong and savage beast; to pastoral society, the tragedy of gods and myth; to all class society, the tragedy of the will of the hero. To early bourgeois society, the tragedy of the will of the prince; to late bourgeois society, the tragedy of the will of Joyce's "Ulysses" and Proust's "I" living in a world wholly of personal phantasy. Tragedy is not in itself tragic; it is beautiful, tender and satisfying—in the Aristotelian sense cathartic. But there is also the spectacle of culture tragically perishing because its matrix, society, has become dispersed and sterile. This is the pathos of art, which cannot be tragic because it cannot resolve its problems in a tragic way, but is torn by insoluble conflicts and perplexed by all kinds of unreal phantasies. This is the tragedy of art to-day in all its dissolution and futility. It is the tragedy of will that does not understand itself; of the unconscious individual who is slave to he knows not what. Art is the privilege of the free.

All art is conditioned by the conception of freedom which rules in the society that produces it; art is a mode of freedom, and a class society conceives freedom to be absolutely whatever relative freedom that class has attained to. In bourgeois art man is conscious of the necessity of outer reality but not of his own, because he is unconscious of the society that makes him what he is. He is only a half-man. Communist poetry will be complete, because it will be man conscious of his own necessity as well as that of outer reality.

That everything which comes into being must pass away; that all is fleeting, all is moving; that to exist is to be like the fountain and have a shape because one is never still—is the theme of all art because it is the texture of reality. Man is drawn to life because it moves from him; he has desires as ancient and punctual as the stars; love has a poignant sweetness and the young life pushes aside the old; these are qualities of being as enduring as man. Man too must pass away.

Therefore the stuff of art endures as long as man. The fountain dwindles away only when men are rent and wasted by a sterile conflict, and the pulsing movement of society is halted. All this movement is creative because it is not a simple oscillation but a development unfolded by its very restlessness. The eternal simplicities generate the enrichment of art from their own bosoms not only because they are eternal but also because change is the condition of their existence. Thus art is one of the conditions of man's realisation of himself, and in its turn is one of the realities of man.

BIBLIOGRAPHY

D'ABRO, A. Evolution of Scientific Thought from Newton to Einstein. 1927.

ADLER, A. The Neurotic Constitution. 1916.
  Individual Psychology. 1924.

ADLER, M. J. Dialectic.

ALDRICH, C. R. The Primitive Mind.

ALLEN, A. H. B. Pleasure and Instinct. 1930.

ALVERDES, F. Social Life in the Animal World.

D'ALVIELLA, E. G. La Migration des symboles. 1891.

APOLLINAIRE, G. Alcools.

APTHORP, W. F. The Opera, Past and Present. 1901.

ARISTOTLE. Poetics.
  Rhetoric.

ARNOLD, M. Introduction to "English Poets". Ward. 1880.

ASHLEY, W. J. Economic Organisation of England. 1914.

ATKINSON, J. J. Primal Law. 1903.

BARTLETT, F. C. Psychology and Primitive Culture. 1923.

BATESON, W. Mendel's Principles of Heredity. 1909.

BELL, CLIVE. Since Cézanne. 1922.

BELL, E. Hellenic Architecture. 1920.

BENEDICT, R. Patterns of Culture. 1935.

BENNETT, H. S. The Pastons and their England. 1922.

BERGSON, H. Essai surles données immédiates de la conscience. 1889.
  Matière et mémoire. 1896.
  L'Évolution créatrice. 1907.

BERKELEY, H. Mysticism in Modern Mathematics. 1910.

BEWER, J. A. The Literature of the Old Testament in its Historical Development. 1904.

BLACK, M. Nature of Mathematics. 1933.

BLOOMFIELD, L. Language. 1935.

BOISSONADE, P. LE Travail dans l'Europe chrétienne au moyen âge. 1921.

BOURNE, H. E. The Revolutionary Period in England. 1914.

BOWDEN, W. The Rise of the Great Manufactures of England, 1919.
  Industrial Society in England towards the End of the Eighteenth Century. 1925.

BREASTED, J. H. A History of the Ancient Egyptians. 1908.
  Ancient Times. 1916.
BRÉHIER, L. L'Art byzantin. 1924.
BRIDGMAN, P. W. The Logic of Modern Physics. 1927.
BROAD, G. D. Perception, Physics and Reality. 1914.
  Scientific Thought. 1923.
BRODETSKY, S. The Meaning of Mathematics. 1929.
BROUWER, L. E. J. "Intuitionism and Formalism" (Bull. Amer.
  Math. Society, vol. xx.). 1913.
BUCHER, K. Arbeit und Rhythmus. 1899.
BUDD, C. Chinese Poems. 1912.
BUDGE, E. A. W. Egyptian Magic.
  Egyptian Religion.
BUKHARIN, N. I. Imperialism and World Economy (trans.). 1930.
  Economic Theory of the Leisure Class.
BUKHARIN, N. I. (and others). Marxism and Modern Thought. 1935.
  Poetry, Poetics and the Problems of Poetry in the U.S.S.R. 1935.
BULLEN, A. H. Elizabethans. 1924.
BURKITT, M. C. Prehistory. 1921.
  The Old Stone Age. 1933.
BURNS, EMILE. Capitalism, Communism and the Transition.
BURROW, T. Social Basis of Consciousness.
BUSHELL, S.W. Chinese Art. 1909.
BUTLER, W. F. The Lombard Communes. 1906.
BUXTON, L. H. D. Primitive Labour. 1924.

CAJORI, F., History of Mathematics. 1919.
CAMPBELL, C. M. Destiny and Disease in Mental Disorders. 1935.
CANNON, W. B. Bodily Changes in Pain, Hunger, Fear and Rage.
  1915.
CARLTON, F. T. History and Problems of Organised Labour. 1920.
CARPENTER, RHYS. The Aesthetic Basis of Greek Art. 1921.
CARSE, A. The History of Orchestration. 1926.
CASSIRER, E. Sprache und Mythos. Leipzig, 1925.
CHAMBERS, E. K. The Medieval Stage. 1903.
  The Elizabethan Stage. 1923.
CHENEY, S. W. Primer of Modern Art. 1923.
CHEYNEY, E. P. Industrial and Social History of England. 1920.
CHILDE, V. G. The Dawn of European Civilisation. 1926.
CLAPARÉDE, E. Recognition et moïeté. Arch. de Psych. 1911.
CODRINGTON, R. H. The Melanesians. 1891.
COLERIDGE, S. T. Biographia Literaria. 1917.

COMMUNIST INTERNATIONAL PROGRAMME. 1929.

CONWAY, B. L. The Condemnation of Galileo. 1910.

CONYBEARE, F. C. Myth, Magic and Morals. 1910.

CORBUSIER, LE. City of Tomorrow. 1929.

CORNFORD, F. H. Origin of Attic Comedy. 1914.
From Religion to Philosophy. 1912.

COULTON, G. C. Social Life in Britain from the Norman Conquest to the Reformation. 1918.

COUTURAT. La Logique de Leibnitz.

COUTURAT (with LEAU). Histoire de la langue universelle. 1907.

CRAWLEY, E. The Mystic Rose. 1927.

CREW, H. and DESALVIO, A. Dialogues concerning Two New Sciences by Galileo Galilei (trans.). 1914.

CROCE, B. Aesthetic (trans.). 1909.

CROUCH, J. Puritanism and Art. 1910.

CUMONT, F. The Mysteries of Mithra. 1903.

CUNNINGHAM, W. Progress of Capitalism in England. 1916.

DALLAS, A. S. The Gay Science. 1866.

DAMPIER-WHETHAM, W. C. A History of Science. 1930.

DARWIN, CHARLES. Origin of Species. 1859.
Descent of Man. 1871.

DAS GUPTA. History of Indian Philisophy. 1922.

DAVIS, W. S. Influence of Wealth in Imperial Rome. 1910.

DEBORIN, A. Lenin and the Crisis of Modern Physics. Leningrad, 1930.

DELAPORTE, L. Mesopotamia.

DEMOLINS, E. Comment la route crée le type social. (2 vols.) 1901–1903.

DEWEY, J. Studies in Logical Theory. 1903.

DIBBLEE, G. B. Instinct and Intuition. 1929.

DIXON, R. B. The Building of Cultures. 1928.

DOWNEY, J. Creative Imagination.

DREVER, J. Instinct in Man. 1917.

DRIESCH, H. The Crisis in Psychology. 1925.

DURKHEIM, E. De la division du travail social. 1893.
Les Règles de la méthode sociologique. 1895.
Les Formes élémentaires de la vie religieuse. 1912.

DUTT, R. P. Fascism and Social Revolution.
World Politics. 1926.

EATON, R. M. Symbolism and Truth. 1925.

EDDINGTON, A. S. The Nature of the Physical World. 1928.

ELIOT, T. S. Poems. 1925.
  Collected Essays.
EMPSON, W. Seven Types of Ambiguity.
ENGELS, F. (see also MARX, K.). Anti-Dühring (trans.). 1878.
  Origin of the Family. 1884.
  Ludwig Feuerbach. 1886.
  The British Labour Movement (trans.). 1936.
ESPINAS, A. Les Origines de la technologie. 1899.
EVANS, A. The Palace of Minos at Knossos. 1921–1936.

FAIRBANKS, A. Handbook of Greek Religion. 1910.
FAY, C. R. Life and Labour in the Nineteenth Century. 1921.
FERGUSON, W. S. Greek Imperialism. 1913.
FIRTH, R. Primitive Economics of the New Zealand Maori. 1929.
FISHER, R. A. The Genetical Theory of Natural Selection. 1930.
FLICKINGER, R. C. The Greek Theatre and its Drama. 1918.
FLUGEL, J. C. The Psycho-analytical Study of the Family. 1921.
FORSYTH, A. R. Mathematics in Life and Thought. 1929.
FORTESCUE, A. The Orthodox Eastern Church. 1911.
FORTUNE, R. F. Sorcerers of Dobu. 1932.
FOX, C. E. The Threshold of the Pacific.
FOX, R. Lenin. 1933.
FRANCOTTE, L'Industrie dans la Grèce ancienne. 1901.
FRAZER, J. G. The Golden Bough. 1911–1915.
FREGE, G. Grundgesetsze der Arithmetik. Jena, 1893–1903.
FREUD, S. Traumdeutung. 1900.
  Ego and the Id. 1919.
  Totem and Taboo. 1919.
  Group Psychology and the Analysis of the Ego. 1922.
  Collected Papers. 1925.
  Introductory Lectures on Psycho-analysis. 1929.
  Future of an Illusion. 1935.
FROBENIUS, L. Der Ursprung der afrikanischen Kultur. 1898.

GARDNER, A. H. Speech and Language. 1932.
GEDDES, P. and THOMSON, A. Evolution. 1912.
GENNEP, A. VAN. Les rites de passage. 1909.
  L'État actuel du problème totémique. 1920.
GHURYE, G. S. Caste and Race in India.
GIRY and REVILLE. Emancipation of Medieval Towns. 1907.
GLOTZ, G. Le travail dans la Grèce ancienne.
  The Aegean Civilisation (trans.).

GODDARD, P. G. The Night Chant, a Navajo Ceremony (*Am. Mus. Nat. Hist.* vi.). 1902.

GOLDENWEISER, A. History, Psychology and Culture. 1933.

GOMME, G. L. Folk Lore as an Historical Science. 1908.

GONNER, E. C. K. Common Land and Enclosure. 1912.

GOODALL, T. C. Athenian Tragedy. 1920.

GORDON, R. G. The Neurotic Personality.

GORIS, J. A. Étude sur les colonies marchandes méridionales à Anvers de 1488 à 1567. 1925.

GOSSE, E. A History of Eighteenth-century Literature. 1911.

GREGORY, T. E. The Philosophy of Capitalism.

GROSSE, E. The Beginnings of Art. 1897.

GUIGNEBERT, C. The Formation of the Church.

HADDON, A. C. Evolution in Art. 1914.

HAMMOND, M. B. The Cotton Industry. 1897.

HARDY, G. L'Art nègre. 1927.

HARPER, R. F. Assurian and Babylonian Literature. 1901.

HARRISON, J. Ancient Art and Ritual.

HART, B. The Psychology of Insanity. 1919.

HARTLAND, E. S. Primitive Paternity. 1909.
The Evolution of Kinship. 1922.

HARTMANN, F. L'Agriculture dans l'ancienne Égypte. 1923.

HASBACH. The English Agricultural Labourer. 1908.

HEAD, H. Studies in Neurology. (2 vols.) 1920.

HECKER, J. Moscow Dialogues. 1933.

HEIBERG, J. L. Science and Mathematics in Classical Antiquity. 1922.

HERBERTSON, A. J. and F. D. Man and his Work. 1909.

HEWINS, W. A. S. English Trade and Finance in the Eighteenth Century. 1892.

HEWITT, E. L. Orenda and a Definition of Religion (*Amer. Anthrop. N. S.* iv.). 1902.

HILBERT, D. Grundlagen der Geometrie. Berlin (7th ed.). 1930.

HINGSTON, R. W. G. Problems of Instinct and Intelligence. 1928.

HIRN, Y. The Origin of Art. 1900.

HOBHOUSE, L. T. Mind in Evolution. 1901.
Morals in Evolution. 1906.

HOBHOUSE, L. T., WHEELER, G. C. and GINSBERG, M. The Material Culture and Social Institutions of the Simpler Peoples. 1915.

HOBSON, J. A. Evolution of Modern Capitalism.

HODSON, T. C. The Naga Tribes of Manipur. 1911.

HOFFMAN, W. I. The Graphic Art of the Eskimo. 1925.

HOLBACH. Système de la nature.

HOLLIS, A. J. The Masai. 1905.

The Nandi. 1909.

HOOP, VAN DER. Character and the Unconscious.

HOPKINS, E. W. The Great Epics of India. 1920.

Origin and Evolution of Religion. 1923.

HOSE, C. The Pagan Tribes of Borneo. 1912.

HULME, T. E. Speculations.

HUME, R. E. The Thirteen Principal Upanishads. 1921.

HUTTON, J. H. The Angami Nagas. 1921.

The Sema Nagas. 1921.

HYNDMAN, H. M. Commercial Crises of the Nineteenth Century. 1892.

IMTHURN, E. Among the Indians of Guiana. 1883.

JACKSON, T. A. Dialectics. 1936.

JAENSCH, E. R. Eidetic Imagery.

JAMES, W. Principles of Psychology. 1908.

JEAN, C. F. La Littérature des Babyloniens et des Assyriens. 1924.

JEANS, J. The Universe Around Us. 1929.

JENNINGS, H. S. Behaviour of the Lower Organisms. 1906.

Genetic Variations in Relation to Evolution. 1935.

JESPERSEN, O. Language, its Nature, Development and Origin, 1922.

JEVONS, F. B. Introduction to the History of Religion. 1896.

JOHANNSEN, W. L. Erblichkut. Copenhagen, 1917.

JOHNSTON, H. The Uganda Protectorate. 1902.

JONES, E. Papers on Psycho-Analysis. 1923.

IOYCE, P. W. Old Celtic Romances. 1861.

Social History of Ancient Ireland. 1914.

JOYCE, T. A. Mayan and Mexican Art. 1927.

JUNG, C. G. Psychological Types.

Psychology of the Unconscious.

Contributions to Analytical Psychology.

Analytical Psychology.

JUNOD, H. A. The Life of a South African Tribe. (2 vols.) 1912, 1913.

KARSTEN, R. The Civilisation of the South American Indians.

KAYE, G. R. Indian Mathematics. 1915.

KEANE, A. H. Man, Past and Present. 1920.

KEITH, A. Antiquity of Man. 1925.

KING, C. D. The Psychology of Consciousness.
KOFFKA. The Growth of the Mind.
  Principles of Gestalt Psychology. 1935.
KÖHLER, W. The Mentality of Apes. 1927.
  Gestalt Psychology. 1929.
KRETSCHMER, E. Physique and Character.
KROEBER, A. L. Anthropology. 1923.
KROPOTKIN. Mutual Aid, a Factor of Evolution. 1902.
KRUMBACHER, K. Geschichte der byzantischen Literatur. 1897.

LADD, G. T. Outline of Aesthetics.
LANG, A. Homer and his Age. 1906.
LANGE, F. A. History of Materialism.
LANGFIELD, H. S. Conflict and Adjustment in Art (in *Problems of Personality*, ed. A. A. Roback). 1925.
LAPIDUS, I., and OSTROVITYANOV, R. Outline of Political Economy. 1929.
LASHLEY. Brain Mechanism and Intelligence. 1929.
LAWRENCE, W. W. Medieval Story. 1912.
LENIN, V. I. Materialism and Empirio-Criticism. 1909.
  The Teachings of Karl Marx. 1914.
  Imperialism. 1917.
  The State and Revolution. 1918.
  "Left-Wing" Communism. 1920.
LEVY, H. (and others). Aspects of Dialectical Materialism. 1934.
LÉVY-BRUHL. Les Fonctions mentales dans les sociétés inférieures. 1910.
  L'Âine primitive. 1927.
LEWIS, C. I. A Survey of Symbolic Logic. 1918.
LEXA, F. La Magie dans l'Égypte antique. (2 vols.) 1924.
LING-ROTH, H. The Tasmanians. 1899.
LORIMER, F. The Growth of Reason.
LOWIE, R. H. Primitive Society. 1920.
  Primitive Religion. 1924.
LUQUET, G. H. Art and Religion of Fossil Man. 1930.

MACCULLOUGH, J. A. The Childhood of Fiction.
MACCURDY, G. G. Human Origins. 1934.
MACCURDY, J. T. Common Principles in Psychology and Physiology. 1928.
  Psychology of Emotion.
MACDONNELL, A. A. Sanskrit Literature. 1900.

U

MacDougall, W. Social Psychology. 1908.
  The Group Mind. 1920.
  Outline of Psychology. 1923.
  Outline of Abnormal Psychology. 1926.
MacKenzie, D. The Migration of Symbols.
  Myths of Crete and Pre-Hellenic Europe.
Mach, E. Die Analysis der Empfindungen. 1885.
Mainage, T. Les Religions de la préhistoire. 1920.
Malinowski, B. Family among the Australian Aborigines. 1913.
  Argonauts of the Western Pacific. 1922.
  Crime and Custom in Savage Society. 1926.
  Sex and Repression in Savage Society. 1926.
  Psychology of Primitive Peoples.
Marett, J. R. de la H. Race, Sex and Environment. 1935.
Marett, R. R. The Threshold of Religion. 1909.
  Psychology and Folk Lore. 1920.
  Head, Heart and Hands in Human Evolution. 1935.
Markey, J. J. The Symbolic Process.
Marston, W.M. Emotions of Normal People. 1928.
  Integrative Psychology.
Marx, K. Poverty of Philosophy. 1847.
  The Class Struggles in France. 1850.
  18th Brumaire of Louis Bonaparte. 1852.
  A Contribution to "The Critique of Political Economy". 1859.
  Capital. (3 vols.) 1867–1894.
  Correspondence.
Marx, K. (with Engels). The Communist Manifesto. 1848.
Mason, W. A. History of the Art of Writing. 1920.
Maudsley. The Physiology of Mind. 1876.
Mead, M. Growing up in New Guinea. 1930.
Meek, C. K. Northern Tribes of Nigeria. 1925.
  Tribal Studies in North Nigeria. 1931.
Meier-Graefe. Modern Art. 1905.
Meillet, A., and Cohen, M. Les Langues du monde. 1924.
Miller, I. The Psychology of Thinking. 1929.
Millikan, R. A. The Electron. 1924.
Mills, J. P. The Lhota Nagas. 1922.
  The Ao Nagas. 1936.
Mitchell. Problems of Psycho-pathology. 1927.
Mommsen, T. The History of Rome. 1877.
Money-Kyrle, R. The Meaning of Sacrifice. 1930.

MOORE, C. H. Development and Character of Gothic Architecture 1904.

MORET, A. From Tribe to Empire.

The Nile and Egyptian Civilisation.

MORGAN, J. DE Prehistoric Man.

MORGAN, LEWIS. League of the Iroquois. 1851.

Ancient Society. 1877.

MORGAN, LLOYD. Habit and Instinct. 1896.

Instinct and Experience.

MORGAN, T. The Mechanism of Mendelian Heredity. 1915.

Theory of the Gene. 1920.

MORRIS, W. Hopes and Fears for Art. 1896.

MOSSO, A. The Palaces of Crete and their Builders. 1917.

MULLER, M. The Science of Language. 1880.

MURCHISON, P. (ed.) Psychologies of 1920.

Psychologies of 1930.

MURPHY. Primitive Man.

MURPHY, G. An Historical Introduction to Modern Psychology. 1929.

MURRAY, G. Rise of the Greek Epic. 1911.

MYRES, J. L. Dawn of History. 1918.

NEEDHAM, J. The Sceptical Biologist. 1929.

NICOD, JEAN. Foundations of Geometry and Induction. 1930.

NIETZSCHE. The Birth of Tragedy.

OGDEN, C. K., and RICHARDS, I. A. The Meaning of Meaning. 1923.

OGG, D. Europe in the Seventeenth Century. 1928.

OSBORN, H. F. Men of the Old Stone Age. 1915.

PAGET, R. Human Speech. 1930.

PARKYN, E. A. Prehistoric Art. 1916.

PARRY, C. H. H. The Evolution of the Art of Music. 1917.

PATTERSON, L. Mithraism and Christianity. 1921.

PAULHAN, F. The Laws of Feeling.

PAVLOV, I. P. Conditioned Reflexes. 1927.

PEAKE, H. The English Village. 1921.

PELLISSIER, G. Le Mouvement littéraire au XIXᵉ siècle. 1908.

PENNIMANN, T. K. The Arunta Religion (Sociol Res.). Jan. 1929.

PERRIS, G. H. Industrial History of England. 1914.

PERRY, W. J. The Megalithic Culture of Indonesia. 1918.

Children of the Sun. 1926.

PETERMANN, B. The Gestalt Theory. 1932.
PETIT-DUTAILLIS, C. The Foundation of Modern Monarchies.
PETRIE, F. Tools and Weapons. 1917.
  Social Life in Ancient Egypt.
  Religious Life in Ancient Egypt.
PIAGET, J. Language and Thought of the Child. 1926.
PIÉRON, H. Thought and the Brain. 1927.
PILLSBURY, W. B. Fundamentals of Psychology.
PIRENNE, H. Medieval Cities. 1925.
PLANCK, M. The Universe in the Light of Modern Physics. 1931.
PLATO. Ion (trans. by SHELLEY). The Republic.
  Laws.
PLEKHANOV, G. V. Fundamental Problems of Marxism.
  Essays in the History of Materialism.
POINCARÉ, H. Science and Hypothesis. 1925.
  (Trans.). The Value of Science. 1907.
  L'Invention mathématique (*Rev. du mois*). July 1928.
POLE, W. Philosophy of Music.
POSTGATE, R. History of the English Working Class. 1926.
PRAZ, M. The Romantic Agony. 1933.
PRÉVILLE, A. DE Les Sociétés africaines. 1894.
PRICHARD, H. A. Duty and Interest. 1929.
PRINCE, M . The Dissociation of a Personality. 1908.
  The Unconscious. 1914.
PROTHERO. English Farming Past and Present. 1912.
PUNNETT, R. C. Mendelism. 1905.

RABAUD, E. Éléments de biologie générale. 1921.
RAMSAY, F. P. The Foundations of Mathematics.
RATTRAY, R. S. Ashanti. 1923.
  Religion and Art in Ashanti. 1927.
READ, C. Origin of Man. 1920.
REAVEY, G., and SLONIM, M. Soviet Literature. 1935.
REED, J. Ten Days that Shook the World.
REICHENBACH, H. Atom and Cosmos. 1932.
REINACH, S. Cults, Myths and Religions (trans.). 1912.
RENAUDET, G. The Birth of the Book.
REVESZ, G. Psychology of a Musical Prodigy.
RIBOT. La Logique des sentiments.
RICHARDS, A. Hunger and Work in a Savage Tribe. 1932.
RICHARDS, I. A. Principles of Literary Criticism.

RIDGEWAY, W. Origin of Tragedy. 1910.
  Dramas and Dramatic Dances. 1915.
RIGNANO, E. Psychology of Reasoning. 1923.
RIVERS, W. H. R. The Todas. 1907.
  Instinct and the Unconscious. 1922.
  Conflict and Dream. 1923.
  Medicine, Magic and Religion. 1924.
  Social Organisation. 1924.
ROBACK, A. A. Psychology of Character. 1927.
ROBERTSON, J. M. Elizabethan Literature. 1914.
ROBERTSON-SMITH, W. Religion of the Semites. 1887.
ROBINSON, J. H. The Mind in the Making. 1921.
ROGERS, T. Six Centuries of Work and Wages. 1890.
ROHEIM, G. Australian Totemism. 1925.
RÓMANES. Mental Evolution in Animals.
ROSTOVTZEFF, M. The Roman Empire: Social and Economic
  Development. 1926.
RUSSELL, A. L. N. Architecture. 1927.
RUSSELL, B. Mysticism and Logic. 1918.
  Introduction to Mathematical Philosophy. 1920.
  Analysis of Matter.
  Analysis of Mind.
  Outline of Philosophy. 1927.
RUSSELL, B. (with A. N. WHITEHEAD). Principia Mathematica.
RUSSELL, D. The Prelude to the Machine Age.
RUSSELL, E. S. Interpretation of Development and Heredity. 1930.

SAINTSBURY, G. E. B. History of Elizabethan Literature. 1887.
  Flourishing of Romance and Rise of Allegory. 1897.
SAPIR, E. Language. 1921.
SAUSSURE, DE Cours de linguistique générale. 1916.
SAYCE, A. H. Science of Language. 1880.
SAYCE, R. U. Primitive Arts and Crafts. 1933.
SCHMIDT, W. The Origin and Growth of Religion. 1931.
SCHOEN, M. (ed.). The Effects of Music.
SCHULTZE. Psychologie der Naturvölker.
SCOTT, G. The Architecture of Humanism. 1914.
SEDGWICK, W. T., and TYLER, H. W. A Short History of Science.
  1917.
SELIGMAN, C. G. The Melanesians of British New Guinea. 1910.
  The Peoples of Africa. 1930.
SELIGMAN, E. R. A. The Economic Interpretation of History. 1924.

SEYMOUR, T. D. Life in the Homeric Age. 1908.

SHAND, A. F. Foundation of Character.

SHELLEY, P. B. A Defence of Poetry (essays). 1930.

SHERRINGTON, C. S. Integrative Action of the Nervous System. 1906.

SIDHANTAY, N. K. The Heroic Age of India.

SIDNEY, SIR PHILIP. An Apologie for Poetrie. 1595.

SINGER, C. Studies in the History and Method of Science. 1917–1921.

SKEAT, W. W. Malay Magic. 1900.

SKEAT, W. W., and C. BLAGDEN. Pagan Races of the Malay Peninsula. 1906.

SLATER, G. English Peasantry and the Enclosure of Common Lands. 1907.

The Making of Modern England. 1915.

SMITH, ADAM. The Wealth of Nations. 1776.

SMITH, D. E. History of Mathematics. (2 vols.) 1923–1925.

SMITH, G. E. The Migration of Early Cultures.

Essays on the Evolution of Man. 1927.

Human History. 1929.

SMITH, W. The Commedia dell' Arte. 1912.

SOLLAS, W. J. Ancient Hunters. 1911.

SOURDILLE, C. The Religious Thought of Greece.

SPEARING, H. G. The Childhood of Art. 1912.

SPEARMAN, C. The Nature of Intelligence and the Principles of Cognition. 1923.

SPENCE, L. An Introduction to Mythology.

SPENCER, W. B., and GILLEN, F. J. Native Tribes of Central Australia. 1899.

Northern Tribes of Central Australia. 1904.

The Arunta: A Stone Age People. 1927.

SPENGLER, O. Decline of the West.

SPINDEN, H. J. A Study of Maya Art. 1913.

STALIN, J. Leninism. 1928.

Preparing for October. 1931.

Stalin Reports on the Soviet Union. 1934.

The Colonial Question. 1936.

STAYT, H. A. The Bavenda. 1931.

STEBBING, L. S. A Modern Introduction to Logic. 1930.

STEIN, A. Innermost Asia. 1928.

STEPHEN, L. History of English Thought in the Eighteenth Century. 1902.

STEPHENSON, H. T. The Elizabethan People. 1910.
STODDARD, LOTHROP. The Revolt against Civilisation. 1923.
STOUT. Analytical Psychology. 1909.
  Manual of Psychology. 1913.
STRACHEY, J. The Coming Struggle for Power.
  The Nature of Capitalist Crisis.
  Theory and Practice of Socialism. 1936.
SUMMERS, M. The Restoration Stage.
SUSUKI, O. T. A Brief History of Chinese Philosophy. 1914.
SWEET, H. Introduction to the History of Language.
SWINDLER, M. Ancient Painting. 1929.

TAWNEY, R. H. The Acquisitive Society. 1921.
TAYLOR, G. Environment and Race. 1927.
THALBITZER, S. Emotion and Insanity.
THOMAS, N. W. Kinship and Group Marriage in Australia. 1906.
THOMSON, A. J. Heredity.
THOMSON, J. Through Masai Land. 1885.
THOREZ, M. France To-day. 1936.
THORNDIKE, A. H. Shakespeare's Theatre. 1916.
  Literature in a Changing Age. 1920.
THORNDIKE, E. L. Human Learning. 1931.
THORNDIKE, L. A History of Magic and Experimental Science. 1923.
THURSTONE, L. L. Nature of Intelligence.
TOUTAIN, J. Ancient Economic Organisation.
TROELTSCH, E. Protestantism and Progress. 1912.
TROTTER. Herd Instinct.

UEXKÜLL, J. VON Theoretical Biology. 1926.
UNWIN, G. Industrial Organisation in the Sixteenth and Seventeenth
  Centuries. 1909.
URE, P. N. Origin of Tyranny. 1922.
USHER, A. P. An Introduction to the Industrial History of England.
  1920.

VANDERVELDE, E. Parasitism, Organic and Social. 1895.
VENDRYES. Language. 1925.
VOSSLER, K. The Spirit of Language.
VRIES, H. DE Die Mutationstheorie. 1900.

WALEY, A. A Hundred and Seventy Chinese Poems. 1918.
  More Translations from the Chinese. 1918.

WALLASCHEK, R. Primitive Music. 1893.

WALTERS, H. The Art of the Romans. 1911.

WARNER, G. T. Landmarks in English Industrial History. 1912.

WATSON, J. B. Behaviourism. 1925.

WEBB, C. C. J. Group Theories of Religion. 1916.

WEBB, S. and B. History of Trade Unionism. 1920.
The Decay of Capitalist Civilisation. 1923.
Soviet Communism—A New Civilisation. 1935.

WEBSTER, H. Primitive Secret Societies. 1908.

WERNER, A. Natives of British Central Africa. 1906.

WESTERMARCK, E. A. Origin and Development of Moral Ideas. 1906.
Ritual and Belief in Morocco. 1926.

WESTON, J. L. From Ritual to Romance.

WHITE, A. D. The Warfare of Science with Religion.

WHITEHEAD, A. N. Principles of Natural Knowledge. 1925.
Science and the Modern World. 1926.

WIEGER, L. Histoire des croyances religieuses et des opinions philosophiques en Chine. 1917.

WILLIAMS, C. T. A. The Rhythm of Modern Music. 1909.

WILLIAMS, M. Social Scandinavia in the Viking Age. 1920.

WILLIAMS. Papuans of the Trans. Fly. 1935.

WILLIAMSON, J. A. A Short History of British Imperialism. 1922.

WINCHESTER, C. T. Life of John Wesley. 1900.

WINDLEBAND, W. A History of Philosophy. 1901.

WIPER, R. Communism and Culture. 1925.

WISSLER, C. The American Indian. 1917.

WITTGENSTEIN, L. Tractatus Logico-Philosophicus. 1922.
Some Remarks on Logical Form (*Aristotelian Socy. Supp.* vol. ix.). 1929.

WOOD, H. T. Industrial England in the Middle of the Eighteenth Century. 1913.

WOODGER, J. H. Biological Principles. 1929.

WOODWORTH, R. S. Contemporary Schools of Psychology. 1931.

WOOLF, L. S. Imperialism and Civilisation. 1928.

WORDSWORTH, W. Preface to "Lyrical Ballads". 1802.

WUNDT, W. Völkerpsychologie. 1900.
Grundzüge der physiologischen Psychologie. (5 Aufl.) 1903.

ZUCKERMAN, S. Social Life of Monkeys and Apes. 1932.

INDEX

Economic differentiation and the
    novel, 21
  foundation of modern culture, 55
  foundation of tragedy, 68 *ff.*
  function of primitive festivals, 27
  individualism, 18
  production, 125, 137 *ff.*, 144, 164
    and consciousness, 165, 166, 171
    and culture, 16
    and freedom, 279
    and ideology, 141, 287 *ff.*
    and individuality, 152
    and language, 139, 196
    and life-experience, 204
    and modern poetry, 111
    and music, 245
    and mythology, 36
    and painting, 252
    and phantasy, 195
    and poetry, 93
    and revolution, 282
    and social organisation, 181
    and the novel, 207
    and the origin of language,
      248–9
    and the working class, 273
    bourgeois revolution in, 55
    capitalist, 61 *ff.*, 64, 121, 271 *ff.*
    capitalist and the poet, 104
    commodity production, 101–2
    industrial, 88 *ff.*
    in the eighteenth century, 84–5
    organisation for, 27
    ownership of the means of, 37,
      39
    struggle with outer reality in, 34
Economics, 77
Economy, bourgeois, 44, 58
  Greek, 49
Education, 177
"Ego," 124, 131, 147, 160 *ff.*, 185,
    186, 189, 190, 220, 221
  and environment, 192
  and external reality, 237, 291, 296
  and insanity, 224 *ff.*
  and neurosis, 238
  W

and the body, 244
and visual art, 250
common, 151, 152, 171, 177,
    179, 184
in dream, 182
Fascism and, 282
mathematical, the, 228
social, the, 222, 236, 237, 242
Egocentricity of poetry and dream,
    208
Egypt, 13, 17, 38, 39, 41, 188
  god-kings of, 40
Egyptian early literature, 13
Egyptian empire, 19
Einstein, 7, 55, 147
Electrical Trades Union, 115
Eliot, T. S., 111, 122
Elizabethan Age, 55, 74 *ff.*, 83, 84,
    117, 120, 202, 239, 295
  blank verse, 86
  court lyrics, 80
  culture, 21
  drama, 254, 257
  poetry, 74 *ff.*, 118, 119
    interest of the Romantic Poets
      in, 96
  tragedy, 257
Emotion, 32, 69, 92, 123, 125 *ff.*,
    134–5, 151, 156, 185, 191,
    199, 203, 206, 214, 217, 291
  and Aristotle's theory of *catharsis*,
    52–3
  and dream, 209
  and extraversion, 227
  and poetry, 217–18, 266–7
  and the purpose of art, 261 *ff.*
  and society, 36, 71
  and sound in animals, 248
  and visual art, 250
  artistic, 267
  collective, 26, 30, 31, 35, 59
  of the schizophrenic, 224
  magic and science, 33
  poetry and dream and, 219 *ff.*
  primitive, 173
  social, 29, 30, 31

X